Contents

List of Tables and Figures

Tables

Figures

All images from *Das Bild* are courtesy of the C. F. Müller Verlag and Hüthig GmbH and Co.

Artists for the Reich

Culture and Race from Weimar to Nazi Germany

Joan L. Clinefelter

Oxford • New York

First published in 2005 by
Berg
Editorial offices:
1st Floor, Angel Court, 81 St Clements Street, Oxford OX4 1AW, UK
175 Fifth Avenue, New York, NY 10010, USA

Berg is the imprint of Oxford International Publishers Ltd.

Library of Congress Cataloging-in-Publication Data
Clinefelter, Joan L.
  Artists for the Reich : culture and race from Weimar to Nazi Germany /
Joan L. Clinefelter.
    p. cm.
  Includes bibliographical references and index.
  ISBN 1-84520-201-5 (pbk.) — ISBN 1-84520-200-7 (cloth)
  1. Deutsche Kunstgesellschaft. 2. National socialism and art. I. Title.

  N6868.5.N37C58 2005
  709'.43'09043—dc22

                                                        2005001813

British Library Cataloguing-in-Publication Data
A catalogue record for this book is available from the British Library.

ISBN-13   978 1 84520 200 2 (Cloth)
          978 1 84520 201 9 (Paper)

ISBN-10   1 84520 200 7 (Cloth)
          1 84520 201 5 (Paper)

Typeset by JS Typesetting Ltd, Porthcawl, Mid Glamorgan
Printed in the United Kingdom by Biddles Ltd, King's Lynn

www.bergpublishers.com

Acknowledgments

This book would never have been completed without a great deal of assistance. Above all, I want to acknowledge the patience, humor and support of Karl-Heinz Dukstein. He has endured a lot over the years and through it all, he always believed I would finish. The book is for him.

James Diehl, my advisor at Indiana University, taught me all about the joys and frustrations of research and teaching. He remains a model for me and I greatly appreciate all the support he has provided. The History and German Studies faculty at Indiana University provided me teaching and research assistantships, which I appreciate still. James Riley and Aron Rodrigue are to be especially thanked for the invaluable experience they gave me as their research assistant. I also benefited from a Max Kade Fellowship, a year of support from the Deutsche Akademische Austauschdienst and a Mellon Dissertation Write-up Grant. My friends from Indiana University should also be thanked individually but this group recognition will have to suffice; you know who you are.

I also want to thank the staffs of the many archives I used. This includes the Berlin Document Center, the Bundesarchiv in Koblenz and Berlin, the Karlsruhe Generallandesarchiv, the Niedersächsisches Hauptstaatsarchiv Hannover, the Niedersächsisches Staatsarchiv Wolfenbüttel, the Sächsisches Hauptstaatsarchiv Dresden and the Thüringisches Hauptstaatsarchiv Weimar. The advice and assistance I received with locating and copying material is enormously appreciated. The library staffs at the Karlsruhe Staatliche Kunsthalle and the Landesbibliothek in Karlsruhe were also very helpful. The staff in the imaging service areas at Harvard College Library and the art library at the University of Wisconsin, Madison were of great assistance. I also very much appreciate C. F. Müller Verlag and their parent company, Hüthig GmbH and Co., for granting me copyright permissions for images from *Das Bild*. I also thank the Landesverein Badische Heimat eV for permission to use the image from *Ekkart*.

My colleagues at the University of Northern Colorado have read earlier versions of this work and provided keen insights. To say that I appreciate their advice and encouragement is completely insufficient. I consider myself to be especially lucky to part of a department that values scholarship and teaching, and whose members are not merely colleagues but friends. Barry Rothaus, Marshall Clough, Ron Edgerton, Fritz Fischer, Erin Jordan, Alexander Knott, Joan Pratt, Don Shaffer, Michael Welsh and Jan Worrall all deserve my sincere thanks. Other colleagues, including David Caldwell, Tom Bredehoft, Rosemary Hathaway and Tracey Sedinger have also helped with advice and encouragement. The University of Northern Colorado Faculty Research and Publications Board generously provided two research grants. The Graduate School and Office of the Provost, under Marlene Strathe, provided a summer faculty fellowship. The Dean of Arts and Sciences, Sandra Flake, approved a sabbatical leave so I could finish the manuscript. Such funding and the faith they reflect aided greatly in the completion of this work. Thanks, too, goes to Jennifer Newman, who helped copy-edit the text.

Finally, a special thank-you to my families, the Clinefelters and the Duksteins, for their love and encouragement.

Joan L. Clinefelter

Introduction

This work focuses on the German Art Society, a *völkisch* artists' interest group established in 1920 that combated cultural modernism and promoted its vision of a racially pure German art. While it may seem reductionist to concentrate on just one organization, the Society offers the opportunity to analyze the connections between culture, race and art from the Weimar Republic through the end of the Third Reich. The German Art Society also demonstrates that the Right's attacks against the avant-garde associated with the republic were not only against aesthetic modernism. The virulent anti-Semitism and anti-democratic values that fueled the assault against Weimar's cultural pluralism were just one side of the culture wars. Right-wing, *völkisch* groups such as the Society also promoted a racialist interpretation of art and culture. The artists associated with the German Art Society termed this the 'German style of art'. They emphasized the artists' supposed racial purity to legitimate paintings and sculpture that rejected modernist styles in favor of adherence to traditional themes and modes of representation. The artists, art professors, teachers and critics who belonged to the Society were committed to promoting representational art that imitated nature and was tied to the styles associated with nineteenth-century salon painting. By infusing such 'old-style' art with racial meaning, Society members sought to legitimate traditional art on a biological basis.

The German Art Society has long been a shadowy presence on Germany's cultural Right and its cultural mission has been briefly described before. However, all previous works have analyzed the Society primarily as a precursor to Nazi culture.[1] The intense anti-modernism and anti-Semitism of the Society's program serve in these works as examples of the cultural currents that the Nazis tapped into during the Weimar Republic and then transformed into official policy after 1933. Hildegard Brenner's analysis of the Society remains the best treatment of the organization.[2] Brenner's study of art's social function in the Third Reich and the cultural apparatus the Nazis constructed to regulate the arts gave rise to a rich and varied literature. Berthold Hinz's exploration of the aesthetics of art in the Third Reich has shaped the common understanding of 'Nazi art' and remains a classic treatment.[3] Most recently, Alan E. Steinweis has explored the Combat League for German Culture (*Kampfbund für deutsche Kultur*) and its role as a mediator between cultural anti-modernists and the Nazi Party. Steinweis's work on the Reich Culture Chamber and Jonathan Petropoulos's analyses of National Socialist cultural politics have contributed greatly to understanding the incredibly complicated institutional and ideological framework of Nazi culture and the role of art in the Third Reich.[4]

This work draws heavily on such scholarship as well as from recent work on the *völkisch* movement and the cultural Right in the Weimar Republic.[5] For the German Art Society was more than just a precursor to Nazi art; and although its notions about culture, race and art are certainly repugnant, the group was more than a lunatic-fringe element in the republic. The history of the Society reveals a strand of continuity in German culture that reaches from the Wilhelmine Empire through the republic and into the Third Reich. As part of the wider *völkisch* movement, the German Art Society offered a radical, right-wing alternative construction of German identity that was grounded in race and culture. Organizationally fractured and ideologically amorphous, the *völkisch* milieu was nevertheless well established before the First World War. In their work on the *völkisch* movement in Wilhelmine Germany, Uwe Puschner, Walter Schmitz, Justus H. Ulbricht and others have demonstrated that the *völkisch* groups were not only a Weimar-era incubator of National Socialism.[6] Even the Nazis themselves recognized they were different from – though also related to – the *völkisch* adherents. Like the *völkisch* movement of which it was very much a part, the German Art Society had an agenda and belief system that deserve to be studied in their own right.

In the first chapter, I examine the early life of the Society's founder Bettina Feistel-Rohmeder to demonstrate how she created an identity as a cultural expert using racialist ideas about culture, art and race. Through her father, Wilhelm Rohmeder, she and the Society were firmly rooted in the *völkisch* movement of the empire. Her concept of a pure German art was also an outgrowth of debates over the nation's culture and modernism's place in it. In particular, I try to show that the understanding of Germany as a nation defined by a common cultural heritage was transformed by the Right before the First World War. By casting modernism and its supporters as foreign outsiders, proponents of a uniquely 'German' culture exchanged the old idea of Germany as a nation of culture for that of a racially defined people of culture. Art that was tied to the *Volk* became a medium that could supposedly integrate Germans into a community conceived as ethnically pure and eternal.

The second and third chapters focus on the German Art Society's campaign to promote its German style of art and combat the avant-garde in the Weimar Republic. I thus argue that the Society's cultural campaign was not only against modernism but for a particular concept of art. That is, their anti-modernism was not just defined negatively by what it was not but also 'positively' by what they believed German art to be. I also offer an analysis of the members who made up the core of the Society. In this way I begin to trace the dense network of alliances and shared memberships that connected the group to the *völkisch* movement. The German Art Society was an affiliate of the German League (*Deutschbund*) and created the Executive Council of United German Art and Culture Associations (*Führerrat der vereinigten Deutschen Kunst- und Kulturverbände*). Through this umbrella organization, the Society united nearly twenty *völkisch* groups, expanded its art journal and cultural news service, and even promoted its first exhibition of 'pure German' art. I also show how the Executive Council, which cooperated closely with the Combat League for German Culture, brought the Society into close contact with the National Socialists.

The last half of this book concentrates on the German Art Society in the Third Reich. The Society's contributions to the Nazis' initial struggles to define the arts in 1933 receive their own chapter. Because the Society did not disband in 1933 but continued and even grew during the Nazi regime, it offers the opportunity to follow a cohort of non-modernist artists through the Third Reich. As I demonstrate, members expected to become recognized experts for the National Socialist regime. The group's first traveling exhibition of pure German art, launched in April 1933, was the first example of what art in the Third Reich might be. German Art Society members played an important role in the local degenerate art exhibitions as well.

Throughout, I suggest that the Nazis' cultural policies directed from above were in turn shaped by the artists from below. Indeed, the notion that 'politics issued orders and art obeyed them' is insufficient on several points.[7] It assumes that the National Socialist leadership got exactly the art it desired. Yet there was widespread dissatisfaction with the kind of painting, sculpture and graphics that developed during the Third Reich. While controls effectively excluded modernist art after 1937, the Nazis were never able to develop a new artistic form that was wholly 'Nazi art'. The 'top-down' explanation for Nazi culture also treats the artists as objects of no agency of their own, as if they had no choice but to follow orders.

The corollary to this idea is the belief that 'real' artists did not collaborate with the regime and that art of the Third Reich is not really art but some kind of aberration. This is a convenient way to avoid dealing with the problem of treating art in Germany between 1933 and 1945 but is ineffective as a way of explanation. Artists are not autonomous from politics, economics or any other aspect of their historical time and place. The so-called German style of art in no way reflects my personal tastes, but the Society's works were well-executed if usually unimaginative landscapes, genre scenes and still lifes. The German Art Society's artists had trained in the leading academies and were members of the educated middle class. They supported National Socialism because it responded to their needs and confirmed their long-held prejudices and fears. And because they expected to profit from the elimination of modernism and the state's endorsement of racially-inspired art.

Indeed, as the final chapters show, the German Art Society sought to shape policy, urging the Nazi leadership to take even more extreme measures to eliminate Jews and modernists. Members were dissatisfied with the pace of cultural reform. The Society's art journal, which began publication in 1934 and continued until early 1944, gave voice to members' discontent with the regime's policies. Many members were old fighters in the NSDAP and their loyalty never wavered. Their journal reviewed the major art exhibitions, repeated the dominant themes set by the party and even held exhibitions that traveled to various German cities after 1933. But the group's journal and exhibitions were also used as opportunities for the Society to critique policy and to point out the lack of results.

The German Art Society and the Nazis recognized that there was some essential difference between *völkisch* and National Socialist art. Just where the boundary between the two is difficult to demarcate, but I attempt to suggest some differences in the final chapter. While I do think that there is such a thing as 'Nazi art', I believe it was defined less by content and style and more by the interpretive gloss placed on the works. By this I mean that there is little inherently National Socialist about a painting, say produced in 1934, of a peasant leading a cow down a country lane. Instead, such a work was 'Nazified' by its placement in a party-approved context – exhibition, art journal, public building or Nazi leader's collection – and by its interpretation by approved art reporters.

Indeed, the Nazis themselves crafted three different themes that sought to cast art in an appropriately National Socialist light. The Society dutifully repeated these themes, but it also manipulated them to suit the members' own interests and even to criticize policy. From 1937 until the war began, the Nazis proclaimed that a new era in German art had begun. The official art journal *Art in the Third Reich* trumpeted the expectation that a new generation of artists would win a new art for the Reich. The Society repeated this interpretation of culture after the first Great German Art Exhibition but only half-heartedly. As members suggested in their journal and meetings, the idea that a new German style could develop was in their view impossible. Art was biologically determined; the German style was eternal. Thus, German art could no more change in terms of style than a person could change eye color. The German Art Society did continue after 1937, but authorities regarded it as a rather backward collection of elderly artists. As a *völkisch* group, it was somehow not sufficiently National Socialist.

However, after the Second World War began, the Nazis argued that the war would spark the creativity they had longed for. The German Art Society picked up the new theme and represented itself as marching in step with the regime. Its artists were winning new territory for the Reich and demonstrating the superiority of German culture. It was not until the last Nazi theme was developed, after the defeat at Stalingrad, however, that the Society really moved from the periphery closer to the center of National Socialist culture. The war, claimed the Nazis, was now for the defense of European culture. Only the Germans could protect Western civilization from the Anglo-American-Bolshevik forces that willfully destroyed European cities and treasures, claimed the Nazis. The Society adapted this interpretation of German art and made it its own. Its last exhibition in 1943 and its leader, Bettina Feistel-Rohmeder, were both recognized by the party leadership at long last as valuable contributors to art in the Third Reich.

Overall, I argue that the relationship between the *völkisch* German Art Society and National Socialism was not as symbiotic or smooth as has been imagined. Similarly, just what made art 'Nazi' remains, I fear, unclear and in need of further exploration. But because the German Art Society enables the examination of the intersection of culture, art and race from the republic through the Third Reich, 1933 serves as neither a beginning nor an end point for cultural analysis here. This provides a longer view of the culture wars associated with the Weimar Republic and increasingly, too, with Wilhelmine Germany.[8] The German Art Society helped to rally artists for the Third Reich and served to integrate them into the regime. Although its members never became the arbiters of cultural authority as they imagined, in the end they did succeed in becoming artists for the Reich, if only by default.

–1–

Bettina Feistel-Rohmeder and the Origins of the German Art Society

Bettina Feistel-Rohmeder was the driving force behind the German Art Society throughout its existence. She founded the organization in 1920, established its cultural news service and journals and served as its business manager until 1944. Whatever one may think of the cause to which she was devoted, one must admit that her career was remarkable (Figure 1.1). Yet it has been largely ignored, with most sources crediting the artist Hans Adolf Bühler for Society ventures.[1] In part, the lack of source materials is to blame. Nearly every work that mentions the German Art Society relies on one source: the 1938 collection of articles from her cultural news service. Entitled *In the Terror of Art Bolshevism*, she included there a brief history of the Society's efforts before 1934, but she downplayed her own role.[2] Society publications also offer few clues; she was never featured as an artist and her personal life was rarely discussed.[3] Although she did create an archive of German Art Society materials, it was destroyed in air raids in 1944.[4]

However, without Feistel-Rohmeder there would have been no German Art Society. Moreover, her early life reveals important clues about the Society and its mission. Her concept of a pure German art grounded in racial precepts was firmly in place by 1905. Her views and the origins of the Society itself developed from the Wilhelmine-era debates about German art and modernism's place in the nation's culture. Feistel-Rohmeder's background also demonstrates that the Society was a product of the empire's *völkisch* movement. From these disparate sources, Feistel-Rohmeder crafted for herself an identity as a cultural leader whose expertise was grounded in race and devoted to the creation of what she considered a cultural renaissance of the pure German racial community, the *Volk*.

She was born Bettina Rohmeder on 24 August 1873 in Heidenheim, near Munich, the only child of Dr (Johann) Wilhelm and Johanna (Barfus) Rohmeder. Her mother remains an unknown quantity; never mentioned by her daughter, it is likely that she died before 1899 when Rohmeder remarried.[5] He was a teacher, school official and *völkisch* activist both before and after the First World War. Nothing is known about Bettina's childhood, but she was deeply influenced by her father's right-wing politics and intense anti-Semitism. Rohmeder chaired the Society for Germandom Abroad for forty years, led the Munich chapter of the

Figure 1.1 Bettina Feistel-Rohmeder. From *Das Bild*, August 1938, p. 231.

anti-Semitic Reich Hammer League and played a dominant role in the German-*völkisch* Defense League.[6] He and his daughter were apparently very close. Rohmeder proudly noted her occupation as an artist in his 1912 and 1922 *Who's Who* entries.[7] He supported his daughter's later efforts as leader of the German Art Society, too. He used his *völkisch* contacts to attract new members and donated funds on at least one occasion.[8]

For her part, Bettina clearly adored her father. He is the only family member she ever mentioned in print and she dedicated her first book to him. His portrait was one of her two paintings ever reproduced in the Society's journal.[9] Perhaps she was drawn to the *völkisch* milieu because it offered her a realm in which she could interact with her father and that could not be shared by her much younger half-siblings (who were about the age of her own child).[10] Father and daughter both belonged to the German League (*Deutschbund*), an elitist anti-Semitic group, joined the Nazi Party (NSDAP) before 1930, and dedicated themselves to the *völkisch* cause.[11]

Feistel-Rohmeder's praise for her father is all the more striking when compared to the complete silence regarding her own family. She married Arthur Feistel in 1896 and they had one child, Charlotte. In the sources available, she never once mentioned her child; nor did she thank her husband in any public speech or writing, even though they remained married until her death in 1953.[12] Sources describe Feistel's occupation only as '*Kaufmann*', a generic term for a white-collar worker.[13] He may have struggled to make a living because between roughly 1900 and 1920 the family moved seven times. It may also be that the family moved in order to accommodate Feistel-Rohmeder's artistic studies; at the very least, she did receive training as an artist after her marriage.

Rather than attend an art academy, an option often denied women, Feistel-Rohmeder studied privately with respected painters, including Adolf Hoelzel, Ludwig Dill, Johann Vincent Cissarz and Bernhard Pankok.[14] She also worked with Dill when he organized an art and garden show in 1907.[15] Judging by the books she cherished, Feistel-Rohmeder was well educated and may have spoken Italian, French and English. She traveled at least once to Venice to study art and published a book on women in the Venetian Renaissance in 1905.[16] Right around that time, she began her career as an art critic in Heidelberg, writing reviews for local newspapers.[17] Feistel-Rohmeder also worked as an independent artist. In 1909, she opened the Mannheim Workshop for Arts and Crafts where she designed book plates, letterheads and advertisements, and helped to produced a postcard series of Heidelberg and Mannheim. She closed this workshop three years later 'due to an illness in the family' and moved to Oberägeri (Zug) in Switzerland.[18] She relocated to Dresden sometime before November 1920, where she remained until moving to Karlsruhe in late 1933.[19]

Her professional training and background so far offer few clues to her hatred for modern art. However, Feistel-Rohmeder's anti-modernism and racialist understanding of art were formulated by at least 1905. She herself traced the origins of the Society's mission to defend pure German art to one Wilhelmine-era art historian, Henry Thode. In a series of lectures at the University of Heidelberg in 1905, Thode demanded that the German artistic tradition be defended from the foreign invasion of modernist art. Feistel-Rohmeder attended these presentations; years later she and other Society members claimed that their aesthetic program had originated in Thode's lectures.[20] In a passionate appeal, he rejected claims that French Impressionism and its German supporters were superior to the tradition-bound academic art favored in Germany.[21] Thode contrasted the current obsession for the newest styles with art that was grounded in technical skill, the faithful representation of nature and accessible to every viewer. Above all, he praised the monumental, fantastical works of Arnold Böcklin and the paintings of Hans Thoma as being especially Germanic in inspiration.

For example, Thode reported that upon seeing Thoma's paintings for the first time he was struck by just one thought: 'that is German! And everything that is German' was found in Thoma's art.[22] His works revealed the very essence of art: the perfect representation of a unified, clear conception of pure feeling.[23] Though ignored by the art establishment, Thoma remained true to his inner vision, painting scenes from nature in shimmering colors. For Thode, Thoma's innate sensibility and technical skill revealed the 'power and meaning of nature'.[24] His landscapes evoked a love of home and the simple pleasures of life. Paintings such as *Miraculous Birds* invited viewers to soar above the land, to glory in nature and its power. True to the tradition of art and to nature, such works transported viewers into a fantastic realm of pure feeling and of oneness[25] (see Figure 1.2).

However, explained Thode, such artists were under attack. The Berlin Secession and other modernists were 'a great party, steadily increasing in power [and] headquartered in Berlin'. These 'fanatic admirers and lovers of French Impressionism, who had gone so far as to call Manet a genius', promoted foreign over native art. A conspiracy was afoot and 'German art and the German character' now had to be 'justified and defended in their own Fatherland'.[26] Thode was especially concerned that the emerging private market of artists, dealers and middle-class patrons was beginning to challenge traditional art institutions.[27] Modernists were routinely excluded from state commissions, awards, even museum collections and positions within academies. However, by 'seceding' from established artist organizations and creating their own groups, exhibitions and journals, they were creating their own niche in Germany's cultural life. New art journals like *Art and Artists* furthered their reputations; modernists began to be regarded as new, innovative and better artists than those who adhered to the older styles.[28]

Unable to prevent their advance, Thode cast the modernists as outsiders who sought to poison the nation's art and break the cultural ties that bound Germans together. This was a common tactic in the culture wars emerging before the First World War and drew upon the established ties between German nationalism and culture. Well before Germany existed as a political entity, the nation was imagined as a *Kulturnation*, literally a nation constituted by its collective cultural heritage. The fine and folk arts, language and literature, even science, industry and the military were widely regarded as physical manifestations of the German character: loyalty, closeness to nature, cleanliness and creativity. German culture was not merely an expression of national identity but the source of identity itself.[29] The stakes over modernism's role in Germany were very high, for according to those who sought to defend art which respected traditional themes and styles, the very essence of German identity was at risk.

Thode's presentations sparked a lively debate in the press, especially with the leading German Impressionist, the painter Max Liebermann. A founding member of the Berlin Secession, Liebermann's outsider status was underscored by his

Figure 1.2 *Miraculous Birds* by Hans Thoma, copyright managed by Corbis.

being Jewish as well. He and Thode harried each other in the newspapers over the summer of 1905.[30] Years later, Bettina Feistel-Rohmeder cast Thode's lectures and Liebermann's response in a radical, *völkisch* light. On one side stood the defenders of German art led by Thode and his ideal German artist, Hans Thoma. On the other were arrayed Liebermann, modernists and their supporters, determined to destroy German art, the very essence of the *Volk*.[31] Another German Art Society member,

Edgar Schindler, described Thode's lectures more starkly: 'one recognized immediately: this was a matter of life and death. Two life principles met each other in battle, Jewish-international liberalism and German nationalism.'[32] The Society remembered the struggle between Thode and Liebermann as a 'foreshadowing of the battle between National Socialist and Bolshevik concepts of art'.[33]

That Feistel-Rohmeder and other Society members connected Thode's defense for traditional art to the Nazis' anti-modernism was not as far-fetched as one might think. Although Thode was no *völkisch* activist, racialist vocabulary and anti-Semitism had insinuated themselves into debates about German art by 1900.[34] In particular, the *völkisch* movement radicalized the old notion of *Kulturnation*, transforming a nation of culture into a cultural *Volk*. That culture, rather than politics, constituted a nation and people remained, but within the *völkisch* movement, cultural identity and the unity it promised were infused with racism. In the arts, works from the Renaissance, the Romantic movement and nineteenth-century salon painting were praised as uniquely 'German'. Albrecht Dürer, Caspar David Friedrich, Wilhelm Leibl and Hans Thoma occupied points on a continuum of the native cultural tradition. By infusing artistic traditionalism with race, art became a medium not only for national integration but also for racial regeneration.[35]

The German Art Society was directly connected to Wilhelmine Germany's *völkisch* movement and this notion of a racialized art. After 1927, the Society was an affiliate of the German League, an influential group founded in 1894 that brought the 'science of race' to the *völkisch* movement.[36] The League spread its ideas through its newspapers and its members, who cultivated 'racist anti-Semitism' in the other organizations they joined.[37] For example, German League members belonged to the Pan-German League, the Navy League, the Society for Germandom Abroad, the Hammer League and the German-*Völkisch* Writers Association. The German League repeatedly sought to organize these and other *völkisch* groups into a more disciplined, coordinated movement. As part of this effort, it used special interest groups, often led by members, to promote all things Germanic and combat the 'Jewish conspiracy'.[38] The German Art Society would become one of these.

Indeed, the very idea for a *völkisch* artists' interest group originated in a German League presentation by Feistel-Rohmeder's father. In 1916, Wilhelm Rohmeder, a leading League member, outlined a plan that illustrated just how *völkisch* beliefs and art could be combined. In his lecture, Rohmeder decried the advance of 'foreign, Jewish' modernists and the retreat of true German artists. He believed that the art market and institutions had been so infiltrated by artists hostile to German culture that racially pure artists had only two choices if they were to prosper. They could abandon the cause of German art, surrender to the will of the art market and 'disown their race and as slaves, hitch themselves to the triumphal chariots of the foreign-blooded'.[39] Or they could resist.

Rohmeder declared it was time to defend German interests in the cultural realm by creating an organization to bring together 'the *true* German artists'. Eventually, 'this could lead to the creation of a separate journal, around which could flock the truly German community of artists and art critics'. These cultural leaders would spark the creation of a network of associations, exhibitions and even a '*völkisch* art publishing house'. In this way the 'economic and commercial interests of the visual artists' would be represented 'free from the influence of foreigners'. Rohmeder advocated that the *völkisch* community organize an alternative cultural milieu to transform art into '*a weapon in the battle for the soul of the German people*'.[40] Rohmeder was convinced that Jewish dealers, critics and artists had infiltrated German culture in order to destroy the healthy sensibilities and racial identity of the *Volk*. Only the coordinated efforts of a *völkisch* elite, a community of racially enlightened experts and activists, offered any chance of salvation.

Rohmeder ended his German League presentation noting that 'leading men' were needed and asked: 'who will place themselves in the service of this great task?'[41] The answer was his daughter, Bettina Feistel-Rohmeder. Although she never admitted to it in print, the German Art Society was modeled after her father's 1916 presentation.[42] But her choice to do so was quite unusual. It was rare enough for a woman to regard herself as a professional artist, as Feistel-Rohmeder did. But she was also an activist in a extremely male-dominated, radical right-wing milieu. Unfortunately no record has been located that describes just how she juggled her roles as wife, mother, artist and later leader of the German Art Society. When she reviewed the work of other female artists, Feistel-Rohmeder did note in passing that some had to stop painting temporarily in order to care for their families. These comments typically appear as asides, yet their tone resonates with a kind of empathy, with a sense that these women had to sacrifice their art in the interest of their families. Feistel-Rohmeder certainly recognized the difficulties female artists encountered in pursuing their craft. However, because she believed that motherhood was a vital female role, she could not fault husbands and children for making it difficult for women to pursue a career in the arts.[43] Building upon her own experience, Feistel-Rohmeder believed that if women wanted to be artists, it was up to them to find a way to accommodate their careers.

Feistel-Rohmeder faced obstacles not just to become an artist but also to be an art critic and managing editor. Both before and after 1918, female journalists were a distinct minority in the profession. In 1925 for example, women accounted for just 78 of the 3,235 members of the National Association of the German Press, 'about 2.5 per cent of the entire membership'. In 1928, there were 170 female journalists; in 1932, there were 222.[44] Unsurprisingly, most of these women were relegated to reporting women's topics rather than politics: childrearing and household tips, reviews of films, theater and music, and local-interest stories.[45] To break the gender barriers and maintain their profession, historian Almut Todorow has argued that these women had to cultivate the bourgeois, male, attribute of 'personality'. That is, they had to acquire both an authorial voice and a presence to lend their work the authority of a complete individual. To do so, female journalists had to jettison their femininity and become more 'male'. As one female journalist explained, the intellectual woman had to follow the 'path to complete masculinity' and occupy a kind of twilight zone of not being female but also not being male.[46]

While this represented one strategy, it was also possible for women to redefine their gender roles and maintain their feminine identity. By at least 1890, even right-wing organizations were forced to reinterpret female gender roles and the female character in light of the woman question. Surveying an astonishing variety of nationalist and *völkisch* organizations in the German Empire and republic, Karin Bruns has demonstrated that there was a call to redefine female roles via patriotic and racial values. Nationalistic publications offered images of 'female heroism, that called upon "Germanic" or "true-German" ideals' including the Valkyries, Kriemhild and especially Germania. 'Models of female combativeness and female leadership arose that were legitimized by references to race, *Volk*, or Fatherland.'[47] Within *völkisch* and nationalist movements there were new models for the engagement of women.

As Bruns has emphasized, these models of active Germanic women were by no means purely anti-modern. Instead 'traditional concepts of femininity were contained within key concepts of modern discourses' and used terms drawn from psychology, science and medicine.[48] When women agitated against alcohol, tobacco, prostitution and illegitimacy, their campaigns were often cast as struggles against influences alien to and dangerous for the German *Volk*. 'In this way, under the perspective of population and cultural-political "threat[s]" even the German woman could participate in the "struggle for survival".'[49]

Thus, some women on the German Right sought 'to imagine a new woman who was completely different from the Weimar new woman, but nevertheless strong and autonomous'.[50] This new German woman was hardly a feminist but she offered a redefinition of female spheres of influence. For example, the author Sophie Rogge-Börner promoted the image of the new Nordic woman, the descendant of early Germanic women who 'participated fully in the economic and political life of their people' by standing beside – not behind – their men. Other Nazi authors, such as Guida Diehl and Paula Siber, reevaluated motherhood by emphasizing its importance to the *Volk*. National Socialist women such as Gertrud Scholtz-Klink used similar ideas as they participated in the Third Reich.[51]

Bettina Feistel-Rohmeder illustrates many of the qualities of this German new woman. Using right-wing and especially *völkisch* ideologies she created for herself an alternative construction of the new woman of the 1920s. She reconstructed gender relations, *völkisch* ideology and racial theories in a way that enabled her to reconcile her cultural and political activism with her identity as a woman.

Two works by Feistel-Rohmeder provide a glimpse of the mental processes by which she could cast herself as a *völkisch* cultural expert. The first is her 1905 book *The Image of Women in the Venetian Renaissance*; the second is an article written in 1933 called 'Racial Self-Awareness'.[52] In both works Feistel-Rohmeder recombined elements of *völkisch* ideology to legitimate her leadership role within the mostly male right-wing milieu.

Building upon notions of womanhood inherited from her Wilhelmine childhood, Feistel-Rohmeder believed that there were real emotional, psychological and biological differences between men and women. She claimed that women were superior to men in many ways. They were always ready to sacrifice themselves for their families, to put aside their own interests, to bear quietly their own pain in order to better serve their families and societies. Women, she believed, were more aware than men of the burdens of life, burdens which were above all bound to the duty to raise one's children only to let them go.[53] She felt that women were tied closer to nature and to their race because of their ability to bear children. Thus, Feistel-Rohmeder insisted that German women held a place worthy of respect on the grounds of both race and gender.

But she did not argue that women should live in a separate realm or leave politics to men. Feistel-Rohmeder would have argued that such an arrangement was unGerman. Racially pure German men and women had to work together. The image she called forth was that of men and women standing beside one another. Just as men had their own duties within the private sphere of the family, women had certain duties to perform within the public sphere. Feistel-Rohmeder's actions demonstrate that she rejected the notion that the home and children should be the sole focus of a woman's life. Her vision of what women were capable of extended far beyond a domestic sphere inhabited solely by women.

This is what she suggested in her book on women in the Venetian Renaissance, one of the few sources in which she commented extensively upon women's roles. In this work Feistel-Rohmeder searched for portraits of what she called the new women of the Italian Renaissance. She believed that these women, as well as the men who made the Renaissance possible, were products of the Aryan race.[54] Feistel-Rohmeder made a clear distinction between the medieval, 'oriental', subservient woman and the new woman who was Nordic and an equal companion of the Renaissance man.

To Feistel-Rohmeder, the women of Venice played a crucial role in the Renaissance. However, she also claimed that few artists of the era gave women their due. For example, she took Titian to task for painting women who sponsored the arts as merely pretty objects. She criticized his portraits of Isabella D'Este, Caterina Cornaro and Eleonora Gonzaga for representing them as being merely generic types of beauty rather than as creative, powerful individuals.[55] Feistel-Rohmeder contrasted Titian's portraits with those by Lorenzo Lotto. Unlike

Titian, she claimed, Lotto never painted women only for their beauty. She praised his portrait of Laura da Pola for its honest depiction of a woman 'strong and true'. Here was a powerful personality, not simply a beautiful woman.[56] Feistel-Rohmeder regarded Laura da Pola as an ideal example of the new women of the Venetian Renaissance. In Feistel-Rohmeder's view, the Renaissance in Venice reached maturity only after such women began to participate fully in the city's culture[57] (see Figure 1.3).

These Venetian women, explained Feistel-Rohmeder, were all blond, racially pure Germans. As such, they were not simply passive objects that belonged to their husbands. Nor did they lounge all day in the sun, plotting their 'victory over men'.[58] Instead, the ideal new Renaissance woman 'was an enchanting creature, full of grace and veiled intelligence, endowed by God in the gentleness of her

Figure 1.3 *Laura da Palo* by Lorenzo Lotto, copyright managed by Corbis.

aesthetic instinct and the self-perfection of her outer personality'.[59] These new women of the Renaissance, argued Feistel-Rohmeder,

> took part in the intellectual fire that ignited their age... [They were] the final, finest flower of awakened humanity, as the new women, who with clear, knowing intelligence could dare to be all woman (*ganz Weib zu sein*), were prepared to break the last rusty chains with their soft hands; [a new woman] who, conscious of her self, created a new ethic in order to live that from which the highest must arise: the love of the perfect woman for the perfect man...[60]

Here, Feistel-Rohmeder appeared to be on the verge of proclaiming female independence but then reattached her Renaissance women to their male counterparts. The Venetian women she imagined participated fully in the cultural rebirth of their age, but that participation ultimately occurred only in relation to men's actions and in support of patriarchy. If the men did not recognize these new women as equals or give them their due, then women knew how to cope with such male ignorance. Female modesty recognized that nagging men would accomplish little, noted Feistel-Rohmeder. Better to persuade men gently and hide their intelligence. True women did not achieve greatness by creating cultural products themselves; rather they inspired men to artistic feats they would never attempt without their female companions. The image Feistel-Rohmeder offered of these Venetian women, who in her view were all fair-haired, Germanic and mothers of the *Volk*, was one of women standing beside their men, urging them forward.[61]

Thus in Feistel-Rohmeder's eyes, she and other women were active partners in the racial and cultural renaissance of their own age. This view provides insight into how she viewed her activities on behalf of the German Art Society. She was a new woman of the Germanic renaissance. As the founder of the artists' interest group, she labored to defend racially pure German art and artists from the cultural degeneration of the avant-garde and the republic. At the same time, she wielded her pen as a dagger, dueling with the likes of Max Liebermann, her arch-enemy. Within *völkisch* ideology, the cultural regeneration of the *Volk* was regarded as the single best way to revive the Germans and to reconnect them to their racial heritage. Feistel-Rohmeder's mission and her German Art Society were legitimated by the emphasis upon cultural renewal and her own notions of Renaissance women participating in the renewal by inspiring men to produce the new culture.

The cultural realm had long been coded as at least partially female. In particular, middle-class women were to be sufficiently cultivated so that they could educate their children and pass on knowledge and appreciation of the arts and the nation's traditions to their children. While (male) artists and intellectuals produced high culture, women reproduced a domesticated version of the nation's cultural values within their homes, securing it for the next generation. However, Feistel-Rohmeder posited a rather different cultural role for women. Rather than simply reproduce the status quo, she envisioned the new German women as contributing to the innovation and further development of the arts. Left to their own devices, men could only capture surface appearances. They needed women to inspire them, to awaken their artistic souls and spark cultural greatness. Thus, the racially aware German woman influenced culture in two interrelated ways. By nurturing their men, the new German women were co-creators of a culture that embraced and passed on racial values; by caring for their children, they transmitted their race's culture to the next generation.

Feistel-Rohmeder claimed this innovative role for the new German woman in 'Racial Self-Awareness'.[62] Feistel-Rohmeder offered here what were for her unusually personal insights to her ideas regarding women, art and race. Race offered her the opportunity to argue for the necessity of a woman's touch in the creation of a new cultural form that would awaken the German people to their national mission.

She began this article by noting that what she was about to offer 'should in no way appear as a "scientific" statement'.[63] Rather than coolly evaluating a group of paintings, she likened her viewing experience to a kind of nature walk during which, she wrote:

> I would like to ramble in the colorful meadows of art in a womanly way and instinc-
> tively, able to pick a flower from here and there. When I have joined them into a small
> bouquet, then I would like to be able to do so not as an art critic, who out of theories
> arranges a beautiful system, but as an artist (*Künstler*) who creates from the inner con-
> sciousness.[64]

Throughout this article, Feistel-Rohmeder created a view of art that is gendered through a binary system of male-female. As a woman, she was not scientific, orderly or bound by theories. As she makes clear by coding them as 'unwomanly' qualities, these are male characteristics. Instead, she presented the image of a woman strolling through a landscape, collecting beautiful things instinctively, as only a woman would. She then claimed that while the male/scientific viewpoint was not necessarily flawed, the female/artistic sensibility was more perceptive, more capable of grasping inner truths:

> The artist's interior empathy is thoroughly unlike pure rational analyses. It is certainly
> possible, that the forms which lend the artist his motif, his design, his inner visions
> are scientifically assailable and fail the test of proportion, number and weight. And yet
> such artistic perception of the world can – can, not must! – contain a kernel of truth that
> has yet escaped the scientist; just as the feminine (*weiblich*) perception of the world
> sometimes *touches* upon the heart of the matter, while the man keeps *researching*.[65]

Feistel-Rohmeder declared that female/artistic perception was often more viable than male perception. He persisted in researching and theorizing, the male work of science; she could perceive through the layers of science's obsession with quantification to intuit the quality of the work itself. The female gaze was thus privileged; women's perceptions were superior to men's. At the same time as she made this claim, Feistel-Rohmeder grounded the superiority of her gender upon the foundations of her race. For if women could experience the world better than men, then the new German women could sense even more.

Feistel-Rohmeder next connected the female perception of the world to racial theories and art by relying upon male experts to legitimate her views. In this way, she legitimized her ideas by grounding them in the discourse of science and psychology. For example, she credited the racial theorist Hans F. K. Günther with providing the *Volk* a new science. His work emphasized the primacy of race for understanding humans and their cultures. He also argued that the Nordic race was the most civilized, the most advanced, as well as the most threatened people.[66]

In her article, Feistel-Rohmeder likened Günther's ideas about the Nordic race to a mirror which enabled the *Volk* to look at itself and its culture in a new way. The image she suggested was that of a woman contemplating her reflection in a looking glass. But rather than reflecting the *Volk*'s physical appearance, Günther's mirror enabled the Germans to look beyond mere surface appearances and consider their racial make-up. Indeed, if one peered closely enough, one's ancestors appeared neatly ordered behind the viewer within the mirror's reflection.[67] However, Feistel-Rohmeder claimed that to go so far into this kind of racial looking glass, one had to be able to 'look' like a woman. That is, one must go beyond the theories and sense the racial content, just as a woman or an artist sensed the world.

However, as some Germans attempted to catch a racial glimpse of themselves, they realized that the mirror's reflection was not always a pleasant one. According to Feistel-Rohmeder, 'the race mixing and cross breeding (*Zerkreuzung*) of the German *Volk* was revealed even to the eyes of the layman!'[68] Feistel-Rohmeder then reinforced Günther's revelations by turning to Ludwig Ferdinand Clauss and his racial psychology. He argued that race determined not only cultural production but also how a people viewed themselves and their world. In essence, all human experience was refracted through the prism of race.[69]

Building on these ideas, Feistel-Rohmeder argued that race determined biological form and psychological content. Art was an expression of both racial biology and psychology. Thus, artistic creations were physical manifestations of the race and its mental universe. Racially pure German artists necessarily painted works that gave form to German racial characteristics and values. Conversely, degenerate artists were biologically predisposed to produce paintings that reflected their racial debasement.

However, the connection between art and race did not end with the artist's creation. Citing yet another male 'expert', Feistel-Rohmeder used writings by racial scientist Friedrich Wilhelm Prinz zur Lippe to discuss the relationship between art, the viewer and race.[70] Whenever a piece of art aroused an emotional resonance in viewers, she argued, it was the correspondence between the viewers' racial self-awareness and the art's racial content that established the connection. If no sudden flash of psychic recognition or empathy was evoked in the viewers, then either the work of art was devoid of racial content (and was hence worthless, even degenerate) or the viewers themselves had become alienated from their own racial identity.[71]

Although she did not mention it in this article, Feistel-Rohmeder also relied upon Paul Schultze-Naumburg's 1928 work *Art and Race* for many of her ideas. In one infamous section of that book, for example, he compared photographs of people who suffered from physical illnesses to paintings by Expressionist artists. He claimed that such photographs proved modernist artists were drawn to diseased types, while German artists were attracted to racially healthy types.[72] Like Schultze-Naumburg, Feistel-Rohmeder made a direct correlation between the artists' and the viewer's racial heritages and their artistic productions and reactions. For example, in a 1932 article published in the *German Art Correspondence*, her cultural news service, she asked:

> How do we know if an artwork is German? That is not even the first question that we are dealing with here. Rather, [the question] is: are *you* German? That is, do you have the clear perception that everything our immortals have given us runs through you like a lively stream, that your essence cannot help but pulse and flow with this primal (*urgewaltigen*) river? If you are German in *this* way, then you do not need to ask [this question] even when you stand before a new piece of art; you already *know*![73]

The so-called experts might argue over who the German immortals were; one day it was Goethe and Schiller, the next Dürer and Rembrandt. But for Feistel-Rohmeder such intellectual uncertainty was so much nonsense. Germans who belonged to the racial community of the *Volk* had no cause for such doubts; they innately knew what was truly German.[74]

Such self-reflexivity was a central component of Feistel-Rohmeder's conception of art as well as of the *völkisch* theorists such as Günther, Clauss and Schultze-Naumburg. Art, like race, provided a point of entry to a new construction of an individual's identity. Identification with the *Volk* placed one in the German racial community. No longer alienated by the modern world, she was part of a larger history and mission. Similarly, when one looked at a painting, one saw there not only the artist's racial 'face'; the viewer also saw his or her own racial identity reflected. Painting – and culture – was thus like a mirror. If one were truly German, one connected with a purely Germanic painting. However, if the viewer identified with a modernist painting, then he was necessarily degenerate. Artistic taste was thus racially prescriptive.[75]

Racial psychology and racial science provided Feistel-Rohmeder with the criteria for evaluating the cultural worth and meaning of any work of art.[76] This science of race was based upon emotion rather than rationality. Feistel-Rohmeder hinted that the theories of Günther, Clauss and zur Lippe provided scientific legitimacy to the female gaze, to looking at art 'as a woman' and in particular as a racially aware German woman. Further, she equated the ability to recognize the racial content of art to the woman's ability to react instinctively to art. Reading a painting for racial content was coded as a female quality. In this way, she utilized gender and race to underscore the legitimacy of her own artistic expertise.

Precisely because the Germans had supposedly lost sight of their racial heritage, organizations like the German Art Society and art critics like Feistel-Rohmeder were of the utmost importance. Both contemporary German art and the *Volk* had become 'psychically rootless'.[77] As a result, examples of Nordic culture had lost their racial resonance among many Germans. People could see Nordic artifacts, Germanic architecture and German paintings, but they could no longer experience their racial content. Not until the Germans rediscovered the primacy of race and reconnected themselves to their racial heritage would the *Volk* recover its ability to perceive the true meaning of things. Such regeneration of the *Volk* lay at the heart of the entire *völkisch* enterprise and Feistel-Rohmeder's German Art Society. For her, this regeneration required the active participation of women.

When writing on the Renaissance women of Venice, Feistel-Rohmeder argued that female participation in a city's cultural renewal was crucial. Similarly, she felt that female participation in the rebirth of the German *Volk* was also absolutely necessary. These beliefs justified and legitimated her leadership of the German Art Society. Throughout 'Racial Self-Awareness' in particular and her activities on behalf of the German Art Society in general, Feistel-Rohmeder created for herself an understanding of race and art that accommodated and even privileged the female gender. For example, the 'racial gaze', first directed at Günther's mirror and then art, was coded by Feistel-Rohmeder as female. Science and men researched racial theories and placed them into an ordered system. But Feistel-Rohmeder claimed that female perception, like artistic perception, saw beyond mere appearances to behold the inner truth. She argued that if one carefully contemplated one's racial make-up or a piece of art, then he or she would be able to go beyond the surface. One would be able not just to see but to experience the connection between the individual, race and culture.

Feistel-Rohmeder's new German woman was thus provided with a central role in the Germanic renaissance. As part of the *Volk*, women were a kind of catalyst that had to be present before men could get on with the renewal of the culture. Her interpretation of gender, race and art in turn supported the power relations between men and women within the *völkisch* community. Like the Venetian women who 'dared to be all woman', the new German women were to stand beside their men and urge them to cultural greatness. At the same time, the alternative construct of the new woman, of which she was an ideal example, enabled Feistel-Rohmeder to create a place for herself within the German Art Society as well as the larger *völkisch* and later Nazi program. She might be female, but as a German-blooded woman, her gender and her racial heritage required that she go beyond traditional female roles in order to promote publicly pure German culture, and to do so as no man could.

Feistel-Rohmeder's understanding of herself as a new German woman also sheds light on her organizational tactics. From her notions of female cultural roles, she developed a strategy that guaranteed her influence within the German Art Society even as it sought other affiliations with the wider, male-dominated *völkisch* movement. Rather than leading the Society in the guise of its chairperson, she served as the organization's business manager. This position gave her a place on the Society's board of directors and made her responsible for the day-to-day affairs of the group. Through her voluminous correspondence, articles and the exhibits she organized on behalf of the German Art Society, she enlisted the support of men who had leverage within traditionalist artistic circles and the *völkisch* and Nazi movements. Thus, she cloaked her own influence within the organization by framing herself with influential men.

This framing tactic is illustrated by the German Art Society's chairmen, Eugen Friedrich Hopf and Heinrich Blume. Both had extensive contacts within the *völkisch* movement that were used to the Society's benefit. Hopf, the Society's first chairman, was a leader in the Wilhelmine-era *völkisch* movement and used his ties to the Pan-German League and the German-*völkisch* Defense League to win the Society members.[78] Blume, head of the German League, was also recognized leader within the *völkisch* community and had close ties with the NSDAP.[79] By securing the German League's affiliation with the German Art Society, Blume made it possible for Feistel-Rohmeder to publish her news service and art journal and even launch the Society's first exhibition. Other important Society members such as Hans Adolf Bühler, Ludwig Dill, Paul Schultze-Naumburg and Max Robert Gerstenhauer provided further access to the *völkisch*/Nazi community and its networks for the German Art Society.

These men 'fronted' the organization while Feistel-Rohmeder worked behind the scenes. This was a most useful tactic on several counts. The men had professional prestige and position that she, as a woman and a minor artistic talent, did not. Feistel-Rohmeder relied on their status and organizational affiliations in order to advance the Society's artists. Indeed, had Feistel-Rohmeder headed the organization it is likely that her gender would have tarnished the German

Art Society's prospects because it could have been regarded as 'only' a woman's group.

But Feistel-Rohmeder's gender was also beneficial. She was an older woman who had already raised her child and had a husband to provide a steady income. This was a supreme advantage for her and for the German Art Society she served. She could afford to be a full-time, unpaid employee for the organization. She was for all intents and purposes the Society's mother. But she was a mother who favored sons over daughters. Feistel-Rohmeder never used the Society to agitate for educational or professional reforms that would provide women greater access to artistic careers. Nor did she actively recruit women to join the Society.[80]

Feistel-Rohmeder's activism thus had its limits. But as her early life demonstrates, her ideas about German culture, art and race were very much products of Wilhelmine Germany. In addition, her background indicates the extent to which the German Art Society as well as other right-wing groups of the Weimar Republic were indebted to and even connected with the pre-war *völkisch* movement. The culture wars so associated with the republic preceded 1918, and went well beyond 1933. Feistel-Rohmeder's activism in both the republic and the Third Reich was possible because she had constructed a notion of herself as a new German woman, a role that enabled her to take on a leadership role within the largely male *völkisch* milieu.

–2–

German Art vs Weimar Culture

Scholars of the Weimar Republic have long understood that the left-wing avant-garde developed in constant tension with right-wing cultural productions. Weimar culture's vibrancy owed its edge and even its bitterness to the culture wars that characterized the period.[1] Modernists and their opponents had engaged each other repeatedly in the empire as they struggled to define the nature of German art and modernism's proper place within the *Kulturnation*.[2] The culture wars of the republic were thus a continuation of aesthetic and professional rivalries from the empire. However, these rivalries intensified after 1918 and the character of the cultural battles changed as the status of modernists and their opponents was reversed. The avant-garde, formerly cultural outsiders, had become the new insiders; although their relationship with the republic was never as smooth or as symbiotic as the Right imagined, the modernists gained new legitimacy as they entered professional institutions and their work found greater acceptance.[3] They never fully displaced the 'old guard' however, and the cultural Right, though fractured, thrived in the 1920s. But the perception was that they were the outsiders, the dispossessed heirs of a German culture now in the hands of communists, socialists and Jews.

The German Art Society demonstrates how some of the traditionalist artists turned to *völkisch* ideology and its movement to defend true German art and artists. In their view, the creation of the republic had confirmed their worst fears. The barbarians, once merely at the gates, had penetrated the sacred garden of German culture. The German Art Society understood itself as an artists' interest group devoted to the defense and promotion of racially pure artists and art. The *völkisch* concept of culture enabled Society members to stake their claims to cultural relevancy and legitimacy on the basis of their race. As racially pure Germans it was their duty to educate the public of the degenerative effects of modernist art and to reconnect the *Volk* to their native culture and hence their racial identity. Only then could Germany recover from the defeat and restore the unity of purpose so sorely lacking. From 1920 through 1929, the German Art Society established itself as a cultural leader on the Right by spinning a loose network of contacts throughout the *völkisch* movement. These *völkisch* contacts provided the Society with the means to establish itself and to launch a concerted campaign against Weimar's modernists.

Bettina Feistel-Rohmeder founded the German Art Society on 15 November 1920 in her Dresden home. She created the organization in response to the worsening economic conditions faced by traditionalist, 'pure German' artists and her belief that German art's very existence was imperiled by the republic. The art market, she believed, favored the modernists over those artists who continued to paint traditional themes in styles accessible to the layperson.[4] To defend their interests, she created the German Art Society to promote German artists and their work. In time, the group expected to establish an art journal and to hold exhibitions to further the careers of its members. Publications and exhibitions would also reconnect the German people with their cultural heritage, awaken their racial sensibilities and revitalize a nation wounded by defeat and internal enemies.[5]

In later accounts of the Society's founding, Feistel-Rohmeder claimed she was inspired by the suffering of an archetypal martyr to the cause of pure German art. In the summer of 1920, Richard Guhr, a painter and professor at the State Arts and Crafts School in Dresden, exhibited his work only to be 'scorned' by reviewers. Yet to Feistel-Rohmeder, Guhr's paintings glowed with the power of the old masters; he was 'a visionary and poet of the German people' who called for cultural regeneration. But 'the Volk did not understand him!' and the press and critics belittled his paintings 'in order to prevent an awakening of the Germans'.[6] The 'liberal press', supposedly dominated by the Jews, had no interest in promoting art which faithfully represented the essence of the Germanic character. Guhr's rejection by the art establishment illustrated the threat which the republic posed to German racial and national identity and to those artists who sought to preserve them.[7]

Feistel-Rohmeder believed that artists such as Guhr who remained true to the eternal precepts of German art were 'condemned to an ineffectual and desperate twilight existence' after 1918.[8] To defend their interests, she decided to create an organization that would promote German art and artists. But as even the Society's founding myth of Guhr's struggle reveals, the battle was about more than just style. Beneath the declarations of purity and Germanness seethed professional resentment and financial pressures. The Society's passionate defense for German art was very real, but it was also propelled by an intense bitterness over the artists' economic competition with the modernists.

It is thus important to remember that the German Art Society understood itself as an artists' interest group. As such, it responded to a series of interrelated crises that faced all German artists after the war. The art market was in the midst of a profound change. Increasingly driven by supply and demand rather than being a protected market of elite patrons, the art market experienced first a boom and then a prolonged bust. During the war and until roughly 1921, art came to be seen as a hedge against inflation. A fever of art speculation set in; prices and sales rose dramatically.[9] But not all profited, and artists became deeply suspicious of each other. Every unsuccessful artist bitterly resented his or her competitors who exploited the boom, the public who purchased tasteless works, and, increasingly, the republic who let this happen.

A deep sense of betrayal encompassed both cultural left and cultural right and drove a wedge between the two. The stylistically conservative artists charged that the only reason for which Expressionist and other 'extreme styles' were selling was that people with far too much ill-gotten wealth and too little cultural understanding were the only ones able to afford art.[10] The corollary to this was the belief that the avant-garde was opportunistically exploiting the market. Such sensationalist art was equated with 'dirty books, spicy food, intoxicating drinks and risky speculation'.[11] All very exciting, but hardly satisfying to the German soul. Accusations that the successful modernist artists were crass materialists, were alien to the *Volk*, were degenerate, Jewish, art Bolsheviks quickly followed.[12] Modernists countered that the traditionalists profited more than they did. For example, the November Group complained that artists like themselves 'who refused to make concessions to the public's tastes' were no longer able to earn even a subsistence living from their art. Instead, they were forced to take up new sidelines, as civil servants, as teachers and even as businessmen in order to make ends meet. Even modern artists charged that 'genuine artists are being psychically destroyed (*seelisch vernichtet*) by this state of affairs'.[13]

As the artists accused each other of crass materialism and impure, economic motives, their profits disappeared. Artists' expenses increased and purchasing power declined over the course of the art boom, but the inflationary spiral of 1921 to 1923 devastated the profession financially. While artists received on average three to five times more for their work in 1921 than they had in 1913, the prices of canvas, paint, and linseed oil had doubled; turpentine and paint had quintupled. In all, if the artist's materials represented 8 percent of the price of a painting in 1913, they now represented 22 percent of the price. Meanwhile, basic living expenses – heat and light, rent and food, transport and clothing – had increased 800 to 1,000 percent.[14] As the inflation worsened, sales plummeted. Prices were so high and sales were so low that many artists had to apply for economic assistance. More than 29 percent of Munich's artists applied for aid from a local artists' assistance league in 1921, compared to less than 13 percent in 1913. In Karlsruhe, the number of artists applying for aid had tripled; in Weimar, it had quadrupled.[15] Older artists in particular faced starvation yet were so humiliated by their new poverty that they refused to apply for relief.[16]

According to Fritz Hellwag, who compiled the above data for the Economic Associations of Germany's Visual Artists (*Wirtschaftlichen Verbände bildender Künstler Deutschlands*), the subsistence level of income in 1921 was 8,000 marks a year for female artists and 15,000 for male artists. In one unidentified 'leading art center', artists reported incomes that revealed fully 87.5 percent of female painters and 34.5 percent of male painters lived below subsistence levels. Hellwag explained that these figures came from a comparatively prosperous region with a strong art market; he assumed that the situation most artists faced was far worse. His figures were also based on 1921 prices and income; the hyperinflation of 1922/23 would only create greater misery.[17]

Germany's artists did attempt to organize themselves in order to represent their economic and professional interests and press the government for relief. The National Association of Germany's Visual Artists (*Reichsverband bildender Künstler Deutschlands*, the successor to the Economic Associations) was the largest such group. Out of a total estimated population of 10,000 German artists, the National Association had a membership of 6,300 artists in 1921 and as many as 9,000 in 1924.[18] Unlike most artists' groups, of which there were more than 500,[19] the National Association did not promote any one particular style. Instead, it sought to organize artists as an economic interest group. Throughout the Weimar Republic, the National Association lobbied vigorously for government support for artists.[20]

Artists, writers, musicians and composers all believed that if they could successfully organize their professions, they would be able to win the kind of support the workers' unions had won.[21] Much of their hostility toward the government was fueled by the knowledge that it offered workers wage support during the inflation. As a result, the educated classes, like the middle class as a whole, blamed the new government for protecting the working class while exploiting the middle classes. Artists protested that art could help revive the economy, enhance Germany's reputation abroad, unify the *Volk* and heal the wounds of the nation.[22] Despite such claims, however, their demands went unrealized. Even when the government belatedly funded the Emergency Society for German Art in the summer of 1923, it was too little, too late.[23]

The artists' situation was part of the much larger crisis faced by the so-called intellectual workers and middle class as a whole.[24] The new social democracy did what it could to alleviate the misery of the inflation, but the workers and very wealthy benefited from governmental assistance more than the middle ranks of society, who felt increasingly ignored and ill-used. The inflation's effect on professors, scientists, artists, authors and their universities, institutes, libraries and publishing houses was devastating.[25] There was a widespread concern that the nation's intellectual and cultural institutions, already hurt by four years of war, were being irrevocably damaged. Because national identity and culture were so inextricably bound together, many feared that nothing less than the soul of the German nation was endangered. From 1920 through 1923, Germany's artists and their supporters agitated for government support and reform.[26] But the new democracy was beset with a host of responsibilities and crises. Compared to the revolts from the Left and the Right, the Versailles Treaty, reparations and the economy, the artists' demands barely registered on the government's list of priorities. The artists' hopes that the state that would guarantee their economic survival and somehow raise them up to positions of authority in cultural matters were wholly unrealistic. As one observer noted:

> And even if there had been a Dürer or a Rembrandt sitting in the cabinet: even to them the nourishment of the people, the demobilization of the army, foreign negotiations and many other questions would have been more important than artistic problems. The new men, in particular the Social Democrats, thus completely lost the goodwill of the artists. Their initially numerous followers among the artists ... vanished to a tiny little heap.[27]

All artists were extremely disappointed that the national and state governments ignored their profession. For her part, Feistel-Rohmeder repeatedly denounced German artists' reluctance to defend themselves from the Weimar 'system'.[28] Nearly every article published by the German Art Society during the Weimar Republic emphasized that the new democracy and its art establishment served the economic needs of only the modernists.[29]

Stirred by the public's rejection of Richard Guhr and by the changes she witnessed in the art world, Feistel-Rohmeder vowed to no longer stand by passively and mutely witness the degeneration of German art. Using her father's 1916 plan to create a *völkisch* support system for artists, she invited a small circle of friends to found the German Art Society. The Society's two major objectives were to establish an art journal and host exhibitions of pure German art. Paintings and sculptures that faithfully continued the traditional precepts of the German style were to be transformed into political weapons to combat modernism and regain control over the cultural realm.[30]

Four men attended the Society's founding meeting, hosted by Feistel-Rohmeder in her home: Georg Beutel, an archivist; the teacher Richard Krause; and the painters Walter Witting and Reinhold Rehm. Soon after this meeting, Eugen Friedrich Hopf, a city health official, agreed to become the Society's chairman.[31] With these initial members, Feistel-Rohmeder established a pattern she followed throughout her career. She cultivated men whose pre-existing organizational affiliations could further the fortunes of the German Art Society. Rehm led the Dresden artists' association, the *Bund* (League). Beutel chaired the local branch of the Pan-German League and Krause led the Dresden chapter of the German-*völkisch* Defense League (*Deutschvölkischer Schutz- und Trutzbund*). Hopf was president of the Saxon Union of Military Associations and chairman of another Dresden art group, the Association of Friends of German Art. Hopf had also long been a leading member of the Pan-German League, the German-*völkisch* Defense League and had experience in coordinating cooperation between *völkisch* groups.[32] Hopf's multiple affiliations with nationalist/*völkisch* organizations made him especially valuable to the German Art Society and accounts for his position as its first chairman.

The statutes of the German Art Society made clear the importance of members' organizational and social contacts by creating two classes of members. Regular members served the Society as practitioners of the German style of art. Honorary members supported the Society's mission financially or used their social status and official positions to aid the organization. These honorary members also lent the Society a certain prestige and by 1929 they included Alfred Rosenberg, Emil Kirdorf, Max Robert Gerstenhauer and Hans F. K. Günther. Membership was by invitation only; all prospective members had to affirm their allegiance to *völkisch* precepts and their Germanic racial heritage.[33]

Despite the support of these men and their ties to the larger *völkisch* movement, the German Art Society fell apart shortly after its founding. From roughly 1921 until 1927, the organization essentially existed only in the minds of its supporters. While planning the Society's first art exhibition of pure German art, the membership split over the question of including the artist Max Liebermann in the show. Long considered the most prominent German modernist, Liebermann symbolized everything that Feistel-Rohmeder intended the Society to combat. However, some members believed that a show of contemporary German art was unthinkable without him.[34]

Feistel-Rohmeder viewed the very thought of including Liebermann as an outright betrayal of the Society's mission. She considered him a degenerate Jew who profited from the defeat of Germany. She derided those members who supported Liebermann's inclusion in the proposed Society exhibit as apostates. Members loyal to Feistel-Rohmeder's vision followed her into a kind of organizational exile as a special section of Rehm's art group, the *Bund*. Assisted as well by Hopf's Association of Friends of German Art, the Society circle exhibited together and organized visits to artists' studios, but little else was achieved for the next several years.[35]

Members later referred to this as the period during which the Society was forced to go underground, a view that reflected the organization's self-image as being under siege. Unable to combat the cultural decay of the republic, the Society retreated to the 'spiritual catacombs' and 'disappeared from public view' until 1927.[36] Throughout this period, the German Art Society continued to search for new supporters. For example, sometime before 1923, the group attempted to finance an art show with the aid of the League of Germans in Bohemia (*Bund der Deutschen in Böhmen*). The Society planned to take advantage of Germany's rampant inflation and use Czech currency, which would have been exchanged at a favorable rate for German marks, in order to finance the exhibition. However the currency reform was introduced before the financial arrangements were completed and so the Society's planned art exhibition went unrealized.[37] For Feistel-Rohmeder, the government's currency reform was just one more indication that the republic conspired against the Society and the German cultural revival.

It was only through the patronage of a national *völkisch* organization that the German Art Society succeeded in establishing a lasting organizational existence. In 1927, the German League, an intensely anti-Semitic nationalistic group, accepted the Society as a branch organization. According to Feistel-Rohmeder, Heinrich Blume, head of the German League, was responsible for securing the German League's support.[38] Blume became the new chairman of the German Art Society, thereby heading both the parent organization and its new affiliate. The German League's influence was reenforced through the Society statutes. Members of the Society's board of directors had to belong to the German League and League approval was required for all changes to the Society's statutes.[39]

Unfortunately, Feistel-Rohmeder never explained just how Blume learned of the German Art Society. However, when she remembered the Society's early years in her 1938 book, she claimed that one event drew the attention of the wider *völkisch* movement and Blume to the Society's mission: the International Art Exhibition Dresden 1926.[40] The offensive nature of this art show was so obvious to Feistel-Rohmeder that she never bothered to explicate her reaction or explain just why *völkisch* adherents would find the show so distasteful that they would turn to the German Art Society. Given that this exhibit included Society members (Richard Müller, Wolfgangmüller, Hans Hanner, and Siegfried Mackowsky) and other artists the organization approved of (Leo Samberger and Sascha Schneider), her outrage is at first glance puzzling.

The International Art Exhibition Dresden 1926 was the first international exposition held in Germany after the First World War. Saxony's cultural ministry hoped it would bring prestige to Dresden and Germany, and help revive the lackluster domestic art market. To fulfill such hopes, the best of German painting and sculpture was sought out for the show.[41] In particular, the show's organizers decided that they would highlight contemporary German painting rather than the old masters. For Feistel-Rohmeder, it was the authorities' definition of contemporary German painting that aroused her ire. In the press, two classes of German artists were consistently recognized: the traditionalists and the modernists. It horrified Feistel-Rohmeder that the press identified traditional painting as the 'older German painting' done by 'older' artists.[42] Although modernists such as Liebermann, Ernst Ludwig Kirchner, Emil Nolde and Karl Schmidt-Rottluff were the same age as some of the so-called older artists, their work was described as modern, new or young rather than as old-fashioned.[43]

Even worse, the modernists won pride of place in the German section of the show and in the press accounts. Liebermann exhibited fifteen works in a special retrospective show; Lovis Corinth was honored with fourteen works set apart in a special memorial exhibition that included his last self-portrait, *Ecce Homo*. Paula

Modersohn-Becker, Oskar Kokoschka, Max Beckmann, Max Pechstein, Paul Klee, Christian Rohlfs: they were all there, all the especial targets of the German Art Society. And what of the Society's heroes, the pure practitioners of the German style? Hans Thoma was honored with only three submissions; Wilhelm Trübner had two works shown; Adolf Menzel and Wilhelm Leibl were completely excluded. And while press reports devoted entire paragraphs to individual modernists, the 'old-style' artists were lumped together and merely listed.[44]

That all this occurred in Dresden, the home of the German Art Society, provoked Feistel-Rohmeder to act. Given her later strategies for securing assistance, the timing of Blume's support and the references she does make to the international art show in Dresden, it is likely that she used the exhibition as evidence for the collusion between the liberal press, the Jewish-run art market and the Weimar Republic directed against the pure German artist. Armed with such proof of the endangered status of racially pure art, she set out to revive the fortunes of her Society by finding equally outraged supporters. Assuming she followed her later pattern of behavior when looking for such support, Feistel-Rohmeder probably fired off a letter to Blume, outlining her organization's mission and seeking German League patronage. If Feistel-Rohmeder wrote such a letter, she would have emphasized her membership in the German League's women's section as well as her father's membership. She could even have drawn Blume's attention to her father's proposal for a *völkisch* artists' group, presented at a German League meeting.[45]

However he did learn of the organization, Blume responded and the German Art Society could not have found a better ally. Not only did he transform the Society into an affiliate of the well-established German League but he also took an active role in all Society endeavors. In later years, Blume referred to the German Art Society as 'his favorite child' and his fondness for the group never wavered.[46] The German League's adoption of the Society was consistent with the organization's practice of working through affiliated organizations specifically created to carry out political or cultural agitation.[47] For example, the League supported efforts of the *völkisch* literary historian Adolf Bartels and his organization dedicated to pure German literature. The League also sponsored a German nativist school in Bad Berka (the *Heimatschule Bad Berka*).[48] By accepting the Society as a branch organization, the German League continued its tradition of operating through affiliated groups. It now had a *völkisch* artists' interest group to promote its vision of a German culture free from all Jewish influence.

With the financial backing of the German League, the German Art Society reestablished itself as a functioning organization and immediately set out to achieve one of its most cherished goals: the creation of a *völkisch* art journal. The result was *Deutsche Bildkunst* (*German Pictorial Art*) which first appeared in early 1927 with Feistel-Rohmeder as its editor. Devoted to the promotion of the German style of painting, *Deutsche Bildkunst* represented the Society's first successful foray into the battle to defend what it viewed as true German art. Early issues of the *Deutsche Bildkunst* are extremely rare. However, if the samples located are representative, the magazine typically featured the lives and works of Society members. Feistel-Rohmeder and the other Society members who contributed articles consistently stressed the artists' ties to their native region and their constant struggle against the art establishment. Artists such as Reinhold Rehm, Elsa Munscheid and Paul Buchhorn won the magazine's praise for their loyalty to the tradition of German art and their refusal to bow to the will of art dealers and the vagaries of the newest style. Features on the approved German artists included reproductions of their work; short book reviews and accounts of members' exhibitions rounded out each issue.[49]

The journal's illustrations were designed to demonstrate by example just what the German style of art was. Most depicted paintings of landscapes and portraits, all done in a realistic style. For example, Buchhorn's *Parsifal's Homecoming* portrayed a lone knight on a weary, white horse riding toward a distant mountain. *Lost Land: Burg Persen* by Rehm depicted a craggy, wooded mountain capped by a fortress, surrounded by more mountains and a sky of billowing clouds.[50] Here was no Expressionism, no abstraction of forms or scenes of social discontent. The German style of painting was really the style approved by the empire's staid academies. But within the pages of *Deutsche Bildkunst*, such works, always paired with an article featuring the life and economic struggle of a true German artist, were transformed into expressions of the eternal essence of German art.

Despite such grandiose claims, however, *Deutsche Bildkunst*'s circle of readers was very small and the journal was by no means influential. In its first incarnation, the magazine appeared quarterly from 1927 to 1930. Printed in runs of 3,000 issues, subscribers were members of the Society and the German League. The League was the sole source of funds for *Deutsche Bildkunst*, covering the costs for paper, printing and distribution. Feistel-Rohmeder and the few other contributors worked for the magazine on a voluntary basis, receiving no pay for their efforts.[51]

As important as the *Deutsche Bildkunst* was to the German Art Society, the organization reached a much wider audience through another of its publications, the *German Art Correspondence*. The *Correspondence* was a cultural news service funded by the German League and written almost exclusively by Feistel-Rohmeder. A typescript collection of exhibition reviews, cultural criticism and Society news, the *Correspondence* was sent free of charge to roughly 100 newspapers about once a month. Feistel-Rohmeder claimed that the following periodicals newspapers used its news service: the National Socialist papers *Völkischer Beobachter* (Munich), and *Der Angriff* (Berlin); the newspapers *Niederdeutsche Zeitung*, and the *Neue Sächsische Landeszeitung* (Dresden); the German League publication, *Deutschbund-Blätter*; Ernst Jünger's *Die Kommenden*, Theodor Fritzsch's *Der*

Hammer and *Flamme* (Stuttgart). At least three foreign newspapers also used the *Correspondence*: the *Rochester Abendpost*, the *Sonntagsboten* (Pittsburgh) and the *Urwaldboten* in Brazil.[52] As these newspapers indicate, the German Art Society's cultural views found resonance in conservative, *völkisch* and National Socialist circles.

Society members' ties with *völkisch* journals and organizations played an important role in disseminating *Correspondence* articles. *Correspondence* material appeared in the newsletter of the Nazi cultural organization, the Combat League for German Culture. The Society joined the Combat League as a corporate member in early 1929,[53] and many leading Society members, including Walther Gasch, Hans Adolf Bühler and August Gebhard, were also Combat League activists. Through his position on the board of the Karlsruhe Combat League chapter, Bühler established a close friendship with Otto Wacker, editor of the local Nazi newspaper *Der Führer*. This newspaper reproduced *Correspondence* materials and published other anti-modernist articles by Gebhard and Fritz Wilkendorf and Josef August Beringer, two future German Art Society members.[54] Gasch worked on *Der Freiheitskampf*, the Nazi paper for Dresden, which used *Correspondence* articles, as did the *völkisch* journal *Die Sonne*, edited by Society members Werner Kulz and Max Robert Gerstenhauer. These periodicals and the Society's *Deutsche Bildkunst* and *German Art Correspondence* enjoyed a symbiotic relationship. The journals and newspapers reprinted articles from the *Correspondence* and the Society's art journal and news service drew its readers' attention to the other periodicals through its reviews.[55]

The *German Art Correspondence* operated as a kind of pendant to the *Deutsche Bildkunst*. While the magazine promoted those artists the Society deemed worthy of support, the *Correspondence* was reserved primarily for vicious attacks against the Society's enemies, the modernist artists and cultural administrators that it associated with the republic. Favorite targets included the artists Max Liebermann, Emil Nolde, Otto Dix and George Grosz, the museum directors Ludwig Justi of Berlin and Ernst Posse of Dresden and the staff of the Bauhaus. Through her articles and reviews, Feistel-Rohmeder accused these men of contributing to the decay of German culture.[56] She also spared no sympathy for female artists. She derided Paula Modersohn-Becker as a neither 'especially pretty nor especially gifted' artist who used her 'sex appeal' to lure men into supporting her.[57] When Käthe Kollwitz was appointed as the first woman to head the master atelier for graphic art at the Prussian Academy of Arts, Feistel-Rohmeder accused her and the academy of driving her predecessor (and honorary Society member) Ernst Moritz Geyger out of Germany altogether.[58] Although the 100 newspapers that received the news service did not always use these articles, they made it possible for the Society to reach a much wider audience than the *Deutsche Bildkunst* and popularized its cultural critique.[59]

With the aid of its publications, the fortunes of the German Art Society advanced to the point where it could finally hold its own art exhibition in 1929. The First Exhibition of Pure German Art opened on 24 May in Lübeck as part of the German League's thirty-fifth annual congress.[60] The German League paid for the show and the industrialist Emil Kirdorf also contributed funds.[61] German League luminaries lent their names and prestige to the exhibition; Blume served as the show's patron and Gerstenhauer was the honorary chairman. Framed by these men and placed in the setting of the League's national meeting, the Society presented its exhibition as the first ever *völkisch* art show.

Like the later Society exhibitions held in 1933, 1937 and 1943, the Lübeck exhibit's primary goal was to define by example what constituted German art. The ability to explain or show just what German art looked like was a perennial problem for both cultural traditionalists and *völkisch* believers. They could readily point to art that was not German – i.e., modernist art – but identifying art of the *Volk* was a much thornier problem. After all, just what constituted 'Germanness' visually? The Society's Lübeck show offered the first attempt to publicly offer an interpretation of racially pure, contemporary German art.

For the German Art Society, the first prerequisite for the Germanic style was that the artists themselves be of pure German blood. To assure such racial purity, only Society members were invited to participate.[62] In accordance with *völkisch* aesthetics, such true German artists necessarily produced art that reflected their racial identity. Thus, the 200 paintings and graphic works submitted by forty German Art Society members were 'German' due to their creators' heritage.[63] However, even Feistel-Rohmeder had to admit that there was a great deal of variation within the supposedly homogenous German style presented in the exhibition. Yet as Feistel-Rohmeder explained to her readers:

> It could not be expected, that all 40 of the artists invited would maintain the same unity and quality of style...; the very fact that we have here art from three generations, prevents this expectation. But that the belief of a spiritual commonality, surpassing all hopes, saw itself verified; that in such strength and immediacy [it] became evident, *what* German painting even today still is; how it is logically built upon the tradition of Dürer, Holbein, the Dutch, the German Romans and the romantics to Böcklin, to Leibl's circle to Trübner, that was a satisfying achievement! No one, who did not walk through this exhibit with bound eyes, could ever again ask: what exactly do you mean by German painting?[64]

Although no catalog from this show has been located, sources suggest that styles ranged from a stark realism to a soft romanticism, from works of distinction to amateurish attempts.[65] Only two works exhibited in the Lübeck show were ever described, yet they offer some further hints as to what consituted the German style. One was reportedly a self-portrait by Rehm. Seated in a 'patrician' room with a painting of a general from the Wars of Liberation behind him, Rehm depicted himself as a German man, complete with a green copy of the anti-Semitic journal *The Hammer* in his left hand. The work evoked a 'dramatic confrontation' between Rehm and his audience and was painted in a 'deeply toned, painterly' manner. It was, declared Feistel-Rohmeder, quite simply a masterpiece.[66]

In later Society literature, a painting by Richard Guhr was fondly remembered as emblematic of the exhibition. Entitled *The German Child Searches his Way*, the painting's focal point is a young, Christ-like child, surrounded by an intense darkness. Blond, with curly hair and a cherubic innocence, the Germanic child's eyes are fixed ahead and to the left. His face and torso are lit from a small glowing dish or urn, suspended by a chain. The child holds this in his right hand and he steps and reaches forward toward some unseen goal. From the dark recesses of the work loom leering, evil figures with glowing eyes that challenge the child's progess. Painted in the tradition of Böcklin's mythical/fantastic works, the child represented 'young life, the eternal-young German soul' seeking its way amidst alien, hostile forces. Such depictions of 'young, Aryan beings' finding their way in the dark, surrounded by images of Jews and death appear to have been a common theme in Guhr's work. Guhr may even have painted one work with Richard Wagner carrying such a child across some deep water, rather like an Aryan version of St Christopher carrying the Christ-child.[67]

Feistel-Rohmeder grandly predicted that art historians would one day recognize the exhibition as 'a starting point' for the creation of 'a German art consciousness'. To Society members the Lübeck exhibition represented a 'deliberate and one-sided nurturing of tradition and [the] rejection of all compromise'; it portrayed only the *German* style of contemporary painting.[68] Blume repeated this theme in his opening speech at the exhibition. For the first time in all of Germany, he declared, true German artists united to present art for the people, consciously rejecting fashionable trends in the arts.[69] The Society, added Gerstenhauer in his remarks, offered an exhibiton designed to combat the the de-Germanization (*Entdeutschung*) of culture. The German style of art was a political weapon wielded to regenerate the *Volk*.[70]

The Society heralded its achievement through the *German Art Correspondence*, sending out show reviews that appeared in *völkisch* and National Socialist newspapers.[71] Feistel-Rohmeder also reviewed the show in the most glowing terms in *Deutsche Bildkunst*. There, she compared the exhibition to a spring stroll through a fresh, newly green landscape after a 'long, miserable winter'.[72] Finally, a show of real German art could speak to the people and promote the true artists of Germany. Like seeds strewn across the German soil, true German art would take root and flourish, reuniting the people with their native culture.[73]

According to Feistel-Rohmeder the exhibition sparked a spirited debate in the Lübeck press, to the point that the show remained opened longer than planned. She claimed the critic A. B. Enns' hostile reviews of the show in Lübeck newspapers were key in bringing the exhibit to the public's attention and typical of her opponents' views.[74] Enns ridiculed the very notion of a singular German art and emphasized the lack of stylistic coherence and quality. In his view, the few decent paintings exhibited in Lübeck were completely overwhelmed by the wild profusion of 'unart'. Far from illustrating anything Germanic, Enns proclaimed that the Society's art revealed 'narrowness of feeling, a hostile sense of nature, superficiality, bombast and technical incompetence... The artistic as well as the national is served up here in a mixture which is not only distasteful' but also completely misunderstood both art and nationality.[75] However, despite (or indeed because of) such harsh criticism, the German Art Society believed it had scored a real success. For its members, the exhibit symbolized the increasing vigor of the German Art Society in 1929.

By the time of the First Exhibition of Pure German Art, the German Art Society had begun to forge organizational ties with *völkisch* organizations. Its vision of German art and its critique of modernism appealed to a variety of anti-modernists ranging from nationalists to *völkisch* adherents and National Socialists. However, the Society's contact with the wider *völkisch* movement remained largely informal, relying on its members' roles in other groups. For example, through its leadership, the German Art Society had ties to at least nine other *völkisch* groups. In 1929, the board of directors consisted of Blume (chairman); the artist Ludwig Dill (second chairman); Feistel-Rohmeder (business manager); and Paul Fritzsche (treasurer). Countess Bettina von Arnim auf Krebstein, the author Wilhelm Kotzde-Kottenrodt, Eugen Schilken, Georg Beutel and the artist Wolfgang Müller (aka Wolfgangmüller) also belonged to the board.[76] As required by the Society's statutes, all were members of the German League. In addition, these board members belonged to: the Stahlhelm; the SA; the National Socialist Teachers' League; the NSDAP; the Combat League for German Culture; the German-*völkisch* Defense League; and the Pan-German League.[77]

This pattern of shared memberships with other *völkisch* and Nazi organizations was repeated in the German Art Society's rank and file. In 1929, the Society had 100 individual members and 13,827 corporate members, that is, people who belonged to organizations that had joined the Society. Corporate members included eight chapters of the German League and the *Junglandbund*, a nationalist youth association.[78] But aside from these corporate members, individual members belonged to and even led a variety of other right-wing organizations. In the absence of detailed membership records, tracing individuals' affiliations with other groups is extremely difficult. However, the German Art Society often noted members' affiliations, occupations and geographic locations in articles, exhibition catalogs and announcements published in the *German Art Correspondence*. Using such sources, it is possible to construct a profile of 100 members of the German Art

Table 2.1 German Art Society Core Members' Organizational Affiliations

Combat League for German Culture	19
German League	19
Other *Völkisch* Associations	18
NSDAP	17
Other Artist Associations	13
Total Number of Affiliations	86

Society who joined before 1933 (46 joined before 1930). These members served in leadership positions, exhibited in Society art shows and remained active well into the Third Reich. Thus, these 94 men and 6 women can be considered the core membership of the Society.[79]

Table 2.1 illustrates both the variety and the number of organizational affiliations held by the German Art Society's core members. These memberships in other groups demonstrate the vital importance of organizational networks and personal contacts that sustained the *völkisch* movement in general and the German Art Society in particular. Each shared membership represented an opportunity for the Society to promote its cultural mission. The Society's strongest ties were with the German League, the parent organization. It also had strong connections to the National Socialists, through membership in either the Nazi Party or the Combat League for German Culture. Often, Society members belonged to the same local Combat League chapter. For example, the Munich, Karlsruhe and Dresden chapters had three, four, and five core German Art Society members respectively.[80]

The Society also attracted members who belonged to other artist associations. The Society's early ties to Dresden art organizations were reflected by members' affiliations with the *Bund*, the Free German Theater Committee and the Association of Friends of German Art. Members also belonged to the Munich *Bund*, the National Association of Germany's Visual Artists, the architectural association the *Block* and the Front Soldiers' League of Visual Artists (*Frontkämpferbund bildender Künstler*). Of these, only the National Association was not a *völkisch* organization.

Table 2.1 also indicates the number of German Art Society connections to other *völkisch* groups. Members belonged to the Pan-German League; the Eagles and Falcons, a right-wing youth group affiliated with the German League; the German-*völkisch* Defense League, the *völkisch* poet Georg Stammler's *Werkland* Circle; the Nordic Ring; the Society for Germandom Abroad (*Verband für das Deutschtum im Ausland*); the National Socialist Teachers' League; and patriotic leagues. These extensive ties with the larger *völkisch* movement enabled the Society to disseminate its message and, eventually, to build a base of support for its mission.

Table 2.2 German Art Society Core Members' Occupations

Artists	60
Professors	18
Teachers	7
Writers/Editors	6
Other Civil Servants	6
Nobility	3

In terms of members' occupations, the vast majority were artists and art educators who felt that the republic's acceptance of cultural modernism threatened both the art they favored and their claims to cultural expertise. As Table 2.2 shows, the predominance of artists (painters, graphic designers, sculptors) reflects the Society's mission as an artists' interest group.[81] According to the Society's art journal, these artists became members for several reasons. First and foremost, they were 'German-blooded' (*deutschblütige*) practitioners of the 'German style' dedicated to the *völkisch* cause.[82] They believed that their racial purity entitled them to determine the proper course for the arts in Germany. Moreover, articles and personal testimonies of Society members indicate a high degree of perceived oppression under the Weimar Republic. Feistel-Rohmeder and the other contributors to Society publications consistently emphasized that these contemporary German masters were scorned by the art establishment, supposedly dominated by Jews in league with the alien republic.[83]

While certainly not all German artists held the Jews and the republic responsible for their economic plight, many did view the artistic profession with a sense of pessimism and gloom. Data on the economic position of artists in the Weimar Republic remain fragmentary, but among artists there was a consensus that there were simply too many painters, sculptors and the like for the market to support.[84] Competition for sales, recognition and teaching positions was intense. Even during the republic's relatively prosperous years, organizations such as the Economic Association of Visual Artists, Southwest Germany *(Wirtschaftlicher Verband bildender Künstler Südwestdeutschlands E.V.*, which became part of the National Association of Germany's Visual Artists) complained consistently about the lack of state support for and understanding of artists' economic situation. In February 1926, for example, the Economic Association hosted an emergency meeting in Baden. State and municipal authorities joined representatives of Baden's artists (including Bühler and Gebhard) and the press in a three-hour discussion of the profession's dire economic straits. As a result, the state's budget to assist destitute artists increased from 10,000 to 30,000 marks. These funds were used to purchase works by local artists.[85]

The use of state monies to acquire paintings by living German artists was one way the government supported artists. State funds also provided small loans to indigent artists.[86] Yet, even taken together, these measures were not enough to alleviate the misery of numerous artists. A pervasive sense of dwindling fortunes and deep pessimism permeated the artistic community. While quantifying the economic decline of the artists lies beyond this study, a qualitative perception of doom resonates in the sources. For example, articles in the National Association of Germany's Visual Artists' journal *Art and Economy* (*Kunst und Wirtschaft*) in 1927 described the arts as a 'dying profession' whose members suffered from an 'epidemic' of pessimism.[87] Worn out by dissillusion, the artists complained of lack of success and state protection. Certainly, the fear that true German artists could no longer compete and make a decent living in the republic's art market drove the creation and growth of the German Art Society. But other artists, even modernists who the Society assumed were profiting, were also deeply troubled by a market glutted with artists, academies filled with eager students about to enter the art market and the general inability to prosper.

Too many artists chasing too few professional posts, teaching positions, state commissions and private consumers had been problems during the Wilhelmine Empire as well. But under the Kaiser, modernist artists were excluded from most avenues of official support. The traditionalist painters and sculptors were virtually guaranteed a protected market.[88] Most German Art Society members had been trained during the Wilhelmine era.[89] As young German artists, they had expected that at the very least their status, prestige and professional prospects would be protected from most competition with the modernists.

But after 1918, such state-sponsored protection was lost even as the ability of the state to support its artists contracted. To Society members, who had entered the art academies expecting to be protected from competition with the modernists, the 'new' competition for resources did not take place on an even playing field. From the art boom, to the inflation, through the 1920s, members were convinced that the republic skewed their chances for success by favoring modernist artists.[90] Thus, artists were generally bitter about their financial situation and wanted both the state and national governments to increase financial aid to artists and to address the needs of their profession. But the German Art Society believed it had an exclusive axe to grind.

The German Art Society behaved as if its artists alone suffered. The group advocated the idea that members suffered not just because they were artists, but because they were a particular kind of artist: artists who recognized the primacy of race, tradition and the German style of painting. Members of the Society believed that they were singled out for mistreatment by the art establishment. In sum, they were not merely miserable, they were persecuted. They blamed their relative poverty and lack of success on the modernist bias shared by the government and the art market, both supposedly run by Jews.[91] The Society provided its members a like-minded community with which they could commiserate, an identifiable enemy (or better yet, enemies) and a coherent plan of action that addressed their professional dissatisfaction.

Ironically, despite members' perceptions of oppression under the republic, many were in fact very successful artists who benefited from the very regime they despised. August Gebhard, for example, was paid unusually well for a painting sold to the Karlsruhe music academy.[92] Professor Richard Müller of Dresden received 9,000 marks when the state of Saxony purchased a painting exhibited at the International Art Exhibit Dresden 1926, the show castigated by Feistel-Rohmeder for its modernist bias.[93]

Additionally, as Table 2.2 reveals, at least eighteen German Art Society members were employed as professors. These men were not ignored by either the government who employed them or the art establishment, of which they were very much a part. Society professors whose affiliations are known taught at leading art academies: four at the Dresden academy; four at the academy in Munich; two at the academy in Karlsruhe; and one each at art academies in Weimar and Berlin. As professors, members such as Bühler, Ludwig Dill, Hermann Groeber and Richard Müller served on juries for state- and city-sponsored exhibitions, thereby having a voice in whose works were shown, rewarded and even purchased for government offices and museums. Art professors also advised state cultural ministries on artistic matters such as nominations to museum directorships, professorships and commissions to decorate public buildings.[94] Those Society members employed as art professors fulfilled all of these tasks over the years; they educated generations of students and won awards, commissions and sales contracts from state ministries. Despite the Society's claims to the contrary, neither the republic nor the art market had marginalized its professor-members; instead, they now shared their influence with their modernist colleagues. And in the eyes of the German Art Society, that was precisely the problem.

Society professors bitterly resented sharing studio space with their pro-modernist colleagues, and believed that art education had been infiltrated by degenerates. They feared that their modernist colleagues held greater appeal to the art-buying public, the critics and students. This was particularly dangerous because professors such as Otto Dix 'corrupted' students into believing that 'perversion was art'. As Feistel-Rohmeder noted, such seduction of the nation's youth was enough to make any mother cry.[95] The Society professors feared that the meaning of their social and professional status was being devalued by the entry of the modernists into the art academies.[96] For instance, when Ernst Moritz Geyger lost his position at the Prussian Academy of Arts to Käthe Kollwitz, he wrote that it was better to feed pigs in Italy than hope for artistic recognition in Germany.[97]

The other German Art Society members who held civil-service jobs shared the professors' cultural fears and professional pessimism. Like the professors, the Society's teachers and the other civil servants owed their jobs to the republic. In rank, the teachers ranged from lower-level instructors to school principals, typically in elementary schools. The other civil servants described in Table 2.2 include city officials (*Stadträte*) and officials in state education and cultural ministries. Taken together, the Society members employed as art professors, teachers, and state and city officials offer yet another example of the prevalence of anti-democratic elements employed in the republic's institutions.

Even the *völkisch* authors and editors who joined the Society found a niche in the Weimar Republic. They included Gerstenhauer and Kulz, editors of *Die Sonne*; author Wilhelm Kotzde-Kottenrodt; and poet Georg Stammler. Stammler and Kotzde-Kottenrodt also had their own organizations.[98] Despite their claims to the contrary, these German Art Society members, like the artists and professors, were very much a part of the cultural life of the Weimar Republic. However, their *völkisch* views and their aesthetic system encouraged an antagonistic relationship with the republic and 'its' modernist culture.

Besides sharing a sense of alienation and professional frustration, these 100 core Society members also formed an apparently close-knit circle of friendship and sociability. As Table 2.3 reflects, members were clustered in Dresden, Munich, Karlsruhe, Berlin and several other cities.

Table 2.3 Geographic Concentration of German Art Society Core Members

Dresden	27
Munich	12
Berlin	9
Karlsruhe	6
Brunswick	5
Weimar	4
Freiburg iB	3
Other[a]	34

[a] Concentrations of 2 or fewer members and unknown residence

In Dresden, the Society's home, members knew each other well because most had joined in the early 1920s, during the so-called underground period. In Munich, Society members Ernst Emil Heinsdorff, Karl Alexander Flügel and Anton Rausch all belonged to the local artists' group the *Bund*.[99] Flügel, Heinsdorff, Rudolf Scheller and Siegfried Czerny formed a circle of friendship around the painter Edmund Steppes.[100] The strength of the Society outside of Berlin, the cultural mecca of the Weimar Republic, offers yet another indication of the members' sense of alienation. Before 1918, the arts in Germany were very decentralized. Munich, Dresden, Karlsruhe and Weimar all had excellent art academies and vibrant artistic traditions. After 1918, Berlin eclipsed these provincial art centers; for anti-modernists, the capital represented all that was wrong with Germany.[101] Members of the Society were thus more likely to live far from Berlin and to identify with the artistic traditions of their cities and regions rather than the republic.

Society friendships also extended beyond their hometowns. For example, core members Stammler, Kotzde-Kottenrodt, Gerstenhauer and Society supporter Adolf Bartels met regularly at Theodor Scheffer's German nativist school at Bad Berka (Scheffer was also a core member); Stammler even taught there.[102] Some Society friendships may also have formed during training at the academies. Of the thirty-three core members whose educational background have been determined, eight attended the Munich art academy, nine the Karlsruhe academy and six the Dresden academy, all at roughly the same time. There were also at least twenty Society members who shared teacher-student relationships. Bühler, Gebhard, Heinsdorff, Czerny and Hans Schroedter studied under Hans Thoma, the painter the Society regarded as a German master. Arthur Bär, Gasch and Siebert studied with Richard Müller; Alois Brunner with Ferdinand Barth; Hermann Tiebert with Bühler. Müller and Emil Hoegg were colleagues at the academy in Dresden, as were Barth and Hermann Groeber in Munich. In Dresden, Franz Hochmann worked at Guido Richter's art school and taught Munscheid and Rehm there.[103] Members even came from the same family; Ludwig Dill and his wife Johanna Dill-Marburg, and the brothers Ernst and Hubert Haider.

As the number and variety of the members' organizational, professional and personal affiliations illustrate, culture on the Right thrived throughout the Weimar period. Through its members and its association with the German League, the German Art Society was clearly a part of the much larger *völkisch* movement. Hostile to the Weimar Republic, the Society's members banded together to defend their claims to artistic legitimacy and cultural leadership. As both pure Germans and members of the educated middle class, they believed that they had the right and the ability to determine just what constituted German art. In their view, it did not matter that the Weimar Republic offered a culture that could accommodate aesthetic modernism and the more traditional styles. Their belief in *völkisch* precepts and racism necessarily condemned the republican form of government and modernity in all its forms, especially in the arts.

By 1929, the German Art Society had successfully established itself as an independent organization with its own art journal and news service, and even its own exhibition. Although its members perceived themselves as victims of a republic that refused to acknowledge their talents, they were actually quite successful and many participated in state artistic institutions like the academies, public schools and state ministries. Yet they perceived themselves as outsiders, derided and exploited by the republic. The German Art Society offered its members a forum through which they could assert their claims to cultural expertise. On both racial and artistic grounds, members argued that they were the legitimate arbiters and producers of the one and only true German culture. Through *Deutsche Bildkunst*, the *German Art Correspondence* and the Society's first exhibition, its artists proclaimed their right to combat the modernists who had usurped the throne from its rightful heirs. From 1920 until 1929, however, such claims to cultural hegemony circulated primarily among the small community of Society members. As important as the Society's affiliations with other *völkisch* organizations were, these ties remained informal, consisting of members' affiliations with *völkisch*, artist, and special-interest organizations. To truly reclaim their cultural authority, the German Art Society's members would have to develop a strategy that would expand their movement and forge an even stronger network of supporters.

–3–

The German Art Society, the *Völkisch* Movement and National Socialism

Throughout the last years of the Weimar Republic, the German Art Society continued to forge its network of *völkisch* alliances through its membership and publications. In 1929, the Society formalized its *völkisch* alliances by creating the Executive Council of United German Art and Culture Associations (*Führerrat der vereinigten Deutschen Kunst- und Kulturverbände*). This group positioned the Society as a leader of what Bettina Feistel-Rohmeder called 'the art-defense movement'.[1] Responding to the ever-fractured nature of the *völkisch* movement, the Executive Council sought to become the umbrella organization that would unify anti-modernist forces on the Right. At the same time, the Executive Council became a vehicle which brought its members and the German Art Society into the National Socialist movement. These connections with the wider *völkisch* movement and the Nazis enabled the Society to thrive during the last years of the Weimar Republic. Especially after 1930, the German Art Society strengthened its ties to the NSDAP in the hope that the Nazi political victory would pave the way for the cultural renaissance the Society envisioned, and intended to lead.[2]

The first step toward assuming this leadership role came in the form of a letter to President Paul von Hindenburg. In late 1928, the German Art Society and six other groups wrote Hindenburg to ask that he reconsider his support for modernist art exhibitions. In particular, the signatories protested the president's willingness to allow himself to be designated as the official patron of the First International Art Exhibition Dresden 1926 and German Art Düsseldorf 1928.[3] The six signatories (and the organizations they represented) were: Heinrich Blume (German Art Society); Eugen Friedrich Hopf (Friends of German Art, Dresden); Max Robert Gerstenhauer (German League); Paul Schultze-Naumburg (the architectural association the *Block*); Guida Diehl (the German Women's Combat League and the Newland Movement); and Professor Malguth (League of *Völkisch* Teachers). In all, they claimed to represent the views of some 10,000 men and women.[4]

The signatories declared that by lending his name to 'modernist' art shows, President von Hindenburg unwittingly supported the destruction of German culture. In making this charge, they drew his attention to three effects modernist exhibitions had upon both German culture and the public. First, they claimed, modernist art denied and defamed the 'German ideal of beauty'.[5] Rather than painting ideal forms, artists such as Emil Nolde and Ernst Ludwig Kirchner distorted the human figure, using degenerates as their models. To add a professional air to this critique, they directly referred to Paul Schultze-Naumburg's book *Art and Race*, thereby 'proving' their claim that modernist artists depicted physically deformed and mentally ill persons.[6]

Second, they claimed that the paintings portrayed base sexual practices, brothels and prostitutes as if these were legitimate topics for art. A proper sense of shame, family values and the honor of decent German men and women were sullied by the exhibition of such works. Finally, the signatories argued that the art exhibited consciously sought to denigrate the honor of all Germans through its horrific and insulting pictures of German soldiers and veterans as crippled and impoverished men.[7] In the name of the German people, the seven groups appealed to Hindenburg to distance himself from such cultural decay and to support true German artists.[8]

The president's office tersely responded that it did not share the signatories' view that Hindenburg's name had been misused through association with the exhibitions.[9] However, the protest letter represented a crucial advance for the German Art Society. For the first time, the Society had won active support from numerous *völkisch* groups. Although this protest did not succeed – or indeed, because it did not – the Society felt that it was time to try a new tactic.

In early 1929, after the Hindenburg letter was published in the *German Art Correspondence*,[10] the German Art Society invited the signatories and other *völkisch* associations to come together in an umbrella group that would unite elements sympathetic to the German Art Society's cultural battle. On 10 March 1929, the Executive Council of United German Art and Culture Associations met for the first time.[11] The Executive Council was a union of *völkisch* groups that provided a forum for cooperation between organizations concerned for the health of German culture. Only organizations (rather than individuals) that supported the *völkisch* worldview, rejected 'the influence of alien (*unvölkische*) powers in German cultural life' and accepted only racially pure (*deutschblütige*) members could join.[12] Like the German Art Society, such groups believed that the regeneration of the German people and state could best be achieved through a revitalization of the *Volk* and its culture. By pulling together their resources and acting in concert, members of the Executive Council hoped to produce an art magazine and sponsor an art exhibition, thereby paving the way for a *völkisch* renaissance. For its part, the German Art Society created this umbrella organization as a means by which it could fulfill its own cultural mission while simultaneously establishing Society members as leaders on the cultural Right.

While historians have long recognized the Executive Council's role in uniting a variety of *völkisch* organizations devoted to the defense of German culture, they have missed the dominant role played by the German Art Society within the Council.[13] The German Art Society sent out the invitations for the first meeting of the then-unnamed umbrella group.[14] At the founding meeting, the Society shaped the Council's statutes and bylaws to ensure its control over the new association. The Executive Council adopted the Society's exhibition guidelines as its own, and the statutes of both groups were virtually identical.[15] The Society also made sure it governed the Council's board of directors: the Society's chairman, business manager and treasurer (Heinrich Blume, Bettina Feistel-Rohmeder and Paul Fritzsche, respectively) served the same functions in the Executive Council.

German Art Society dominance continued at the committee level as well. Society board members were to be active in the Executive Council's exhibition, art journal and artists' assistance committees 'in sufficient numbers'.[16] Only an honorary or board member of the Society could chair the exhibition committee.[17] All Executive Council committee decisions were subject to final, unanimous approval of the Society's board of directors.[18] Not only did the German Art Society have effective control over the Council but the Council also adopted the Society's goals as its own: to sponsor a purely German art exhibition; to found a *völkisch* art magazine; and to defend German artists and art against the poisonous influence of alien art forms.[19] In essence, the Executive Council represented an expansion and formalization of the German Art Society's *völkisch* network.

From March 1929 until 1932, the bulk of the German Art Society's work was accomplished within the framework of this new organization.[20] Feistel-Rohmeder justified the Society's dominance within the Executive Council by claiming that as 'the only art experts' organization (*Fachorganisation*) in greater Germany based on *völkisch* principles', the German Art Society and its members had proven, professional credentials and experience.[21] By forging a *völkisch* alliance, the German Art Society became a national organization and used its new contacts to achieve its objectives. At the same time, the Executive Council enabled the Society to strengthen its claim to possess artistic expertise and hence cultural legitimacy.

At the first meeting of the Executive Council, held in Weimar, a combination of groups formerly affiliated with the German Art Society joined newcomers to the art-defense movement. The Society's old friends, the German League and two Dresden artists' groups, the *Bund* and the Association of Friends of German Art, were all founding members. The other Council organizations included three more signatories of the protest letter sent to Hindenburg a few months before: the *Block*, the League of *Völkisch* Teachers and the German Women's Combat League. Also present were representatives from the Nordic Ring and the Ring of Black Houses (*Schwarzhäuser Ring*). Alfred Hugenberg's cultural organization, the Defense League for the Intellectual Property of Germany, was unable to attend but sent its best wishes.[22] The Dresden, Karlsruhe and Weimar chapters of the Combat

League for German Culture also joined the Executive Council. Within the year, six other organizations became part of the Executive Council: the Eagles and Falcons, a youth group affiliated with the German League; the Berlin Association Germandom in Art (*Verein Deutschtum in der Kunst*); the Karlsruhe chapter of the Bayreuth League of German Youth; the German school (*Deutsche Heimatschule*) at Bad Berka, also affiliated with the German League;[23] the poet Georg Stammler's *Werkland* Circle; and the Dresden Free German Theater Committee. In all, at least eighteen *völkisch* organizations joined the Executive Council.[24] In early 1931, Feistel-Rohmeder claimed that the Council comprised nearly 250,000 people.[25]

Cultural, political and economic considerations all played a role in bringing these organizations to the Executive Council. As part of the *völkisch* movement, all of the Council members shared the German Art Society's anti-Semitism, racial ideology and abiding concern for German cultural purity. By allying with the Council, the other organizations maintained their individuality while creating a unified force against artistic degeneracy and the democracy which supposedly made it possible. Indeed, throughout the wider *völkisch* movement there was a sense of urgency in the late 1920s as more right-wing groups, including the National Socialists, searched for common ground upon which they could rally to bring down the Weimar Republic. This renewed impetus to overcome the inherently fractured nature of the *völkisch* movement may well have been sparked by the elections of 1928.

While the Weimar Republic has been regarded as doomed to fail, contemporaries in 1928 did not know that the depression, the ensuing political gridlock and parliamentary breakdown were just a few years away. In 1928, the democracy appeared to be succeeding. The May elections represented a victory for the political parties most closely associated with the Weimar Republic. The success of the Great Coalition of the SPD (which won an impressive 29.8 percent of the vote), 'Center, BVP, DDP, and DVP' severely disappointed the German Right.[26] The *Völkisch*-National Block failed to win a single Reichstag seat; the NSDAP garnered only 2.6 percent of the vote, despite a concerted propaganda campaign.[27] Although Feistel-Rohmeder and the Society left no record of their reaction, the elections appear to have spurred forces of the Right to greater action and cooperation. For example, shortly after the elections, Feistel-Rohmeder noted in the *German Art Correspondence* that more organizations had been established to rescue German art.[28] The Executive Council of United German Art and Culture Associations was an expression of a renewed impetus to encourage cooperation between *völkisch* groups.

Certainly the 1928 elections had a important effect on the National Socialist movement. After the elections, Adolf Hitler reconsidered his strategy to focus upon urban centers and woo the workers with his brand of socialism. Recognizing that the 'success of the Left and the weakening of the bourgeois parties offered the

NSDAP the opportunity' to consolidate nationalist, *völkisch* and other disenchanted middle-class voters, Hitler and the National Socialists changed tactics. The more socialistic appeals were dropped or toned down while the NSDAP placed new emphasis upon a 'more traditional, conservative, and nationalistic' propaganda line.[29] As the message was increasingly refined, new special-interest groups were formed to attract future votes from the bourgeoisie. Between October 1928 and November 1929, the Nazis created the Association of National Socialist German Lawyers, the National Socialist Association of Doctors and the National Socialist League of Students. At the same time, the Hitler Youth redirected its efforts away from winning over worker youth to attracting middle-class boys.[30]

To recruit members of the educated and propertied middle classes, the Nazis also began to exploit the potential of the cultural wars of the Weimar Republic. The Combat League for German Culture, proposed in 1927, became a primary tool for the Nazis to 'penetrate the German upper bourgeoisie more effectively'.[31] Officially a non-party organization, the Combat League offered a way to support cultural anti-modernism without joining the National Socialists. Once in the Combat League, however, the artists, intellectuals and art lovers learned more about the Nazi movement and were encouraged to join or support the NSDAP. In this way the Combat League served as an intermediary between middle-class Germans with culturally conservative/*völkisch* views and the Nazi Party. Across Germany, local chapters held meetings, sponsored lectures and encouraged individuals to join its struggle against the 'cultural decadence' of the republic and for the *völkisch* 'connection between race, art, and science'.[32] While it sought individual members, the Combat League also invited whole organizations to join, preparing for the eventual absorption of entire groups into itself and the Nazi movement.[33]

Although the Executive Council did not itself become a corporate member of the Combat League, it did increase contact between the German Art Society and the Nazi group. The Society became a corporate member, as did other Executive Council groups, including the German League, the Bayreuth League, the Eagles and Falcons, the *Bund* and the Nordic Ring.[34] Society/Executive Council officers Walther Gasch and Hans Adolf Bühler led local Combat League chapters in Dresden and Karlsruhe; in turn, those chapters joined the Council as did the Combat League's Weimar chapter.[35] In June 1930, the German Art Society and five other members of the Executive Council participated in the Combat League's congress held in Weimar.[36]

The relationship between the local Combat League chapters and the Executive Council was thus a symbiotic one. Both groups believed they could use the other to spread their message and bolster their ranks. The National Socialists realized the potential cultural issues offered in attracting the interest and votes of the middle classes. By cooperating with other *völkisch* groups through the Combat

League, the Nazis sought to win new converts to their cause even as National Socialists assumed leadership of the wider *völkisch* movement.[37] For their part, the Executive Council and the German Art Society hoped to win Nazi support for their cultural mission. Just as Nazis sought to use groups like the Executive Council to advance their political goals, the Society thought it could use National Socialism to achieve its cultural aims. The Executive Council thus offered a perfect forum for both *völkisch* adherents and committed National Socialists.

Economics also played an important role in encouraging groups to join the Executive Council. Although established before the Great Depression hit Germany, the economic crisis encouraged the continued cooperation between *völkisch* groups that made the Council possible. By combining their efforts, *völkisch* organizations could better utilize the resources available to them. Moreover, for the supporters of the German Art Society and the Council, the depression brought the cultural crisis into sharper relief. Many anti-modernists had long argued that the state and the art market favored modernist artists, leaving the *völkisch* artists with at best a precarious existence. Now, the depression threatened to push the true German artists over the edge; they simply would not survive and the last defenders of German culture would disappear. More than anything else, the depression made the defense of true German art a necessity for those groups that believed German culture was both the source and expression of German national/racial identity.

Economics accounted for the participation of *völkisch* artists' associations in the Executive Council, too. Few artists even in the best of times earned a steady income from art sales and teaching, and the ranks of impoverished artists, often referred to as the art proletariat, swelled throughout the Weimar Republic.[38] As the economic crisis worsened and Chancellor Brüning's deflationary policies eliminated state subsidies to artists and art groups, artists' economic situation deteriorated rapidly. 'The Reich, state and local governments severely curtailed or altogether eliminated many of the grant programs that had provided a modicum of support to thousands of artists.'[39] As potential buyers were hit by the depression, the private art market shrank and prices for paintings dropped to alarming levels. As historian Alan E. Steinweis has explained, '[u]nemployment rates among artists climbed higher than those affecting most other branches of the economy. However, artists constituted less than 1 percent of the total unemployed and therefore lacked a strong political voice.'[40] By joining the Executive Council, *völkisch* groups who feared for the plight of German artists and culture could contribute to their defense.

Feistel-Rohmeder also did her part to castigate publicly the government's inability to manage the crisis and to voice the artists' growing insecurity, fear and suspicion. Her articles in the *German Art Correspondence* (or the *German Art Report* as it was renamed in 1932) resonated with a growing sense of panic over the precarious financial and professional lives of German artists. Although modern artists were just as hard hit by the depression, Feistel-Rohmeder was convinced that her beloved contemporary German artists suffered more profoundly. Through the *German Art Report*, she informed Council and Society members as well as the general public about the republic's failure to safeguard contemporary German culture. The conditions she described help to account for other pro-German cultural associations' decision to work with the Council rather than relying solely upon government support or just hoping for an economic recovery.

For example, in January 1931, Feistel-Rohmeder noted that the National Association of Germany's Visual Artists received 40,000 RM to assist destitute artists; the authorities claimed they could offer no more. She then identified 30,000 RM allocated to the art historical institute in Florence and 10,000 RM to a library in Rome, an institution started by a Jew, she claimed. Surely such funds would be better spent in Germany.[41] In February and April, she pointed to the government's financial support for the German Art Community (*Deutsche Kunstgemeinschaft*). A 'pro-modernist' artists' interest group based in Berlin, it had so far received 'half a million' marks from the government.[42] The German Art Community used at least some of this money to purchase art and thus support artists. Feistel-Rohmeder noted that most of the funds went to Berlin artists and everyone knew, she insinuated snidely, just what kind of artists lived in Berlin. Nor did such offenses occur only in the republic's capital. In November 1931, Dresden's Ernst Arnold Gallery sold a painting by Oskar Kokoschka for 600 marks; the same gallery sold drawings by two 'German' artists for 100 to 160 marks.[43]

With each passing month, Feistel-Rohmeder's attacks became more rancorous. In a March 1932 *German Art Report* article, she reported that in Berlin an art dealer offered artists a mere 22 to 64 marks (or 5 to 15 dollars) for copies of seventeenth-century English paintings. Yet another dealer offered 20 marks for oil paintings of roughly 27 x 36 inches. Such shameless exploitation of artists' desperation by foreign, blood-sucking art dealers was just another indication of how the republic failed to protect its most creative members, fumed Feistel-Rohmeder. To underscore her point, she indignantly noted that Ludwig Justi, the Berlin National Gallery's director, sought to purchase a painting by Vincent van Gogh for 249,000 RM. Rather than pay such enormous sums of money for a painting by a deceased 'French' painter, Feistel-Rohmeder demanded that the funds be used to support living, contemporary (as opposed to modernist) German artists. Many artists were outraged by this purchase, including the 2,300 members of the National Association of Germany's Visual Artists in the Munich region.[44] But even this national artists' interest group could not save itself from the depression. In October 1932, the National Association briefly suspended publication of its official organ, *Art and Economy* (*Kunst und Wirtschaft*), due to lack of funds.[45] But Feistel-Rohmeder and the German Art Society continued their campaign against the modernists and the republic.

The Executive Council was created for precisely this purpose. At the very first meeting, Feistel-Rohmeder had declared that the Council, 'armed with expertise and the power of numbers, will be in the position to represent effectively the interests of the German visual arts from *both within and without*'.[46] This dichotomy, from within and without, was repeatedly used by Feistel-Rohmeder to identify two of the main tasks required for the defense of German culture. She believed alien powers existed outside of the German community; they were intent upon poisoning the *Volk*'s culture through the promotion of a people-less (*volkslosen*) art. These outsiders had to be confronted with a force from within the German community; *völkisch* 'insiders' who could both represent and regenerate the arts. The Executive Council of United German Art and Culture Associations would pull together these insiders and become an institution to battle for the defense of the *Volk* and its culture.

According to Feistel-Rohmeder and the other Council members, the *Volk* was surrounded by hostile, alien forces bent on its destruction. But within the German community itself all was not well. Distracted by the outsiders, the *Volk* had lost contact with its cultural heritage and required cultural reeducation. This could be achieved by bringing the German community into contact with pure German art and artists through an art magazine and exhibitions. Then the healing process would begin; the German community would be regenerated and recognize itself as a powerful force. Once the *Volk* awakened from its numb slumber, the German arts, and the members of the German Art Society, would prosper once again.[47] To this end, the Executive Council devoted itself exclusively to the promotion of pure German art. 'From within and without, all powers, who work [in the arts] in Greater Germany shall be brought together', declared Feistel-Rohmeder.[48]

Establishing a German art journal, organizing an exhibition of truly German art by racially pure German artists and organizing economic relief for the artists: these were the goals of the Executive Council of United German Art and Culture Associations. Meeting at least twice a year, the Executive Council had a fairly simple organizational structure. The board of directors consisted of a chairman, vice-chairman, business manager, treasurer and other two members.[49] Executive Council board members included Blume, Fritzsche, Feistel-Rohmeder, Ludwig Dill, Eugen Friedrich Hopf and Hans Adolf Bühler.[50] The board supervised the Council's three committees, responsible for organizing an exhibition, creating an art journal and assisting struggling artists. By looking more closely at each of these committees, the extent to which the Executive Council was wholly a creature of the German Art Society becomes clear. Such a focus also demonstrates that the Executive Council, like the Society, relied upon its members' organizational and professional contacts to further its goals.

The exhibition committee worked to organize the Council's German art show, planned for 1930, and arrange its funding. As the statutes stipulated, Society members played leading roles in the exhibition committee. Of the nine exhibition committee members named in the sources, eight belonged to the German Art Society. The Society's first chairman, Hopf, headed the group. As the Executive Council representative for the Dresden Free Theater Committee and the Association for the Friends of German Art, Hopf had extensive contacts within the Dresden art community that could be used to further the Council's goals. Walther Gasch, Karl Quark, and Willy Waldapfel, all Dresden painters, were to help attract potential exhibitors. The other members of the exhibition committee represented groups that were also likely to find interested artists: Kurt Guratzsch, chairman of the Dresden Free Theater Committee (and the only non-Society member); Reinhold Rehm, Council representative for the *Bund*; Feistel-Rohmeder for the Society; and Major [Moritz] Müller, representative for the Combat League's Dresden chapter.[51] All of the exhibition committee members lived in Dresden. Ready access to each other and long acquaintance, if not friendship, made it much easier for the committee to meet.

At the first Executive Council meeting, Feistel-Rohmeder explained the vital need for the exhibition committee to attract 'German capital' to finance the exhibition and estimated that 20,000 RM would be required for the Council's show.[52] Assisted by Guratzsch, Gasch, Quark and Waldapfel, Hopf planned to contact political parties, the *Landtag* (presumably of Saxony) and various local communities for financial support. He was also to contact potential individual sponsors, including Alfred Hugenberg and leading Dresden personalities. Executive Council chairman Blume sought out the wealthy conservative industrialist Emil Kirdorf, who had helped with the Society's Lübeck show, for a donation.[53] However, raising so much money for an art exhibition during the worsening depression proved extremely difficult. Only in late 1932 did the exhibition committee finally win sufficient backing to realize the show.

While the Executive Council planned its own exhibition, the German Art Society opened its pure German art show in Lübeck during the summer of 1929. The Council did not play a role in the Lübeck exhibit.[54] Since the exhibition opened less than two months after the Executive Council's establishment, there was little time for it to become involved. However, the Council's assistance committee (*Unterstützungsausschuss*) did help sell the exhibit's artworks. Headed by Society/ Council treasurer Paul Fritzsche, the assistance committee created a purchasing scheme designed to make the Lübeck artworks more affordable. In effect, the committee became a sales agent for the Society's exhibitors, arranging installment payment plans for interested purchasers. The painting's price, according to the amount, was divided into 12, 18 or 24 monthly payments of at least 10 RM. Any member of the German League whose local chapter guaranteed payment was eligible to purchase works through this payment plan. Other purchasers who provided some sort of collateral (securities and bonds were suggested) to the assistance committee's office in Halle could also participate.[55]

The assistance committee's payment plan had two main functions. First, it enabled art lovers to purchase works they could not otherwise afford. And second, once a painting was sold, the monthly payments provided the artist a reliable source of annual income. The Council hoped the payment method would enable true German artists to continue working, despite the hardships of the economic depression. This was one of the most concrete responses to the depression made by the Society and the Executive Council. To advertise both the Lübeck exhibition and the payment method, the assistance committee prepared a brief catalog and a slide collection of the Society paintings. The committee also enlisted the aid of the German Art Society's *Deutsche Bildkunst*. Its December 1929 issue reportedly reproduced a large number of Lübeck works available for sale through the Council. Fritzsche suggested that members have their friends peruse the December issue and select the painting they desired. Members could then purchase Society artwork through the payment plan as special Christmas presents.[56] Due to the lack of source material, it is impossible to tell how successful this sales tactic was. Feistel-Rohmeder claimed that the support group made several sales but provided no details. Most likely, the increasing severity of the economic depression made even the small payments impossible. It is, however, important to note that any sales benefited the German Art Society artists more than the Council itself. Successful sales provided a regular income for the artists, but the Council did not profit financially. The committee members worked voluntarily and charged a registration fee of only 3 RM for arranging sales.[57] Once again, the Society used the Executive Council as a tool to fulfill its mission to defend German art.

The extent to which the German Art Society exploited the Executive Council's resources is demonstrated further by Feistel-Rohmeder's manipulation of the Council's art journal committee. As head of this committee, Feistel-Rohmeder played a decisive role in winning Council support for the expansion of the Society's own art journal, *Deutsche Bildkunst*, which she had founded and edited since 1927. Initially the Executive Council planned to create its own journal, *German Art (Deutsche Kunst)*.[58] By December 1929, however, the journal committee abandoned this plan and agreed to adopt *Deutsche Bildkunst* as its journal. In light of the economic crisis, it made more sense for the Executive Council to expand a pre-existing periodical with an experienced editor who was willing to work for free and an established circle of readers rather than start a new journal. The decision also benefited Feistel-Rohmeder and the Society. Feistel-Rohmeder kept her position as editor and 'her' magazine was expanded in length and in readership.[59]

The expansion of *Deutsche Bildkunst* was achieved by marshalling Council resources. Heinrich Hendriok, Council representative for the Eagles and Falcons, promised that his Berlin publishing house would publish the magazine if the organization assured him 900 subscribers. He also offered to cover all of the promotional costs until the Executive Council was able to do so. The *völkisch* coalition's member organs rallied to support the subscription drive. The German League newspaper (*Deutschbund-Blätter*), the Combat League newsletter, the Newland Movement organ (*Neulandblatt*) and the League of *Völkisch* Teachers' journal (*Völkische Schule*) published announcements seeking *Deutsche Bildkunst* subscriptions. The Society's *German Art Correspondence* and the *Deutsche Bildkunst* itself also announced the expansion of the journal and its urgent need for subscribers.[60] Although the deal with Hendriok's firm fell through after the first issue, financial support from the German League and from loyal Society members enabled the journal to continue. For example, Feistel-Rohmeder noted that some members made small donations or willingly paid twice for a subscription in order to support the journal.[61] From late 1930 until early 1933, *Deutsche Bildkunst* appeared on a fairly regular quarterly basis, no mean accomplishment during a period where other journals folded or severely curtailed their activities.[62]

Through its Executive Council of United German Art and Culture Associations, the German Art Society built a number of bridges between itself and the wider *völkisch* movement. However, working with a *völkisch* coalition like the Executive Council was also extremely difficult. Coordinating eighteen different groups and eliciting their participation in the Council was a challenging task. The Association for Germandom in Art, the *Bund*, the Women's Combat League, the League of *Völkisch* Teachers and the *Schwarzhäuser Ring* all missed the Council's second meeting in December 1929; Schultze-Naumburg's architectural organization left the Council within a year.[63] This suggests that the membership of the Executive Council was fairly fluid and perhaps unreliable. Despite the German Art Society's best efforts, the *völkisch* movement remained a splintered collection of interest groups.[64] Gradually, the German Art Society realized that the Council, useful though it was, could never win the cultural influence necessary to usher in a German renaissance.

The Executive Council continued to exist until 1933, but after the Nazi Party's breakthrough in the 1930 elections, the German Art Society realized that the Nazis offered the political means by which its cultural mission could be achieved. Judging by the Society's activities in the last years of the Weimar Republic, its members believed a Nazi regime would implement policies favoring pure German art and artists, especially those who had proven their loyalty. Leading Society members joined the Nazi Party between 1929 and 1932, in part out of belief, but also in part out of the anticipation of power and influence. As members of the Combat League and the NSDAP, Society members served as cultural advisors to the Nazi Party. Gasch served as visual-arts advisor to the NSDAP in Dresden; Siegfried Czerny did the same in Munich and Heinrich Blume was arts advisor to the party for the Gau Hesse-Nassau.[65] The Society expected that the Nazis would recognize and reward both the organization and its members as old fighters in the battle for German art when they finally attained power.

Such dreams appeared to have come true in early 1930 when Wilhelm Frick became Thuringia's state minister of the interior and education. For the first time, a Nazi Party member had the political means to implement cultural policy. Aided by cultural advisors drawn from the ranks of the Combat League, Frick promulgated a ministerial directive entitled 'Against Negro Culture – For the German Race' which used established laws to legislate against modernist culture. According to Frick, alien races had for years gained dominance over the entire spectrum of German culture. Jazz music, 'Negro dances' and 'Negro songs' poisoned German sensibilities. In the interest of maintaining and strengthening the German race, he ordered that all instances of 'Negro culture' be suppressed. Permits for theatrical and musical productions were approved only if the authorities believed that German morals and culture were being well served. As result, works by Hindemith and Stravinsky disappeared from concert halls, and classical dramas replaced modernist works.[66]

In the visual arts as well, Frick's tenure as a state minister foreshadowed what was to come in the Third Reich. He appointed the architect, racial theorist and Society/Executive Council/Combat League member Paul Schultze-Naumburg to head the State Academy for Architecture, Crafts and the Visual Arts in Weimar, formerly home to the Bauhaus. Immediately, he used his position to attack modernist art. He ordered the destruction of Oscar Schlemmer's murals which graced the halls of the Weimar art academy and demanded the removal of some seventy modernist artworks from the *Schlossmuseum* in Weimar.[67] Schultze-Naumburg also embarked on a speaking tour, presenting his lecture 'The Battle for Art' to large audiences. The struggle for German art, claimed Schultze-Naumburg, was part of the larger struggle for the German race to survive.[68] The art-defense movement, once promoted only by the German Art Society, was receiving national attention.

Frick, Schultze-Naumburg and their cultural policies were vehemently attacked and debated in Thuringia and throughout Germany. Art, theater and film organizations decried the censorship of the arts. For example, National Association of Germany's Visual Artists criticized Frick's policies and Schultze-Naumburg's destruction of the Bauhaus murals.[69] For Feistel-Rohmeder, such criticism of Frick and his policies represented pure hypocrisy. Defending Frick through her cultural news service, she argued that in the rest of Germany, state governments and the national leadership regularly promoted modernist art. Now a minister in one state actively defended German culture and was censured for his efforts. The intellectuals of the 'democratically ruled German Reich' could 'lecture, preach, drum and scream' in defense of modernism, but let one man speak out in favor of German art and culture and he was cruelly attacked.[70] Nevertheless Feistel-Rohmeder predicted, Frick and his policies would prevail and serve as a model for all of Germany.[71]

As genuine as Feistel-Rohmeder's defense of Frick was (she joined the Nazi Party in 1929) it was also motivated by self-interest. In a letter to Frick sent on behalf of the Executive Council of United German Art and Culture Associations and the German Art Society, she congratulated him for his courage to use his position to further the interests of the German race and its culture. She then went on to argue that the Executive Council and Society had combated the 'Negroization' (*Verniggerung*) of culture for years.[72] Throughout paragraphs of effusive praise, she strategically included references to the Executive Council and Society's ties to the Nazi movement, the *Völkischer Beobachter*, the Combat League for German Culture and Schultze-Naumburg. Only at the very end of the letter did she get to the heart of the matter. She requested that Frick support *Deutsche Bildkunst* and its effort to win 900 subscribers. This request was granted thanks to the intercession of Society member Schultze-Naumburg. Now director of the leading art school in Thuringia, he recommended that the state ministry of culture and all the art schools subscribe to the magazine.[73] The German Art Society's devotion to the cause of *völkisch* culture and its network of organizational and personal alliances were beginning to bring results.

Frick's tenure as interior and cultural minister of Thuringia lasted barely a year, but his cultural policies and the modest support he offered convinced the German Art Society that an alliance with the National Socialists represented the best chance to realize its mission. The Society did continue to use the Executive Council of United German Art and Culture Associations. The *völkisch* coalition provided the funds necessary to publish *Deutsche Bildkunst* and it enabled the Society to claim the support of numerous organizations. Increasingly, however, the Executive Council was relegated to the position of a German Art Society affiliate rather than an active organization pursuing its own goals. The Society came to favor the Combat League for German Culture and the Nazi Party over its *völkisch* allies.

The best evidence of the Executive Council's decline and the Combat League's advance within the Society's esteem is provided by the final preparations for the groups' proposed exhibition of pure German art. The Executive Council had planned the exhibition for 1930; two years later, the show was still unrealized. The Council had simply been unable to find the means necessary to host the show. However, in the fall of 1932, another Nazi Party member became a state minister of education: Dietrich Klagges won the post in Brunswick. Blume and Feistel-Rohmeder hoped Klagges, like Frick, would support cultural policies defending pure German art, and asked for his support. Such hopes were reasonable. Klagges was not only a fellow Nazi Party member but also a fellow member of the German League. Mindful of these connections, Blume and Feistel-Rohmeder downplayed the role of the Council in their letter to Klagges and highlighted the Nazi and League connections. Although they mentioned the Executive Council, Blume and

Feistel-Rohmeder now represented the Traveling Exhibition of Pure German Art as a joint venture of the German Art Society, a branch of the German League, and the Combat League for German Culture.[74]

In the very first line of their letter, Blume and Feistel-Rohmeder represented themselves as fellow 'insiders', opening with the cryptic initials 'I.D.N.H!' which only a fellow German League initiate would recognize as its sacred motto: 'On behalf of Germany, Heil!' (*Im deutschen Namen Heil!*). They then went on to emphasize their connections with the German League as well as the Nazi Party. As a fellow League brother and party member, they hoped Klagges would use his ministerial position to assist the Society, an affiliate of the German League.[75] Pointing to Society members who served as cultural advisors to the Nazi Party, Blume and Feistel-Rohmeder implied that the Society had broad support within the Nazi Party and the Combat League for German Culture.[76] After detailing the shared cultural mission of the Society, the German League and the Nazi movement, they asked Klagges to help, requesting that he provide free exhibition space for the show's appearance in Brunswick, promise state funds for the exhibition itself and assure the ministry's purchase of some of the art displayed.[77]

Klagges's first inclination was to decline the request but he soon agreed to help the German Art Society secure the means necessary to bring its show to Brunswick.[78] Due to the deflationary policies and fiscal limitations placed upon his ministry, Klagges could not promise any substantial financial support. However, he could make rooms in the Burg Dankwarderode available for the show, if the Society were willing to wait until early 1933. In turn, Klagges expected the Society to cooperate with the local Brunswick chapter of the National Socialist Culture Association.[79] Thus by a stroke of good fortune, the German Art Society could now plan to hold a traveling exhibition of pure German art in 1933. Moreover, Klagges agreed to lend his name, and hence prestige and authority, to the exhibit by serving as the show's patron (*Schirmherr*). The German Art Society's shared memberships and cooperation with *völkisch* and National Socialist groups was about to pay off in the guise of its first national, traveling exhibition. Little did they know that the exhibition would be held in an entirely different political climate.

By late 1932, the German Art Society had successfully created an organizational network of *völkisch* groups, first through the Society's membership and then through the Executive Council of United German Art and Culture Associations. These *völkisch* contacts enabled the Society to thrive during the last years of the Weimar Republic, propagandize against the 'republic's' culture and agitate for a cultural renewal. At the same time, the Society increasingly cooperated with the National Socialist Party and the Combat League for German Culture. As a result, the Society was well positioned when the Nazis came to power in 1933. The Executive Council and its *völkisch* allies had enabled the German Art Society to survive the republic; its Nazi partners would allow it to weather the transition from the republic to the Third Reich.

−4−

Artists for the Reich, 1933

When Adolf Hitler became chancellor on 30 January 1933, the German Art Society was poised to take full advantage of the new cultural climate. The Society's First Traveling Exhibition of Pure German Art, scheduled to open in Brunswick in April, was one of the first exhibitions that attempted to define just what art in the Third Reich might be. Members had high hopes that they would soon be rewarded with positions of authority in the new regime's cultural apparatus. The German Art Society believed that as the oldest *völkisch* artists' organization it was only a matter of time before the National Socialists would enlist the group in a decisive battle against the avant-garde. The Society was sure that the Nazis would need its members' expertise as new policies were developed. In sum, the German Art Society believed it was on the verge of a breakthrough.

Although the German Art Society did achieve a surprising degree of influence particularly in Baden, 1933 proved to be frustrating and even disappointing. In its members' eyes, the battle for German art in the first year of the Third Reich was hardly a victory. Rather than witnessing the wholesale destruction of cultural modernism, they instead were stunned to see National Socialists join some modernists to proclaim that Expressionism and other modernist styles were national, Nordic and even National Socialist. Unlike the Nazis, who were willing to at least consider adapting modernism to the Third Reich's needs, the German Art Society's rigid definition of pure German art provided no such flexibility. The Society lived 'in the terror of art Bolshevism'.[1] This position both aided and hindered the group's fortunes.

The continuation of the German Art Society's battle for German art and against modernism in 1933 illustrates a feature of art and culture in the Third Reich that has been long recognized. For at least the first several years, National Socialist cultural policy was haphazard and inconsistent, an extended improvisation that developed out of multiple power struggles both inside and outside of the party.[2] Just about the only thing that could be agreed was that German culture, however defined, remained a central component of national identity. Thus who would control the shaping of that identity was a vital issue for the Nazis.

And for the artists, too. Artists had professional, economic and very personal interests in the ability to assist in the redefinition of German culture. State and party support of the arts offered the promise of employment and even authority within the emerging Nazi cultural administration. Reforms in art education, in the profession's ability to represent its interests and in the government's support for the arts had been hoped for in the first years of the Weimar Republic. Many artists looked to the Third Reich to realize reforms the republic had been unable to effect. But this was not simply passive expectation; artists across the political spectrum participated actively in the debates over culture in 1933. The struggle to define art and culture in the first years of the Third Reich was not just a question of orders promulgated at the top. Old rivalries between artists and over the German content of culture also shaped the arts in the Third Reich from below. As the German Art Society aptly demonstrates, not all artists had to be coerced into supporting the Nazi regime. They enthusiastically embraced the new regime, and demanded that it respond to their calls for a cleansing of German art.

The first months of the Third Reich offered the German Art Society unprecedented opportunity for action. Because the Nazis did not establish their own cultural ministry – the Reich Culture Chamber – until the fall, the spring and summer of 1933 represented 'a kind of interregnum' period for the artistic sector.[3] As cultural institutions were purged of their modernists, *völkisch* and Nazi art experts stepped into the power vacuum with enormous enthusiasm and wide latitude for action at the local level.[4] The German Art Society was in an ideal position to take full advantage of the interregnum period. Unlike other groups, the Society was not delayed by the process of *Gleichschaltung*. For organizations, this typically entailed affiliation with an approved Nazi group, the elimination of all non-German (i.e. Jewish) or politically unreliable (socialist and communist) members and the election of NSDAP members to the board of directors. The German Art Society had fulfilled all of these prerequisites well before 1933. Because the Society had joined the Combat League for German Culture in 1929, it was already part of the Nazi movement. There was no need to purge Jewish or leftist members, for none had ever been permitted, and the Society's board was already dominated by party members.[5] The German Art Society also had access to its *völkisch* coalition, the Executive Council of United German Art and Culture Associations, at least until June 1933 when it disbanded.[6] Through its news service and journal *Deutsche Bildkunst*, the group had access to an audience already convinced of and committed to the purification of German art.

The Society's exhibition was the first exclusively 'German' art show held in the Third Reich and National Socialists welcomed it an expression of the 'new' German culture. Planned in 1932, the exhibition committee brought together leading members of the German Art Society, cultural advisors to the Nazi Party and the Combat League for German Culture.[7] Over the course of the spring, the exhibit's organizing committees had been expanded further as newly-appointed state and city officials eagerly agreed to support the show's appearance in their regions. By April 1933 when the exhibition opened, its various committees included state and city officials from Berlin, Brunswick, Darmstadt, Munich and Weimar. Other artists' organizations also joined in the venture. Regional chapters of the National Association of Visual Artists and the Association of German Art Leagues (*Verband Deutscher Kunstvereine*) in Munich, the League of War-Wounded Artists (*Bund kriegsbeschädigter Künstler*) in Berlin and the National Socialist Culture Association (*Nationalsozialistische Kulturvereinigung*) in Brunswick participated.[8] The show's appearances in Mannheim, Karlsruhe and Frankfurt am Main reflected a similar level of participation by government officials, party members and local artist associations.[9] Such official support not only helped to finance the show, it also bolstered the German Art Society's claim that it occupied a central position in the Reich's cultural life.

Just where the exhibition appeared was determined by the level of support offered by local German League, Combat League and Society chapters.[10] In Brunswick the local German League and Combat League chapters co-sponsored the exhibition. In Frankfurt am Main, the exhibit was held in conjunction with the German League's annual meeting.[11] Wherever the show was held, a combination of officials from city councils, the Combat League, the German League and other *völkisch* cultural organizations helped finance the exhibition. State culture and education ministries also provided funds. For example, Dietrich Klagges, as education minister in Brunswick, provided 500 RM; the education minister in Weimar offered 100 RM. The show's hosts were required to provided exhibition space and cover the shipping costs either to or from the exhibit. Depending on the local level of funding, the Society then divided the receipts from the entrance fees.[12] Any deficit was covered by the Society's parent organization, the German League or funds from supporting state ministries.[13]

When the First Traveling Exhibition of Pure German Art opened in April, the German Art Society had achieved its most cherished dream. Not only had the republic been destroyed and its culture discredited, but the Society was convinced that the new regime fully supported its mission. For thirteen years the Society had labored to rescue art and combat modernist culture. At long last, the alien parliamentary democracy had been defeated. Art and politics could now combine in a way that favored the real Germany. This viewpoint, once held by radical individuals and groups on the fringes of German political and cultural life, was becoming the norm; indeed, it represented the increasingly dominant perspective.

At the show's opening ceremony held on 30 April 1933 at the Burg Dankwarderode in Brunswick, all of the speakers trumpeted the First Traveling Exhibition of German Art as a first example of Nazi cultural policy. The interdependence of pure German art and National Socialist politics was the main theme of nearly all the speeches. Again and again, the invited guests were reminded that the alien

Weimar democracy had supported and was in turn supported by an equally unGerman culture. Under the National Socialists, a truly German regime would promote only German art. The poet and Society member Wilhelm Kotzde enthusiastically praised the 'heaven-sent Führer Adolf Hitler and the art that he favors, an art full of creative power and the profundity of God'.[14] Society chairman Heinrich Blume, who spoke on behalf of the German League, proclaimed that Dietrich Klagges, the show's official patron, represented 'the National Socialist cultural will'. Blume hoped that the exhibition would open the eyes and hearts of the German people who would recognize the art as creations 'of their own blood and race'.[15] City councilman Dr. Benze and the artists Hans Adolf Bühler and Walther Hoeck (both Society members) also emphasized that this exhibition represented a new start for German culture and a glimpse at what the future held. Throughout their speeches, German Art Society members implied that their cultural mission had won the endorsement of the Nazi state.

Such endorsement was embodied in the person of Dietrich Klagges. When the Society first won his support, he was the education and interior minister for Brunswick. In the spring of 1933, however, he had been appointed minister-president of Brunswick, a post he would hold for the duration of the Third Reich. Klagges was thus a high-ranking state official and a well-known old fighter for the Nazi Party. In his remarks, he stressed the interconnection of art and politics in Hitler's Germany. Noting the symbolic importance of the show's appearance in the Burg Dankwarderode, he declared that 'politics and art have always belonged together'.[16] Thanks to the tradition of the medieval martyr-king of Brunswick, Heinrich the Lion, the Burg symbolized the ancient Germanic connection between art and politics. In recent times, Klagges argued, both politics and art had become unGerman; art had become a 'dangerous ally' of a destructive political system.[17] Now under the National Socialist government, art would be reunited with the German people. German art as revealed in this exhibition, predicted Klagges, must show the way to the future and contribute to the reawakening of Germany.

Despite these grandiose claims, the art displayed in the Society's exhibition contributed nothing new to the art world. Scenes from peasant life, idyllic landscapes and historical themes predominated, all painted in styles reminiscent of those in the late nineteenth century.[18] Here was none of the Impressionism, Expressionism or New Objectivity which had taken over German art in the past forty years. But there was also virtually nothing specifically Nazi, either. The traditionalist or *völkisch* landscapes and portraits, out of favor in the Weimar Republic, became expressions of the German awakening and the National Socialist cultural will. Overall, the art displayed in the Society's exhibition bore great resemblance to the art that later graced the walls of the Munich 'Great German Art' exhibitions.[19]

One work exhibited in the Society's show was featured in press reports as indicative of a possible new German art: Hans Adolf Bühler's portrait of his teacher, Hans Thoma. According to one review, Thoma appeared before the viewer as if he wished to deliver a message. An elderly man with a snow-white beard, Thoma walked under a stormy sky in a billowing 'magic cloak of moss green'. In his hands, he sheltered a precious, lidded goblet of glowing amber. 'Does he not shelter in his hands the very essence of German art from the inclement weather of the age?'[20] the reviewer asked. Bühler had transformed Thoma, revered by Society members as the last great German master, into a protector of racially pure art (Figure 4.1). The full-page review of the show in the local Brunswick newspaper featured Bühler's portrait. Thoma appeared in the center of the page, flanked by Wilhelm Haller's *Bethlehem*, Walther Hoeck's *Praying Farmer*, Ludwig Dill's *Harbor* and Karl Alexander Flügel's *Landscape*.[21] With these and similar paintings, the Society's art show consciously celebrated its Germanness and its connections with the Germanic artistic tradition. Previously ridiculed as backward, the 'German style' of art could now flourish in the new cultural climate.

Like Bühler, all of the other artists exhibited in the traveling exhibition had shunned the artistic experimentation of the Weimar period, painting in

Figure 4.1 *Thoma* by Hans Adolf Bühler. From *Ekkart: Jahrbuch für das Badner Land* 15 (1934), p. 24.

traditionalist, academic styles throughout the republic. Their allegiance to clear, easily understood styles and to their German heritage assured these artists a place in the exhibition. The number and identity of the exhibitors also suggests that the Society's cultural program had won over new converts to its mission. Unlike the Lübeck show, the traveling exhibition included artists who did not belong to the German Art Society. According to the catalog printed for the Brunswick station, the exhibition consisted of 140 works by seventy-seven artists. Just over half of the exhibitors were members of the German Art Society: thirty-nine members contributed a total of seventy-one art pieces. Eleven of the exhibitors became members shortly after the show. Only eleven of the artists had participated in the Society's 1929 show in Lübeck.[22]

For a little over one year, the Society's exhibition toured Germany, appearing in Brunswick (30 April to 28 May 1933), Kassel (July), Darmstadt (August to September), Karlsruhe (9 September to 15 October), Mannheim (opened 28 October) and Frankfurt am Main (25 May to 30 June 1934).[23] At each station, the exhibit was lauded by Nazi officials as an example of cultural regeneration. In Karlsruhe, Otto Wacker, the state minister of education, culture and justice, and Bühler, head of Baden's state art museum and academy, incorporated the show into an official celebration of Nazi, German and local culture, the Borderlands Rally held 9 to 27 September.[24] In Mannheim, *Reichsstaathalter* Robert Wagner acted as the local patron and Josef August Beringer, an official of the local art league and Society member, made the opening remarks. Prince Philipp of Hesse sponsored the Darmstadt showing.[25] Gau Leader and Minister-President Sprenger served as the show's Frankfurt patron and Mayor Krebs, chairman of the local Combat League, also offered the show his support.[26] Such official endorsements enhanced the prestige of the Society and its exhibition enormously. Wherever it appeared, the First Traveling Exhibition of German Art proclaimed itself to be a model for the future, the artistic antidote to the poison of the art of the Weimar Republic.

It was, however, not enough for the German Art Society to offer an aesthetic balm; the group was also determined to eradicate the cause of the nation's cultural disease. Throughout 1933, members of the German Art Society and local chapters of the Combat League for German Culture launched a cleansing campaign directed against modern art and its supporters. The most spectacular expression of this effort was the degenerate art exhibitions created to defame the art associated with the Weimar Republic. Newly appointed administrators eliminated Impressionist, Expressionist, abstract and other modernist works from the regular exhibition rooms. Paintings, graphics and sculpture by artists such as Emil Nolde, George Grosz, Wilhelm Lehmbruck and Max Liebermann were then put on display in so-called 'chambers of horror' that derided the art as unGerman assaults against tradition, decency and morality. Branded degenerate, modern art and by extension the artists themselves were publicly pilloried as visual representations of the Weimar Republic. By ridiculing and defaming modernist art as a 'Jewish conspiracy' to ruin German culture, the shows discredited the failed democracy and legitimized further the Nazis' seizure of power.[27]

The German Art Society played a leading role in the creation of these early degenerate art exhibitions. Indeed, the initial idea originated with Bettina Feistel-Rohmeder. In March 1933, she published a battle plan that contained all of the components of the later degenerate shows. Released through the *German Art Report*, Feistel-Rohmeder claimed that she knew, as the program's title made clear, 'What the German Artists Expect from the New Government!'[28] This call to action represented German Art Society members' intent 'to make their particular interests, which they labeled "National Socialist," the basis for general policy'.[29] Extreme in its aggression and militancy, the declaration began by equating the cultural battle with the political. According to Feistel-Rohmeder, the German artists expected

> that in art, too, there will be from now on only *one* guideline for action, a philosophy drawn from a passionate national and state consciousness anchored in the realities of blood and history! Art should serve the growth and strengthening of this *völkisch* community...
>
> They [the artists] expect not only that materialism, Marxism and communism will be politically persecuted, outlawed and eradicated but also that the spiritual battle, that the *völkisch artists* have led through more than a decade *without any help from the state*, will now be taken up by the people as a whole and that Bolshevik nonart and nonculture will be doomed to destruction – *whereby it is a point of honor for the state to place proven soldiers of this cultural battle in the front ranks!*[30]

The German Art Society expected that its members would be such cultural soldiers for the Third Reich. Feistel-Rohmeder clearly anticipated that the *völkisch* believers would be allowed to have their revenge against their artistic rivals.

Continuing her call for action, Feistel-Rohmeder carefully outlined in five points the exact nature of the artists' vengeance. Museum administrators should withdraw all modern art – vaguely defined as 'products of a cosmopolitan or Bolshevik nature' – from their institutions. They should then exhibit the offensive art in order to educate the public on the extent of the cultural and political poisoning Germany had endured. The price paid for each piece and the name of the officials responsible for its purchase were to accompany the art on the pillory. Afterwards 'only one useful function remain[ed] to these works of nonart: namely as kindling for the heating of public buildings'.[31]

The museum directors 'who sinned against a needy nation ... by their shameless waste of public funds' were to be dismissed. She recommended that the very names of those 'artists subscribing to Marxism and Bolshevism' disappear from all printed matter. Even modern architecture and sculpture were not to be spared. Artists expected that 'apartment blocks or churches that resemble greenhouses with chimneys or glass boxes on stilts' would be destroyed and 'that ways will be found to claim restitution from the criminals who grew rich perpetrating such insults against our native culture'. This attack, clearly directed against the Bauhaus, was partially realized with the closing of the famous art school and the dismissal of the entire teaching staff. Finally, Feistel-Rohmeder demanded the demolition of all offensive sculpture which 'still desecrate[d] public squares and parks'.[32]

The 'old law of an eye for an eye, a tooth for a tooth' had to be put into force once again, advised Feistel-Rohmeder. Positive art forms and true German artists needed to be supported and nurtured, even as a 'radical negation' of the 'nightmare of the past years' was carried out. In this way, the people's love for art, immobilized by the '*terror of art Bolshevism*' would be reawakened.[33] The government had only to call upon the *völkisch* artists for assistance. Innumerable forces, capable of guiding the regime in questions of art policy, awaited Hitler's orders. Throughout this manifesto, Feistel-Rohmeder walked a fine line between claiming the right to lead the Nazis onto a new cultural path and proclaiming the artists' obedience to the new regime. But whether as leaders or adherents, she clearly hoped that members of the German Art Society would find favor with the National Socialist government.

Although both contemporaries and the secondary literature unanimously agree that this program struck a responsive chord in the artistic community, just how Feistel-Rohmeder's manifesto was disseminated remains unknown.[34] Through the Council's news service, the program was presumably released to roughly 100 newspapers and journals but neither the *Völkischer Beobachter* nor other Nazi newspapers appear to have printed 'What the German Artists Expect'. However, less than a month after its publication, the proposal's main tenets served as guiding principles for members of the Society who organized local degenerate art exhibits.

The importance of 'What the German Artists Expect' lay in how influential it was among Society members who won positions of cultural authority in the spring of 1933. The March elections and the Enabling Act had ushered in the Nazi dictatorship. In April 1933, the Law for the Restoration of the Civil Service legislated the dismissal of civil servants who were of 'non-Aryan descent' (i.e. Jewish) or politically suspect (communist or socialist). This did not eliminate all supporters of modernism from cultural institutions, but across Germany, museums, academies and ministries had to find qualified replacements for the purged staffs. Drawing upon personnel from the Combat League for German Culture and the 'art political advisors of the of the party's Gau leadership', Minister of Interior Wilhelm Frick appointed art commissioners and gave them authority over national, state and local art institutions.[35]

Because many of the German Art Society's leading members were also members of the Combat League and art advisors to the NSDAP, they had acquired influential positions. Its chairman, Heinrich Blume, advised the NSDAP on cultural matters in Gau Hesse-Nassau; in Baden, August Gebhard, and in Munich Siegfried Czerny served the same function. Walther Gasch was appointed art commissioner for the city of Dresden. Bühler and Werner Kulz served in the cultural ministries of Baden and Hesse-Darmstadt respectively.[36] As Feistel-Rohmeder had hoped just one month earlier, the National Socialists placed its 'proven soldiers' 'in the front ranks'[37] of the cultural struggle.

Armed with their new positions of authority, German Art Society members worked to realize Feistel-Rohmeder's March program by ridding local museums of their modernist art and defaming the works in degenerate art shows. In these actions, new cultural officials could display their loyalty and enthusiasm for the Third Reich even as they positioned themselves as activists worthy of future promotion. They also had the opportunity to settle old scores. The Karlsruhe degenerate art exhibition illustrates the combination of Nazi purges with bitter local rivalries between artists. It also demonstrates the extent to which the German Art Society was able to translate party membership and professional credentials into some influence in Baden.

The Society's prominence in Baden was due to positions in the state's cultural apparatus held by two Society supporters: Otto Wacker and Hans Adolf Bühler. After the March elections, Wacker, an old fighter and editor of the local Nazi Party newspaper, became minister of education, culture and justice.[38] Bühler, the Society's vice-chairman, was the director of the Baden state art museum in Karlsruhe and was appointed head of the state art academy as well.[39] Wacker and Bühler had known each as fellow board members of the Karlsruhe Combat League chapter. Now, they set out to implement Feistel-Rohmeder's March program by planning one of the first degenerate art exhibitions.

In mid-March, Bühler gave Wacker and other state officials a tour of the Karlsruhe art museum, a tour which convinced Wacker that the art collection had to be purged of its degenerate art. Apparently Bühler and Wacker wanted to set the tone for the rest of the Baden by ridding Karlsruhe, the capital, of its cultural decay. But simply eliminating the artworks was insufficient. Wacker ordered that an exhibition of art from the period between 1919 and 1933 be organized. Following Feistel-Rohmeder's recommendations to the letter, he demanded that degenerate works purchased by the previous government be publicly displayed, complete with the price paid and the name of the cultural minister responsible for the purchase of each piece.[40] Bühler had the museum's modernist collection evaluated by Gerda Kircher, later a frequent contributor to the Society's art journal.[41] Because the Karlsruhe art museum had few Expressionist paintings, Impressionist works by artists such as Max Liebermann and Lovis Corinth were selected as examples of cultural degeneracy. Bühler also used the exhibition as an opportunity to attack his longtime artistic rivals, including August Babberger, Karl Hubbuch and Alexander Kanoldt, now defamed as degenerate.[42]

The show, Government Art 1919–1933, was held from 8 to 30 April 1933. As Feistel-Rohmeder had advised, the works were displayed with the prices paid and the names of museum directors and gallery officials responsible for their acquisition. Because many of the artworks had been purchased during the inflationary period of 1922–23, the prices paid appeared to be astromonical. The exhibition's displays emphasized that millions of marks had been squandered on meaningless, hideous dabs of paint. Bühler included an 'erotic cabinet' in the show as well. There, artworks by dismissed academy faculty and students were displayed as obscene examples of the detrimental effect the republic's modernist artists had on art students. The danger of degenerate art to young Germans was implied further by prohibiting entry to people under eighteen years of age, a tactic which heightened the degenerate art exhibition's sensationalism. As a healthy counterpoint to the degenerate show, Bühler exhibited photographs of German masterpieces that previous museum directors had either exiled to store rooms or exchanged for modern works. Society member August Gebhard and Fritz Wilkendorf, later a contributor to the Society's art journal, reenforced this accusation in the press and reviewed the show in glowing terms.[43]

From the Baden cities of Karlsruhe and Mannheim (which hosted the first degenerate art show),[44] degenerate art exhibitions appeared across Germany. In all, twenty-two local degenerate art exhibitions were organized between 1933 and July 1937, when the national Degenerate Art show opened in Munich. Although the styles of art branded degenerate ranged from Impressionism to New Objectivity, the method of defamation mirrored exactly Feistel-Rohmeder's recommendations. Designed to completely discredit the works displayed, these shows exhibited the paintings, sculptures and graphics not as art but rather as documents of the Weimar Republic. Often the exhibits' titles made the connection between the degenerate art and the failed republic explicit: Government Art 1919–1933 (Karlsruhe); The November-Spirit: Art in the Service of Decay (Stuttgart); or Art of Two Worlds (Hagen).[45] These shows charged the artists with crimes against the German people and equated the art with communism, the 'Jewish conspiracy' and parliamentary government. The degenerate art exhibitions illustrated visually the complete break with the Weimar Republic. They also made a great pretense of returning German culture to the people and restoring traditional, national values.[46]

The degree to which these degenerate art shows were coordinated has been the subject of some debate.[47] However, it appears most likely that the shows were the initiative of individuals who had been part of the *völkisch* cultural movement during the Weimar Republic. These individuals were leading members of local Combat League for German Culture chapters, the German Art Society and the

Executive Council of United Art and Culture Associations who won positions within the Nazi Party. For example, the first degenerate art exhibition, in Mannheim, was organized by Gebele von Waldstein, a Combat League member, and Josef August Beringer; a Combat League and Society member, it is very likely that the latter was friends with Bühler.[48] The Mannheim show then traveled to Munich and Erlangen.[49] Bühler, organizer of the Karlsruhe show, belonged to the Combat League, the Society and the Executive Council. Wacker was also a Combat League member and at the very least a Society supporter. As state minister for culture, education and justice, he had jurisdiction over cultural events in both Mannheim and Karlsruhe. Feistel-Rohmeder implied he had a hand in both those cities' degenerate art shows.[50]

In a brief account of the Karlsruhe show, Feistel-Rohmeder had asked: 'Who will hold a court-day in Berlin, in Munich, in Dresden, in Düsseldorf and even in Hamburg?'[51] Richard Müller, Walther Gasch and Willy Waldapfel, all members of the German Art Society and the Executive Council (Gasch belonged to the Combat League as well) answered her call, and organized the Dresden degenerate art show.[52] They were able to do so because, like their friend Bühler in Karlsruhe, they had been appointed to positions of cultural authority. Müller had become director of the Dresden art academy, Gasch was an art commissioner and Waldapfel had become a city official (*Stadtrat*).[53] Planned in June 1933, the show was held twice in Dresden: from 23 September to 18 October 1933, and again in August 1935. Hitler, Joseph Goebbels and Hermann Goering all attended the 1935 show, and Hitler was so impressed he declared that the show had to be shown throughout Germany. Between 1934 and 1936, the Dresden collection of degenerate art appeared in Hagen, Nuremberg, Dortmund, Regensburg, Munich, Ingolstadt, Darmstadt and Frankfurt am Main.[54] Overall, of the twenty-two early degenerate shows, German Society and Executive Council members played a leading role in organizing thirteen.[55] The German Art Society as an organization did not initiate these shows. However, it is clear that leading, longtime members of the Society, who also belonged to the Executive Council, the Combat League and the Nazi Party, did put into practice the ideas expressed in Feistel-Rohmeder's 'What the German Artists Expect'.

The degenerate art shows and the First Traveling Exhibition of German Art convinced the Society that it was only a matter of time before the National Socialist regime would soon anoint its members as artists for the Reich. In the meantime, Society members used their status as old fighters to win new positions and power within local arts administrations. This was especially true in Karlsruhe. Bühler headed both the state art academy and the state art museum. In July, he and Society members August Gebhard and Hermann Kupferschmid used the *Gleichschaltung* of the Baden art league to have themselves voted as the new Nazi Party members of the board of directors.[56] Bühler and Gebhard also served on the board of the southwest German division of the National Association of Germany's Visual Artists.[57] Thus by the summer of 1933, Society members held leading positions in the most important artists' associations in the state of Baden.

Society members often used their new power to advance the fortunes of fellow members. For example, Society members came to dominate the Baden art academy in Karlsruhe. As director of the art school, Bühler had the authority to dismiss old rivals and hire new faculty. Bühler purged his faculty of its modernists, most of whom had been artistic enemies since the 1920s. The artists August Babberger, Karl Dillinger, Karl Hubbuch, Wilhelm Schnarrenberger and Georg Scholz lost their teaching positions.[58] Bühler replaced them with members of the German Art Society: Erwin Aichele, Beringer, Czerny, Gebhard, Müller-Ewald, Georg Siebert, Otto Schliessler and Kupferschmid. 'With this reorganization the influence of the "German Art Society" reached its zenith in Karlsruhe.'[59]

Nor was Karlsruhe an isolated example. In Dresden, Society member Professor Richard Müller, now director of the academy there, accomplished a similar feat, hiring longtime Society members Richard Guhr, Willy Waldapfel and Hans Hanner as professors. Other Society members rose in the ranks of the civil service; for example, Dietrich Klagges promoted Heinrich Blume from the position of teacher to an official within the state education ministry.[60] In this way, Society members redressed their grievances with the republic's cultural institutions. They were beginning to be recognized as art experts and became part of the Nazi cultural administration.

However, neither the German Art Society nor the Nazi purge of cultural modernism went unchallenged. By the summer, defenders of modernist art began to rally and find their own supporters. The battle between modernist and German art, so bitter during the Weimar Republic, continued throughout 1933. Some modernist artists were quite willing to cooperate with the Third Reich and there were National Socialists who believed that there was something uniquely German in the art of those modernists who were racially and politically reliable. The debate between those who sought to incorporate aesthetic modernism into the Third Reich by interpreting it as 'German' and the staunch defenders of cultural purity raged throughout the summer of 1933.

For example, on 29 June the National Socialist German Student League of Berlin hosted a public meeting at the Humboldt University and openly declared its support for the 'Nordic' Expressionists, including Ernst Barlach, Emil Nolde, Ernst Heckel and Karl Schmidt-Rottluff. The students did not want a return to the artistic academicism of the Wilhelmine period and rejected the attempt to regulate art. Before a packed auditorium, Otto Andreas Schreiber, head of the Berlin Nazi student league, attacked the Combat League for German Culture's defamation of Expressionism. His critique of Alfred Rosenberg and the Combat League emphasized a generational difference in the understanding of what constituted German art:

The attempt by uncreative men to enforce an art historical dogma looms like a nightmare over all young artists of our movement. The National Socialist students are fighting against artistic reaction because they believe in art's capacity for vital development ... National Socialist youth ... believes in nothing so firmly as the victory of quality and truth.[61]

The audience burst into applause. Shortly thereafter, student groups from across Germany sent in declarations for support for Schreiber's defense of Expressionism.[62]

Clearly, such support for modernism should not be mistaken for a rejection of National Socialism. Rather, the students, some Nazi Party members and some supporters of modernist art sought to adapt modernism to the ideology of the Third Reich. The Berlin students earnestly believed that modern art could be 'German'. Thus, they organized the exhibit Thirty German Artists in Ferdinand Moeller's Berlin gallery to demonstrate that Emil Nolde, Ernst Barlach and others visually represented the Nordic spirit. Schreiber even created *Art of the Nation* (*Kunst der Nation*), a new journal designed to represent Expressionism as suitably Nordic and racially pure. Founded in October 1933, *Art of the Nation* had around 3,500 subscribers. It continued to publish until 1935, and it was by no means alone in its attempt to reconcile modern art to the Third Reich. The language of blood and race had entered mainstream art criticism even before 1933; now art journals argued that Expressionism, like Italian Futurism, embodied the spirit of the new, National Socialist era.[63] For example, *Art for All* (*Die Kunst für Alle*) observed that it was not a question of national versus international art, or Impressionism and Expressionism versus German art. Instead, all art produced by Germans had to have some elementally Germanic character. The task at hand was to identify that element, distill it and then embark on a new, wholly German path.[64]

Thus the battle over just what constituted German art continued in the Third Reich. Throughout 1933, those who wished to accommodate modernism to the Third Reich and the *völkisch* purists such as the Combat League for German Culture and the German Art Society battled each other in rival publications, exhibitions and lectures. In part, the struggle intensified because the artists themselves understood that much more was at stake than just style. If the modernists were to continue to be part of the artistic profession, they had to find a place in the culture of the Third Reich. Similarly, the *völkisch* activists sensed that the elimination of modernism was finally within their grasp.

The impetus for the continued contest for cultural authority did not only come from below from the artists' ranks. It also came from above, from within the Nazi Party itself. Hitler had always understood the importance of German culture in the national psyche. His self-identification as an artist and his personal tastes influenced the arts in the Third Reich to a great degree.[65] Moreover, his loyal paladins sought to win his favor and increase their power by initiating cultural policies or actions they hoped reflected his views. The arts in the Third Reich were quickly entangled in party infighting and nearly every powerful National Socialist became involved at one time or another. Wilhelm Frick, minister of the interior, Bernhard Rust, minister for science, education and culture, Robert Ley, head of the German Labor Front, even Hermann Goering and Heinrich Himmler were all involved with defining and promoting 'German' culture.[66]

However, the most important rivalry for authority in the cultural realm was between Alfred Rosenberg and Joseph Goebbels. As editor of the *Völkischer Beobachter*, party ideologue and self-styled cultural expert, Rosenberg led the Combat League for German Culture in the Weimar Republic. He expected to be rewarded with authority over cultural matters after the Nazi Party came to power. He was thus bitterly disappointed when Hitler named Goebbels minister of propaganda and president of the Reich Culture Chamber. All artists who wished to practice their craft in the Third Reich had to be approved by and maintain membership in the Culture Chamber.[67] Such authority might not have been so galling to Rosenberg if Goebbels shared his hatred for modern art. But he did not. Ever the tactician, Goebbels believed that modern art produced by Aryans would lend the Reich both prestige and greater acceptance.[68] To this end, he allowed modern artists who could prove their racial purity to join the Chamber of Culture. Goebbels thus supported those who sought to define Expressionism as Germanic and National Socialist. For instance, he approved *Art of the Nation* for publication and he even contributed articles to the journal.[69]

The Rosenberg-Goebbels competition for cultural authority was further complicated because it was part of the much larger struggle within the Nazi movement between the revolutionary and the more conservative wings. Rosenberg drew attention to this division within the party when he attacked the students in Berlin as revolutionaries and Schreiber as a 'cultural Otto Strasser' who attempted to bring revolution into the visual arts.[70] Adherence to tradition, claimed Rosenberg, not revolution, was what German art required. But such pronouncements did little to resolve the controversy. Even Hitler refused to help. At the 1933 Nazi Party congress, he declared that the Nazi movement and state would not allow 'the representatives of the decay' to convert to National Socialism in order to gain influence in the cultural realm 'to suddenly become the standard-bearers of the future'.[71] The traditionalists, like Rosenberg, claimed that this meant modernists had no place in the Third Reich. However, the 'Germanic' modernists countered that they had always worked for a pure German art, not cultural degeneracy.[72]

Feistel-Rohmeder was furious that modernists managed to find supporters even in the Third Reich. Throughout the art summer of 1933, the Society loudly supported Alfred Rosenberg, an honorary Society member since 1929, the Combat

League and the *völkisch* definition of German art. Through the Society's cultural news service, Feistel-Rohmeder released a barrage of articles that attacked the Berlin students and Otto Andreas Schreiber as radicals who had no respect for their elders or for the Nazi movement. How dare they usurp 'our revolution', she asked, indignantly observing that the German Art Society had been fighting for German art when these upstarts were just children.[73]

The issue of age was especially annoying to Feistel-Rohmeder (who was sixty herself). Schreiber was not even twenty-six years old and yet he pretended to know something about art, she complained. As if that were not frustrating enough, the students' Thirty German Artists show once again saw modernists lauded as young and fresh, in contrast to the supposedly old, backward German artists the Society favored. Feistel-Rohmeder sarcastically noted that in the students' exhibit, '22 of the 30 exhibitors were born back in the previous century, [and] that horrible Christian Rohlfs is even a forty-eighter – 1848, yes!'[74] Barlach and Nolde, the leading examples of 'young' art were in their seventies. These were the students' new heroes of German art?

Feistel-Rohemder observed that the 'art summer' of 1933 looked more like a battlefield than a field ripe for harvest.[75] Every advance made by German art and artists was countered by the modernist camp. The 'chambers of horrors' had revealed to the public the danger of artistic degeneracy and the officials responsible for wasting huge sums on such art. Museum directors such as Max Sauerlandt in Hamburg, Gustav Hartlaub in Mannheim and even the Reich Commissioner of Art (*Reichskunstwart*) Edwin Redslob had been fired. However, as Feistel-Rohmeder noted angrily, the Berlin Secession now claimed that it would continue its tradition as the 'shock troops (*Stosstrupp*) of German art' and would work with the new regime. Artists such as 'Rohlfs, Schmidt-Rottluff, Heckel and Pechstein were treated quite tenderly (*recht liebvoll*) by the *Angriff*', published by Goebbels;[76] and Nolde, Beckmann, Barlach and all the rest were still allowed to exhibit. Even the show Thirty German Artists had been allowed to reopen.[77]

Eventually, predicted Feistel-Rohmeder, Adolf Hitler himself would destroy those who dared to wrap modernist art in swastikas and rehabilitate degenerates as Germans. Until then, the Society would continue its battle. Let the fools debate the identity of German art in their articles, speeches and exhibits. The German Art Society, she declared,

the first organization that took a stand against the spook of November art, who since 1920 has lived for only one goal, to lead the German *Volk* back to its native art, will fight side by side with all good forces of the nation, until cleanliness and German morality rule even in the artistic realm. [The Society] knows what *sacrifice* means, because it has already sacrificed half a human lifetime in the service of German art, with no reward other than the knowledge that it has done its very best in this endeavor.[78]

The battle for art in the summer of 1933 thus served as a justification for the Society to continue. The National Socialists had come to power, but they needed the Society's assistance in defeating the modernist enemy and reclaiming a pure German art for the *Volk*.[79]

However, the Society's continual attacks against modernism coupled with its members' success, especially in Baden, put the organization at considerable risk. Since the Nazis themselves were divided on the issue, it was dangerous for the Society to proclaim to anyone who would listen that it knew what German art was even if the National Socialists did not. Particularly as it became clearer that the party was unable to resolve the debate, those artists attacked by the German Art Society appealed to officials for assistance. They warned that the Society and its members behaved as if they determined policy in the arts, not the Nazi Party. In Karlsruhe artists and supporters of a more pluralistic culture protested to the cultural ministry that a tiny clique was using its Nazi ties to monopolize power and control the local art community. These reports derided the Society's traveling exhibition as a ploy to ingratiate itself into the Nazi cultural realm. The degenerate art shows organized by Society members were not only repugnant, argued critics, but they also enabled the Society to carry out a vendetta against longtime Society opponents. Respectable artists such as Alexander Kanoldt were included in the degenerate art shows in Mannheim and Karlsruhe only because Bühler despised them. Attacks against the Society were often veiled as condemnations of Bühler's poor performance as director of the academy and art museum. Bühler and his clique, claimed Baden artists, were abusing their power and ruining local artistic institutions and traditions. In their appeals, Society opponents went so far as to draw Wacker's attention to the fact that Bühler and other members contradicted the vision of Nazi culture formulated by Joseph Goebbels.[80]

In September 1933, one Th. Butz sent the Baden Ministry of Education and Culture a lengthy analysis of the German Art Society's exhibition of pure German art and the growing influence of Society members in Baden.[81] Butz took particular aim at the exhibit's claim to represent those who had suffered as cultural outsiders during the republic. As Butz forcefully noted, many of the artists exhibited in the traveling show, especially Bühler and Gebhard, had been not the victims but the beneficiaries of the old system.[82] Above all, Butz feared that the Society's exhibit represented the means by which its creators sought 'to place themselves in a position of authority in artistic matters'.[83] They desired nothing less than the right to determine what was 'German' in German art and their primary consideration had less to do with quality than with who their friends and enemies were.

The German Art Society's success was winning it enemies and it had not yet won any powerful allies who would consistently support it. Leading National Socialists and cultural officials had sponsored and praised its traveling exhibition as well as the degenerate art shows organized by some Society members. However, Alfred

Rosenberg, the one Nazi leader the Society actively courted, paid no attention to the Society. Even worse, by the end of the year the Society's continual campaign to oust all modernists from the cultural realm risked alienating the Reich Culture Chamber. After all, the Chamber and Joseph Goebbels were to set cultural policy, not some small circle of *völkisch* artists.

The Society soon realized that in order to continue its battle for German art, it needed to find its own place within the emerging Nazi cultural administration. If the German Art Society were to survive the charges of being a petty clique that cloaked itself in National Socialist colors only to exact revenge on old enemies, if it were to continue as a *völkisch* organization in the Third Reich, it had to find a protector with enough power to shield it or at least a niche from which it could operate. Proud of its traveling exhibition, the degenerate art shows and the new-found prestige and authority of its members, the German Art Society was also bginning to learn what would be a painful lesson: the Nazi victory in Germany would not necessarily mean the victory of the German Art Society. Society members considered themselves to be the natural artists for the Reich, but it was not at all clear whether the Third Reich would want them.

The German Art Society in the Third Reich, 1934–1938

After the heady days of the art summer 1933, debates over art in the Third Reich quieted considerably. For the next several years, the Culture Chamber, the NS-Culture Community (*NS-Kulturgemeinde*) and other Nazi institutions consolidated their control over culture. At the same time, the Nazis gradually developed an artistic direction that they believed would be wholly theirs. By 1937, even limited tolerance for modernism ended and the regime proclaimed that a new German art would flourish. In between those years, however, the German Art Society still had a role to play. Its members were fully integrated into the cultural apparatus of the Nazi state. The Society belonged to the Culture Chamber; contributors to its art journal were approved critics. Its members did win some influential positions, particularly within academy faculties, and its art journal highlighted the exhibitions sponsored by the regime, enabling its writers and artists to participate in Germany's cultural life. However, much to the Society's obvious annoyance, the organization never become a major influence in the Nazi regime.

After 1937, the Society entered a period of crisis from which it never fully recovered. The Nazis were able to transform their definitions of art according to pragmatic needs. Ultimately, they were less concerned with aesthetics than with using art as an instrument to support their ideology and regime.[1] The interparty struggle over just which art form would become the official art for the Reich largely disappeared from public view after 1934; in 1937, the Nazis announced that modernism would be banned and a new artistic style would be developed. But the German Art Society remained mired in its fear of art Bolshevism and in its own *völkisch* vision of German art. The ban on modernist art and the National Socialist effort to chart a new direction for arts in the Third Reich undercut the Society and left it without a clear purpose. In short, the group's great expectations for itself under Nazi rule dissolved into bitter disappointment and not a little defiance.

The primary reason for which the German Art Society survived throughout the Third Reich was its ability to establish an identity beyond that of a *völkisch* artists' interest group through the expansion of its art journal, *Deutsche Bildkunst*. Published by the German Art Society from 1927 until 1930, it had been adopted by the Executive Council of United German Art and Culture Associations during the Weimar Republic. When that was forced to disband in June 1933, Hans Adolf Bühler, director of the state art academy in Karlsruhe, negotiated with the Baden Ministry of Culture, Education and Justice to have the academy sponsor and completely revamp the journal.

This support was won by late 1933.[2] *Deutsche Bildkunst* was renamed *Das Bild* (*The Image*): *A Monthly Publication for German Art in the Past and Present* (Figure 5.1). Published under the authority of the Karlsruhe art academy, the staff and content were greatly expanded. Bühler became the managing editor. Long-time members of the German Art Society staffed the editorial board, including Robert Max Gerstenhauer, Heinrich Blume and Siegfried Czerny. Bettina Feistel-Rohmeder, who had managed *Deutsche Bildkunst* largely on her own, became the editor of medieval and contemporary art. Both she and the headquarters of the

Figure 5.1 Cover of *Das Bild*, May 1941.

German Art Society, which operated out of her home, moved from Dresden to Karlsruhe in late 1933.[3]

The new art journal also won the invaluable support of Otto Wacker, Baden's Minister for Education, Culture and Justice. Wacker had been a friend of Bühler's since their days on the board of the Karlsruhe Combat League for German Culture chapter. He and Bühler had worked together on a number of ventures that enhanced the Society's profile in the state, including the opening of the German Art Society's First Traveling Exhibition of German Art in Karlsruhe during the National Socialist Borderland Rally celebrations in late 1933.[4] Now, both Bühler and Wacker leveraged the expansion of the Society's art journal.

Wacker officially announced the creation of *Das Bild* and its association with the art academy in a directive dated 31 December 1933.[5] He used this opportunity to make it clear that he personally endorsed the new journal. In the directive, Wacker proclaimed that he placed 'the greatest value' upon the use of the magazine as an educational tool in the state's schools. The education minister 'expected the academies, institutes of higher learning, technical schools as well as the district and city school administrations to subscribe to the journal as an indispensable tool for instruction'.[6] Wacker ordered principals to circulate subscription lists and encourage their staffs to subscribe. To ensure that they would see the first issue of *Das Bild*, the ministry sent 1,500 copies out to schools for their inspection. As an added incentive, the ministry subsidized the school subscriptions. The regular price of a single issue, 1.25 RM, was reduced to 0.60 RM for schools and teachers, a subsidy of 48 percent.[7]

In this way, the German Art Society's expanded art journal became required reading for Baden's teachers and reached a much wider audience than ever before. A combination of 2,195 schools and instructors received the first *Das Bild*, published in January 1934.[8] Within the schools, *Das Bild* could be found in libraries and faculty lounges; teachers used the journal for personal reference and as a teaching tool in art education and drawing classes. In the eyes of these teachers, *Das Bild* was a National Socialist publication, endowed with the authority of the NSDAP and the state education ministry.[9] Minister Wacker himself reinforced this view by contributing a lengthy article on the connection between the National Socialist movement and the German style of art to the first issue of *Das Bild*.[10]

The relationship between the Baden Ministry of Education, Culture and Justice, *Das Bild* and the state art academy was, however, short-lived. In July 1934, Bühler, managing editor of *Das Bild*, resigned from the directorships of the Karlsruhe art academy and the state art museum. After just eight issues, the art academy severed its ties with *Das Bild*.[11] It is likely that the ministry discontinued its subscription subsidy for Baden teachers. However, the ministry did not rescind its recommendation that teachers use the art journal and teachers' subscriptions continued to be processed through the ministry (rather than directly through the publisher) as late as 1943.[12] Yet, Bühler's resignation strained his relationship with Wacker, who had little to do with the German Art Society thereafter.[13]

Surprisingly, the loss of the ministry's support did not seriously affect the journal. *Das Bild* simply became the organ of the German Art Society. The group persuaded the journal's publisher, C. F. Müller Verlag of Karlsruhe, to continue its association with *Das Bild*. Hermann Fecht, director of the publishing house, joined the Society's board of directors; two years later he began his long tenure as chairman of the organization. Bühler, who remained on the academy's faculty, continued to serve as the head editor until 1941.

From its first issue in January 1934 until the last one in the spring of 1944, *Das Bild* provided a forum for German Art Society members and supporters to promote their vision for a pure German art and to represent themselves as cultural experts. Appearing monthly, *Das Bild* was published on glossy paper and measured about 8 by 11.5 inches. Each issue was roughly thirty-six pages long with an average of thirty black-and-white reproductions. Some issues included one or two images printed on heavier stock, at times in color; these could be removed and then framed.[14] The *German Art Report* became a supplement to the journal and kept members up to date on promotions and exhibitions, birthdays and deaths[15] (Figure 5.2). The journal probably relied heavily on subsidies from the German Art Society, the German League and the C. F. Müller publishers.[16] The Society's membership, with 731 individual and corporate members in 1936, was too small to support the journal alone.[17]

In the absence of more detailed subscription and publication information, circulation figures provide some indication of *Das Bild*'s success. Circulation of the journal ranged from over 7,000 in 1934 to just under 2,500 in 1939, the last year for which figures are available.

Given the specialized nature of *Das Bild*, the figures represented in Table 5.1[18] were respectable numbers which suggest that an interested public purchased and read the journal. Even when compared to other culturally oriented periodicals, *Das Bild* did well. For example, the journal *Das Innere Reich (The Inner Reich)*

Table 5.1 Circulation Figures, *Das Bild*, 1934–1939

first printing, 1934	7,000
1st quarter 1934	7,826
1st quarter 1936	4,960
3rd quarter 1937	3,373
4th quarter 1937	3,246
1st quarter 1938	2,956
1st quarter 1939	2,561
3rd quarter 1939	2,435

Figure 5.2 Sample page from the *German Art Report*. From *Das Bild*, May 1934, unpaginated.

offers a useful comparison. Also published from 1934 until 1944, *Das Innere Reich* was a literary journal that occasionally treated the visual arts. Like *Das Bild*, *Das Innere Reich* was not sponsored by a Nazi agency. *Das Innere Reich* did support some artists branded as degenerate by Feistel-Rohmeder, but on the whole it offers one way to put *Das Bild* into a wider context.[19]

Das Innere Reich first appeared in April 1934, and by June the press runs stabilized to around 6,000 per issue, declining to a range between 5,800 and 5,000 until 1939, the last year for which data is available. This was in line with two other cultural journals published during the Third Reich. The *Neue Rundschau*'s (*New Review*) monthly figures ranged from 4,200 in 1935 to 1,700 in 1939. The *Deutsche Rundschau* (*German Review*) went from a high of 7,000 issues in 1933 to 3,800 in 1939.[20] In terms of size and ability to survive, *Das Bild* compared favorably to other cultural journals.

Das Bild was intended to showcase the German Art Society's expertise in evaluating and producing German art. Generally, over fifty different authors contributed articles in each of the pre-war years. Contributors came from across the Third Reich and many were professors of art or art history, or critics who held doctorates. These included German Art Society members Franz Hofmann (Munich and Berlin), Josef August Beringer (Mannheim), Emil Hoegg (Munich), Paul Schultze-Naumburg (Weimar) and Emerich Schaffran (Vienna). Membership in the German Art Society was apparently not a prerequisite for writing for the journal, but many of its most prolific contributors had belonged to the Society since before 1933. A few contributors had also written for *Deutsche Bildkunst*, including Beringer, Feistel-Rohmeder, Kurt Luther and Edgar Schindler.

Most of the *Bild*'s contributors were men, but a few women did write for the journal. In 1934, three women (out of a total of forty-seven authors) wrote 25 of the 95 attributed articles, or 26.3 percent; in 1938, six women (out of a total of fifty-five authors) contributed 27 of the 111 attributed articles, or 24.3 percent.[21] Because Feistel-Rohmeder was so prolific – she wrote sixteen articles in 1934, twelve in 1938 – she was largely responsible for the high percentage of articles by women. However, Gerda Kircher, Klara Trost and Erika Günther were also frequent contributors before the war. Kircher, who held a doctorate, had volunteered at the Karlsruhe state art museum during the republic and assisted Bühler with selecting art for the 1933 degenerate art exhibition.[22] Trost, from Hanover, and Günther were identified as art critics in the tables of contents. More women did write for *Das Bild* during the war, but the overall percentage of contributions by female authors remained relatively stable over time at 25 to 30 percent.

Each year, these authors surveyed the paintings, graphic works and sculpture of over 100 artists. The journal's favorite artists, featured repeatedly over the years, were members of the German Art Society: Hanns Bastanier, Sigfried Czerny, Walther Gasch, Richard Guhr, Ernst Emil Heinsdorff, Richard Müller, Georg Siebert, Hermann Tiebert and Wolfgang Willrich. All of these artists had belonged to the Society before 1933. The only woman whose work was shown more than once or twice was Etha Richter, a sculptor from Dresden and probably a long-time friend of Feistel-Rohmeder.[23] Feistel-Rohmeder had just two of her paintings reproduced in *Das Bild*, and while there were articles and poems dedicated to her, she was never featured as an artist.[24] Non-Society members who were regularly mentioned included Josef Thorak, Arno Breker and Albin Egger-Lienz.[25] Albrecht Dürer, Hans Holbein, Lucas Cranach, Caspar David Friedrich and Hans Thoma were regularly featured in *Das Bild* as proof of the unbroken line of German-creators.[26] This artistic heritage was cast back even further through the journal's focus on early Germanic artifacts and medieval architecture and sculpture.

From the very first issue in January 1934, *Das Bild* proclaimed that the German art was vital to the life of the *Volk*. Racially pure art expressed the eternal characteristics of the German people and offered the best medium to effect the unity of all Germans. As an early announcement of *Das Bild*'s creation proclaimed:

> Nothing is so all-encompassing and penetrating at once as art. Art has no prerequisites like science; with [art], there are no laypersons or initiates. Similarly, it is shared by the poor and the rich, the 'educated' and the 'uneducated'... There is no more moving language than the language of art – there is no stronger enticement or more powerful compulsion as the spell of art for good or for bad – because sensibility and the soul are one in a work of art.[27]

Art integrated Germans into a united Third Reich. Thus the notion of Germany as a *Kulturnation* was continued. Class and other divisions could be overcome through an art connected to the *Volk* and serving the Nazi regime. *Das Bild* would reacquaint Germans with their cultural heritage and introduce them to contemporary masters of the German style. In this way, the nation would be brought closer together and the German people would come to realize that they were a creative, powerful race.[28]

The German Art Society believed that *Das Bild*'s mission to promote the eternal, pure German style was particularly important in light of the debates over artistic policy within state and Nazi Party institutions. The Society became a member of Joseph Goebbels' Visual Art Chamber sometime before October 1935, but it by no means approved of the cultural and propaganda minister's apparent tolerance for modernist art.[29] As it had throughout the Weimar Republic, the German Art Society remained steadfast in its definition of the German style of art. Indeed, a dramatically new direction in the visual arts was impossible according to the Society's definition. *Das Bild* repeatedly explained that the *Volk* was characterized by physical characteristics and spiritual values that were racially determined and thus constant over time. Similarly, artistic style and taste were also expressions of race; as long as the race endured, the German style would also continue to represent elemental, racially determined visual forms. The most basic elements of German art were thus eternal.

The German style of art was characterized by three key components (Figure 5.3). The artist had to be racially pure and free of any political taint. The content of his or her art had to be easily recognized by the layperson or *Volk.* This vague requirement meant no abstract works; the topic could be fanciful but people had to look like normal people (no green stripes on noses or orange faces) and landscapes had to look natural. That the public could easily understand the art was proof that German art was an expression of their race. Both the artist and the public inherited their innate attraction for clear, healthy, uncomplicated images. These images, in turn, reflected the values of the German race: honestly and integrity, purity and cleanliness and an inner sense for order and nature.[30]

Figure 5.3 *Maienzeit* by Erwin Aichele. From *Das Bild*, March 1936, before p. 65.

Stylistically, the works ranged from photographic exactitude, to traditional salon painting, to a kind of generic realism. But overall, the content was easily recognizable. Landscapes were the most popular topic, followed closely by portraits of peasants, craftsmen and other pre-industrial workers. Genre scenes, especially of peasant life, flowers and animals were also favorites. Industrial workers and urban sights were extremely rare. Most issues also featured either a German master or an artifact like a bowl, a bracelet or a sword from the bronze age or the early medieval period. These past masters and cultural remnants demonstrated the continuity of the German style and the existence of a racially determined German essence or character over time.[31]

Despite the journal's pretensions to know exactly what the German style was, articles in *Das Bild* explicated the style not by describing paintings or sculpture in detail, but rather by describing the artist's life and character. In *Das Bild,* it was important to put the artist in his or her proper racial and political context; because the artwork was a natural product of race, explaining that often made a description of the work superfluous. Thus, in the course of a review, an artist's name would appear in emphasized typeface; his or her formative, racial experiences would be described; the titles of a few works would be given; and floating above the text, a representative piece by that artist filled the rest of the page.

The reviews always highlighted connections between the artist, racial heritage and the *Volk*. Articles began with an account of the artist's family ties to the current city of residence. Ideally, the artist's grandparents and parents had lived and worked in the region and the artist had spent his or her childhood in the nearby woods or meadows. A typical example can been seen in one of the many reviews of *Das Bild* favorite Walther Gasch. According to the journal, Gasch was descended from craftsmen and farmers in Saxony. His maternal grandmother was a well-known herbalist; skilled in the lore of healing and poisonous plants, she traveled from village to village with a cart pulled by two enormous dogs. 'From her and from his mother, the youngster was not only introduced to ... the local flora, but more important, to the whole mysterious force of nature', as he gathered herbs at the river's edge.[32] Such familial and regional ties informed Gasch and other artists' work. They were also a source of suffering, often because the artist's purity granted him a kind of prophecy. For example, even before the First World War, the artist Richard Guhr realized that 'uncountable German tears would flow' before the Germans would be able to break the power the Jews held over the land.[33] Time spent away from home either for school or the First World War served to strengthen the bond between the artist, his homeland and the *Volk*.[34]

Reviewers also repeatedly emphasized the artists' suffering during the Weimar Republic. Even successful artists were cast as victims of an art establishment supposedly controlled by Jews, greed and the desire to corrupt the *Volk*. For instance, professors Georg Lührig and Richard Müller, both of Dresden, returned from the trenches in 1918 only to find 'red Saxony' overrun with the likes of Otto Dix, Emil Nolde and Oskar Kokoschka. As teachers, they entered the 'battle against the despisers and destroyers of authentic culture', waging war with art Bolsheviks, all for the benefit of an uncaring public.[35] They found kindred spirits in their students Richard Guhr, Hans Hanner and Fritz Kampf. Others artists joined the Nazi Party, sacrificing even their art in service of the National Socialist movement.[36] Such tales of personal struggle encouraged the reader to identify with the artist's struggles and underscored the cultural redemption realized by the National Socialists. And, since most of these artists were German Art Society members, their early Nazi activism lent the organization some prestige.

In *Das Bild*, the artist, his work, the *Volk* and the Third Reich were all connected, all part of the same cultural and racial community. The artist physically embodied the characteristics of a region; his or her painting gave form to those characteristics, which in turn typified the German race. It was the artist's ties to home that established his links to the German public at large and to the Fatherland. In the pages of *Das Bild*, all 'spiritual-artistic creation' was anchored in the powers of *Heimat* (homeland). The very goal of all cultural works was to reveal the connections to the homeland, not only for the artists but for the readers as well.[37]

This devotion to *Heimat* was an article of faith for *Das Bild* and a crucial aspect of the German style. Most reviews grouped several artists together in articles that focused on a region or city, such as the Saar, the Rhineland, Dresden or Munich.[38] Artists represented their regions with their very names: Siegfried Czerny-Heidelberg; Katharine Krabbes-Dresden. Regional identity even served as a way to organize the journal. With the exception of January and the rare special-topic issue, each month was devoted to a region or group of regions. The typical pattern, starting with the February issue, was: the Upper Rhine, the Middle Rhine (or the 'Westmark'), Swabia, the 'East Mark' (*Ostmark* or *Ostrich*, generally southern Germany and Austria), Franconia, Bavaria, Hesse, Thuringia, Saxony, the Rhineland, Westfalia, Lower Saxony, Berlin/Northern Germany and the Eastern Reich. The combinations varied according to space and the number of issues published for the year, but every issue had a regional identity.

The Society wanted nothing less than its German style to become the official style of the regime. To this end, the Society sought to win the support of Alfred Rosenberg. Widely known as the staunch opponent of Goebbels' tolerance for some modern art, Rosenberg repeatedly criticized the Culture Chamber for harboring Jews and modernists. While Rosenberg's Combat League for German Culture had none of the power of the Culture Chamber, it did merge with the National Association of German Theaters to form the NS-Culture Community (*NS-Kulturgemeinde*) in 1934. This reorganized group became part of Robert Ley's German Labor Front, but it continued to be identified with Rosenberg and the anti-modernist camp.[39]

Rosenberg remained a favorite of the German Art Society even in later years[40], but particularly before 1937, the group sought to attract his attention through articles in *Das Bild* and in Society meetings. The Society's apparent expectation that Rosenberg would become a powerful, National Socialist ally for the organization reflects its grandiose opinion of itself as a preeminent circle of artists, but members' hopes were not entirely without merit. The German Art Society had named Rosenberg an honorary member in 1928.[41] Many Society members had been active in the Combat League for German Culture during the republic and from 1934 through 1937, local Society and NS-Culture Community chapters shared members and co-sponsored programs especially in Munich and Berlin.[42]

Das Bild used both text and images to make NS-Culture Community exhibits appear to be Society shows. A favorite tactic was to draw attention to Society members' participation in NS-Culture Community exhibitions by adding '(DKG)' (*Deutsche Kunstgesellschaft*) next to their names or using emphasized typeface;

Figure 5.4 *Forest Workers* (*Waldarbeiter*) by Hans Schrödter. From *Das Bild*, June 1936, p. 196.

such lists of names often ran for several pages. Reviewers then claimed that there were many more participants who belonged to the Society but the limited space made it impossible to name them all.[43] Reviews also emphasized that the German Art Society had long fought to promote the very kind of painting now seen in NS-Culture Community shows. This often led to ridiculous claims. For example, in his review of the 1936 NS-Culture Community exhibit The Forest, Kurt Luther reminded his readers that the theme 'forest' had been treated in *Das Bild* and in *Deutsche Bildkunst* over forty-five times as well as in the Society's 1929 and 1933 exhibitions[44] (see Figure 5.4). When illustrating works exhibited in these NS-Culture Community shows, *Das Bild* always highlighted those by prominent Society members such as Bühler, Siebert, Gebhard and Willrich.

The German Art Society also used *Das Bild* to appeal directly to Rosenberg on at least one occasion. On 11 January 1935 in Munich, the German Art Society hosted a lecture, 'Bolshevism in Politics and in Art' by Franz Langheinrich.[45] This lecture repeated themes emphasized by Rosenberg in December 1934, in which he attacked 'artists of Marxism'.[46] Langheinrich's audience was so taken with his presentation that '[w]ith great enthusiasm' the assembly unanimously decided to send Rosenberg a letter declaring its readiness to join his fight. In the letter, the Society members wrote that they, like Rosenberg, 'the loyal paladin of the Führer, the stalwart champion for German culture', were convinced (as they quoted from his speech), that it can no longer be tolerated, that artists, who for fourteen years were impressed (*geprägt*) by Jews and Marxists, will be touted to us today by certain instinctless men and quite decidedly political players (*Hintermännern*) as the artists of the Third Reich.[47]

Just as Feistel-Rohmeder had declared the Society's willingness to serve the Third Reich in her March 1933 manifesto, the Society once more sounded the call against cultural modernism and alerted Rosenberg to their desire to join him:

> Out with the imported fungus of putrification (*eingeschleppten Fäulnisschwamm*) from the art of the awakened Germany! And out with all those who not only tolerate the renewed invasion of art Bolshevism in the new Reich, but in part even encourage it. Here is the root of evil, and here it will above all be necessary to effect a transformation and remove the remnants of the pathetic Bolshevik legacy of the System and art Bolshevism.[48]

Only two men, Hitler and Rosenberg, claimed the Society members, recognized the danger art Bolshevism presented to the Reich and the desperate need for a pure German art. Every one of the sixty-two signatories placed him- or herself at Rosenberg's complete disposal in order to fight 'for the new German ideology, for the prosperity of German life and therefore for German art'.[49] Despite such devotion, however, Rosenberg apparently never responded to the Society's appeal.[50]

In addition to courting Rosenberg, the German Art Society also used *Das Bild* to represent itself and its members as influential partners with the Nazi regime. The *German Art Report*, now positioned in the first and last pages of *Das Bild*, faithfully noted members' appointments to academies and state and party offices.[51] In 1936, several full-page advertisements for *Das Bild* reproduced favorable reviews of the journal by ten leading newspapers including the Nazi Party papers *Völkischer Beobachter* and *Der Führer*.[52] By emphasizing such examples of National Socialist approval of its members and journal, the German Art Society sought to appropriate some of the party's authority for itself, thereby legitimizing the group and its mission.

The German Art Society even attempted to improve its physical proximity to power by shifting its center of gravity from Karlsruhe to Munich. Munich had long been the headquarters of the NSDAP and in 1933, Hitler had proclaimed it to be the city of German art. The German Art Society wanted to associate itself with the new art capital. The shift to Munich was also due to the large concentration of members there (over 100). From 1934 until 1936, the Society's Munich chapter played an increasingly important role within the organization. The head of the chapter, Professor Bruno Goldschmitt, became the Society's new chairman. More Munich members joined the staff of *Das Bild* and in 1935, the Munich chapter hosted the German Art Society's fifteenth anniversary celebration.[53] However, this move did not improve the Society's fortunes. Despite the German Art Society's best efforts, neither the Nazi Party nor the Munich cultural agencies paid much attention to the *völkisch* artists' interest group.

German Art Society members simply did not understand why the National Socialists refused to avail themselves of the Society's obvious expertise. Articles in both *Das Bild* and the *German Art Report* alternately attacked and bemoaned the continued presence of modernist artists. Interspersed with reviews of members' careers and recommended exhibitions were continual reminders that the degenerates had not yet been completely rooted out. Repeatedly Feistel-Rohmeder and Otto Troebes pointed out that Max Pechstein, Emil Nolde, Paul Klee and others still exhibited work. Private galleries, especially the Dresden Gallery Ernst Arnold, offered 'system art' for sale, and the journal *Art of the Nation* attempted to rehabilitate Expressionism for the Third Reich.[54]

These criticisms of Nazi cultural policy abated somewhat in *Das Bild* after 1935, but the German Art Society continued to strike an aggressively anti-modernist stance at its meetings. At times, members were barely able to contain their anger toward a regime that neither embraced the Society nor rounded up its enemies. For example, the German Art Society's fifteenth anniversary, a chance to celebrate its many accomplishments, became an opportunity to voice its deep concern over art in the Third Reich. Held on 15 January 1935 in Munich, the event was attended by a large number of members and special guests, including a Gau representative from the propaganda ministry. An orchestra began the festivities with selections from Handel, Bach and Haydn. Then the keynote speaker, Munich gallery director Franz Hofmann, presented 'The German Art Society and the Cultural Task of the Present'.[55]

Hofmann began by recalling the days before 1933, when he worked on the *Völkischer Beobachter*, back when with the exception of the *German Art Report*, *Deutsche Bildkunst* and a few other papers, there was virtually no defense raised for German art. In Berlin's National Gallery, in Mannheim, and in Dresden, art had become communist propaganda spread by the likes of Grosz, Dix, Barlach and Klee. After the Nazi seizure of power, Hofmann had hoped that such artists would be sent to Dachau, but that had not been the case![56] Instead, socialists and communists redoubled their efforts to hold on to the arts, disguising themselves in swastikas. German art was not yet free from its Bolshevik enemies; 'the international forces, with their unlimited means continue to attempt even today' to reassert their power, he warned. German art in the Third Reich had made some gains, admitted Hofmann, but the Nazis needed to act more decisively. The modernists had to be eliminated; the impoverished German artists required more assistance. These problems, admitted Hofmann, were 'the concern of the large organizations of the state and the party'.[57] Eventually, they would find a solution.

In the meantime, the German Art Society's mission remained unchanged. As in 1920, the Society would continue the '*battle and the clarification and deepening of the German art consciousness!*'[58]

The mixture of defiance toward and fear of remaining modernists and impatience with the Third Reich expressed at the fifteenth anniversary appears to have been a common feature of German Art Society gatherings. In May 1936, the Society's Berlin chapter held a meeting described in the *German Art Report* as 'Anxiety (*Sorge*) over the Path of German Art'. The first order of business was to address the rumors that were being spread about the editor of *Das Bild*, Hans Adolf Bühler. As had been reported in the April issue, chapter head Otto Troebes assured members that the journal was not a 'Catholic action'. Nor had successful searches discovered that Bühler was a Freemason or that he sympathized with democrats and pacifists. Troebes urged members to report to the Society if they learned of the rumors' source.[59] Such attacks against Bühler and *Das Bild* hint that the Society's insistence on behaving as if they could actually shape policy was still earning it some enmity. But as troubling as such attacks were, being ignored was even more disturbing to Society members.

For nearly two hours, the Berlin chapter members passionately discussed what was to be done to cleanse art of its degeneracy and to strengthen the Society's position. The members noted that modernists understood how to use their art as propaganda for their cause; the Society had to do the same. They agreed that they had to do more to reach out beyond their small circle and educate the public. If the Society remained true to the precepts that had guided its mission since 1920, then they could eliminate all those forces that injured the *Volk* and contaminated pure German art.[60] The implication throughout the meeting was that unless the Society mobilized its forces more fully, modernism would remain a blight on the arts, even in the Third Reich.

The threat of modernists and the need to promote pure German art thus offered Society members an enemy to combat and a cause to champion. However, from 1934 through 1937, the Third Reich increasingly pushed modernists to the cultural periphery until they were wholly banned from public view. The German Art Society took issue with the pace of the modernists' exclusion, but what it failed to understand was that once their enemies were gone, half of their mission would be fulfilled. And, once the Nazi state determined just what kind of art was appropriate for the Third Reich, the German Art Society's entire purpose would be taken over by the state. That is, once the Nazi regime finally determined just what 'German art' was, the Society would have no reason to continue.

Over the course of 1934 and through the summer of 1937, the Third Reich's attitude toward modern artists hardened. At the Nazi Party congress in 1934, Hitler had declared that the Futurists, cubists and Dadaists would not be tolerated in the Third Reich; however, he also refused to endorse the 'backward-looking' artists favored by the *völkisch* camp. Instead, the Führer wanted a new German art that would translate the National Socialist world view into visual form.[61] As the artists and cultural administrators struggled to discover just what such a new German art might be, Nazi institutions increasingly regulated the arts. Goebbels purged his Culture Chamber of insubordinate and unreliable artists, musicians and actors. Eugen Hönig, who had allowed 'Nordic' modernists such as the circle around the journal *Art of the Nation* to exhibit and publish, was replaced as president of the Visual Art Chamber by Adolf Ziegler, an old fighter and opponent to modernism. The propaganda ministry and the Culture Chamber extended their control over artists, exhibitions and private galleries, and censorship intensified.[62] In late 1936, Goebbels even abolished art criticism. Because only art acceptable to the regime was permitted, there was no longer any reason to judge artworks; they were by definition all worthy of being called art. Henceforth, only 'art reporters' certified by the regime would be permitted to describe art and elucidate a work's National Socialist content or value.[63] Although Goebbels had hoped that a few modernists might find a place in the Third Reich, by at least late 1935 he abandoned his more culturally diverse course. In light of attacks by the likes of Alfred Rosenberg and Hitler's personal hatred for modern art, Goebbels adopted a strictly anti-modernist line and made it his own.[64]

Most importantly, by 1937 the regime had consolidated its control over culture and had enough confidence in its program to publicly proclaim both the end of modernism and the beginning of a new art for the Third Reich. This 'new' National Socialist cultural policy was proclaimed in the contrasting art shows held in Munich in July 1937: the Great German Art Exhibition (*Grosse Deutsche Kunstausstellung*) and the Degenerate Art (*Entartete Kunst*) show. After days of celebrations and parades, Hitler opened on 18 July the first annual Great German Art Exhibition in Munich's new House of German Art, dedicated to a German art cleansed of modernism. In a scathing tirade presented on the steps of the House of German Art, Hitler declared that:

> the end of artistic lunacy in Germany and … the cultural destruction of our people has begun. From now on, we are going to wage a relentless cleansing campaign against the last subversive elements of our culture… From now on – and this I promise you – all those cliques of gossips, dilettantes and artistic cheats will be sought out and suppressed.[65]

After four years of National Socialism, Hitler had come to 'a final judgement'.[66] In 1933, when he had announced the creation of the House of German art, critics had urged patience; German art could not rise like a phoenix from the ashes but had to be developed over time. A new art for a new Germany would reveal the soul of the *Volk* and express the national will.[67] The promise of 1933 was now proclaimed to have been realized. From 1937 until 1944, the Great German Art Exhibitions highlighted the best in art that the regime had to offer.

However, it was not enough just to offer a positive definition of art in the Third Reich. To underscore the break with the past, the National Socialists also had to publicly defame modernist art once and for all. The day after the first Great German Art Exhibition opened, the Degenerate Art show debuted in the cramped rooms of Munich's Archeological Institute. Hundreds of Dadaist, cubist and Expressionist works were put on display as documents of the cultural degeneracy fostered by the Weimar Republic. More than any policy pronouncement, it was these two contrasting exhibits that delineated National Socialist cultural policy.[68] Although the Nazis were still unclear as to just what constituted German art, they were certain that the annual Great German Art Exhibitions would cultivate a new artistic form that represented the Third Reich. After four years of Nazi rule, it was time to leave the past behind and start cultivating new, younger artists who could provide the regime with a new German art.[69]

This new path represented a real crisis for the German Art Society. According to its understanding of German art, a new direction was impossible. German art could be infused with a renewed impulse, its Germanic qualities could be brought out further, but German art could no more change its basic nature than German blood could. Moreover, the Society's members, most of whom were in their late fifties and sixties, hardly qualified as the kind of fresh young talent the regime hoped to attract. The members had expected to become the new leaders of the Nazi cultural program endowed with the authority to shape the next generation of artists. But it had all gone terribly wrong. The German state had taken up the cause of pure German art; the Nazi Party was finally ready to carry out the purge against modernism. Yet the German Art Society had been completely left behind.

The 1937 delineation of Nazi cultural policy presented the German Art Society with a dilemma it was never ever really able to resolve. The Society's mission to promote pure German art and to combat cultural modernism had been fulfilled. The National Socialists now claimed these two goals as their own. However, if the Society acknowledged its victory, the organization no longer had any reason to continue. Even Bettina Feistel-Rohmeder had to acknowledge that the artists' interest group would henceforth play a more limited role.[70] But what was that role to be? The German Art Society was eager to serve as artists for the Reich, but the Third Reich had little use for the group. What purpose did the German Art Society now serve? The Society was left with two choices: accept victory and disband, or recast its identity. In 1937, the organization decided on the latter course.

The sense of crisis and bewilderment that seized the German Art Society after the Nazis declared the battle for German art to be won was most painfully displayed at the Society's Second Traveling Art Exhibition in the fall of 1937. Just four years before, the First Traveling Exhibition had toured Germany, welcomed by Nazi officials and praised as a model to be emulated. Now, however, the second Society exhibit was just another small art show. Neither *Das Bild* nor the *German Art Report* mentioned any official support. It appears that no catalog of the show was published; even Feistel-Rohmeder's review was unusually brief and did not identify the exhibitors.[71] Although the Second Traveling Exhibition toured the art leagues of Munich, Stuttgart, Karlsruhe and Heilbronn from October 1937 until early spring 1938, it simply could not compete with official, National Socialist exhibitions.[72]

Precisely because it could not compete, the German Art Society attempted to place its second exhibition within the context of a National Socialist cultural triumph. *Das Bild*'s review of the exhibit was positioned in the middle of an extended report of art shows in Berlin, Baden-Baden, Munich and Heidelberg, and of the world exposition in Paris.[73] Society members' participation in these shows as well as the Great German Art Exhibition and others was emphasized throughout the text, the reproductions and even the *German Art Report* supplement.[74] Feistel-Rohmeder reported that 'more than a quarter of the works exhibited in the House of German Art were directly connected' to the Society's mission.[75] In fact, out of the seventy-seven artists who exhibited in the Society's 1933 exhibition, seventeen exhibited in the first Great German Art show.[76] Ever capable of putting the best possible spin on the Society's fortunes, Feistel-Rohmeder insisted that the German Art Society had not been pushed aside; rather, both it and its second traveling exhibit were basking in the afterglow of a Nazi victory.

Though the Society put on a brave face, deep down it could not deny its crisis of legitimacy. It clearly worried that it had to justify itself and its exhibit. *Das Bild* did both by providing the full text of Society chairman Hermann Fecht's speech delivered at the show's opening. A rambling oration that alternated between pride in the organization's past, defensiveness toward its current status and fear of the future, Fecht's speech gave voice to the sense of crisis in the organization. Fecht offers a glimpse into the Society's self-image just four months after its cultural 'victory'.

In his justification of the German Art Society, Fecht stressed the organization's loyalty to the cause of pure German art. For years, he reminded members, they had fought without recognition or outside help. Surrounded by enemies during the republic, the Society had continued to fight after 1933. While such an account of the nearly insurmountable odds the organization once faced was a required element in all Society histories,[77] Fecht here carried the struggle into the Third Reich. Referring obliquely to the Nazis' confused artistic policy between 1933 and 1937, Fecht explained that the Society's struggle

actually became increasingly difficult in the last four years, because the opponents [of pure German art] misunderstood the Führer's quiescence and became ever bolder until finally in this year the Führer's incomparable patience was exhausted and he spoke words of redemption at the opening of the House of German Art.[78]

Fecht implied here that even when the Nazis hesitated, the German Art Society took action despite the cost to itself. At the same time, the chairman tied the Society to Adolf Hitler and the renewal of German cultural policy.

Fecht then turned to the matter at hand, the Society's art exhibition. He acknowledged that people might well wonder what purpose the Society's small art show could possibly serve in light of the official Great German Art Exhibition. His explanation revealed the Society's defensiveness as well as its sense of self-importance. The organization was determined to hold this exhibition because, said Fecht, it wanted to honor

> the old guard, which has always labored unyieldingly in the spirit of our Führer, in the spirit of the Third Reich, and has fought for many years in our German Art Society against everything foreign and above all, against the powers of decay...[79]

This exhibition thus honored Society old fighters by showing their works and by reminding the public of the battle they had fought and won.

The rest of Fecht's speech, which continued for more than a page in *Das Bild*, turned to what became the German Art Society's main justification for its existence after 1937: the absolute necessity to protect German art from the now-hidden proponents of modernism. Since 1920, Fecht reminded the audience, the German Art Society had dedicated itself to leading the *Volk* back to its own art, to promoting artists whose talent, character and selfless devotion to the cause promoted pure German art. Even the creation of Nazi art institutions could not obviate the need for the continued existence of the Society:

> Now many will say once again: admittedly, your pretty appeal is legitimate, but in the future public art institutions (*öffentliche Kunstpflege*) will remove you from this task. No – precisely because the Führer has proclaimed the inviolability, to say nothing of the infallibility, of this [task], we believe that our work can not be taken from us; rather, [our mission] has become even more necessary.[80]

Had not the German Art Society proven its value repeatedly? Was it not true that no Society member found a place in the 'temple of degenerates'? Was the Society not well represented on the walls of the Great German Art Exhibition? Surely this proved the quality of the Society's artistic judgement and expertise.

The organization's fear that it would become superfluous in the new artistic order was evident here and rang out in Fecht's closing remarks. Speaking for the German Art Society, Chairman Fecht sincerely hoped that the more official art institutions knew of the organization's efforts in behalf of pure German art, the more they will not only not hinder our work but also treasure and support [it]. For the enemy is still in our midst, powerful in number and financial means, extremely capable of disguising itself, of setting traps, of surrounding itself with a saintly appearance. We must therefore continue to hope that our combat troops will become ever more numerous, ever more unassailable, and that our German artists, even if they often lack unity among themselves, will at least reject the enemy, reject mediocrity and decay, so that from our model garden [i.e. the Society's exhibit] the German Fatherland will finally arise.[81]

While it is certainly understandable that German Art Society members feared for their organizational existence after 1937, the degree of paranoia exhibited in Fecht's speech is remarkable. Members had always pointed out the existence of the modernist enemy in their midst; but now, at the very moment when the enemy's defeat seemed certain, the organization was terrified that the modernists would somehow rise again. This paranoia, however, served a useful function. From 1937 until at least late 1944, the German Art Society fed itself on the terror of the potential return of art Bolshevism and it remained a constant refrain throughout *Das Bild*, Society meetings and members' correspondence. The Society's paranoia was even reflected in Feistel-Rohmeder's collection of *German Art Report* articles published in book form by Fecht's C. F. Müller publishing house under the title *In the Terror of Art Bolshevism*. Published in 1938, Feistel-Rohmeder began her book by reminding readers that the battle against art Bolshevism had not yet been won; indeed, she believed that many 'old fighters' would not live to see the final day of victory.[82]

At every opportunity, Society members reminded themselves that they had been waging the battle for German art and against modernism since 1920; that they were the first organization dedicated to this mission; that the Society acted on its own, with great sacrifice, long before even the Nazi Party took up the fight. This identity became ever more precious as its members felt increasingly unappreciated by the Third Reich and members would defend it at any price. In responding to the rumors about Bühler, *Das Bild* had warned that insulting a party member could have unpleasant consequences, implying that they could defend the honor of a party member in the Nazi Party Court.[83] In 1937, Bettina Feistel-Rohmeder actually turned to the Nazi Party Court to defend the reputation of the *German Art Report*, *Das Bild*, and herself, and from no less a critic than the Nazi Party newspaper, the *Völkischer Beobachter*.

In May of 1937, just months before the Great German Art Exhibition and the Degenerate Art show, the *Völkischer Beobachter* favorably reported the opening of the new Munich branch of the Dresden Gallery Ernst Arnold, headed by Ludwig Gutbier. Bettina Feistel-Rohmeder regarded it as outrageous that the Nazi Party newspaper approved of the gallery. Both the Gallery Ernst Arnold and Gutbier were longtime enemies of Feistel-Rohmeder and the Society. During the Weimar Republic, she had castigated Gutbier's exhibitions of Emil Nolde, the *Brücke* and other modernist artists. After 1933 the attacks continued, with the *German Art Report* articles demanding that the pro-Expressionist gallery be closed.[84]

In June 1937, Feistel-Rohmeder used the *German Art Report* to attack the Gallery Arnold yet again. But this time, she also went after the *Völkischer Beobachter* for its favorable review of the gallery's Munich opening. She furiously reminded her readers of Gutbier's support of Expressionists during the 'period of decay'. She then imprudently declared that supporters of the German Art Society recognized this enemy of German art, even if the Nazi Party newspaper did not:

> Our reports on Gutbier's support of Pechstein, Kokoschka, Dix, Kandinsky, Nolde and all the other greats of the System, surely remain in the memories of longtime *German Art Report* readers… In its Munich edition of 26/27 May the *Völkischer Beobachter* greeted the opening of this now Munich Gallery Ernst Arnold under the headline 'A New Gallery Begins', with a vibrant report on the gallery's beautiful arrangement and a reference to the owner's '*decades [of] fruitful work*' in Dresden. (Emphasis ours. The editor.)
>
> We assume that Germany's artistic circumstances between the end of the war and the seizure of power are unknown to the reviewer and [we would] gladly place at his disposal our abundant material, especially regarding Gutbier's 'fruitful' activity here and abroad.[85]

As might be expected, the Nazi Party newspaper did not welcome Feistel-Rohmeder's offer to lend her expertise to its staff.

In October 1937, the *Völkischer Beobachter* angrily responded to Feistel-Rohmeder's criticism in a letter directed to the editors of *Das Bild*. The *Völkischer Beobachter* informed *Das Bild* that the Gallery Ernst Arnold review in the *German Art Report* was 'arrogantly critical in tone' and that it had misquoted the *Völkischer Beobachter*. *Das Bild* had thus allowed the reviewer to 'publicly reprimand' an experienced *Völkischer Beobachter* contributor.[86] The Nazi Party newspaper assured *Das Bild* that its reporter was not only well-informed regarding the gallery's past but that, unlike the *German Art Report*'s author, was not guided by personal sentiment and one-sided opinion. Furthermore, the Nazi Party organ absolutely refused to be reprimanded by 'some in no way authorized private circle's little newsletter' and threatened to take action against the complete lack of party discipline exhibited by the editors of *Das Bild*.[87]

Enraged by this letter, Feistel-Rohmeder did not wait for the *Völkischer Beobachter* to act. Instead, she initiated a suit in the Bavarian Nazi Party Court against the *Völkischer Beobachter* correspondent. Feistel-Rohmeder filed her lawsuit on the grounds that the party newspaper's letter to *Das Bild* had insulted her both personally and professionally. Her honor as a Nazi Party member, an old fighter and an experienced art expert were all at stake. From the materials she assembled in her defense, it is clear that she also sought to defend the German Art Society and its mission. In the eyes of the party court, the suit was between Feistel-Rohmeder and [I.?] Berchtold, who eventually took responsibility for the letter sent to *Das Bild*; but in Feistel-Rohmeder's mind, it was a lawsuit between the *Völkischer Beobachter* and *Das Bild*, two rival art experts.[88]

In the materials gathered for the suit, Feistel-Rohmeder represented both herself and the German Art Society as valuable contributors to the development of German art in the Third Reich. She submitted copies of dozens of articles – many had originated in the *German Art Report* – to prove that newspapers such as *Der Freiheitskampf*, the *Vossische Zeitung* and the *Neue Sächsische Landeszeitung* also regarded the gallery with suspicion.[89] She also noted that an earlier art critic for the *Völkischer Beobachter*, Franz Hofmann, valued the Society's efforts to combat modernism.[90]

Even as she sought to defend *Das Bild* and the *German Art Report*, Feistel-Rohmeder also defended her own reputation. As the other critiques of the gallery proved, her review was not due to one-sided, personal sentiment. In one packet of lawsuit materials entitled 'The Insult', Feistel-Rohmeder detailed the abuse she had suffered as a result of the *Völkischer Beobachter*'s attack.[91] As a member of the NSDAP and the National Association of the German Press (a division of the Reich Culture Chamber), she was deserving of respect. The editor who wrote the letter had insulted, as she modestly described herself, 'a personality who was the first to take up during the November Republic the battle against art Bolshevism and for German art and has waged that battle for more than 18 years'.[92] That this battle still needed to be fought was demonstrated by the party newspaper's endorsement of the pro-modernist Gallery Arnold.

It was clear that the *Völkischer Beobachter*'s description of the *German Art Report* as an unauthorized, unimportant newsletter particularly rankled Feistel-Rohmeder. In the documents she submitted, she haughtily informed the party court that the *German Art Report* was a supplement to *Das Bild*. Vastly inflating the journal's circulation figures, she claimed the *Report* was read by '3–4,000 readers' a number 'which according to the normal use of the German language, cannot be described as "some private circle"'.[93] She noted that if it were so insignificant, then the head of the Nazi Party Archive would not have been so pleased to receive a complete collection of the *German Art Report* for its collection.[94] Feistel-Rohmeder went on:

> Is it possible to refer to an art journal that has existed for 11 years as 'in no way authorized'? Foreign countries maintain of the German press, that only the party press is 'authorized'! Until now, the Third Reich provided even non-party, self-supported organs the opportunity to express a candid opinion based upon expert knowledge.[95]

Even the *Völkischer Beobachter* itself had used material from the *German Art Report*, written by Feistel-Rohmeder.[96]

By marshalling such proof Feistel-Rohmeder sought to demonstrate her steadfast loyalty to the Nazi Party while simultaneously casting *Das Bild* in an appropriately National Socialist light. Throughout the lawsuit's materials, Feistel-Rohmeder declared that the German Art Society's views were wholly in keeping with the 'artistic will' of Adolf Hitler, Alfred Rosenberg, Wilhelm Frick and the president of the Visual Art Chamber, Adolf Ziegler.[97] Feistel-Rohmeder also did her best to tie the German Art Society to old fighters prominent enough to capture the court's attention. For example, she claimed that the German Art Society was 'under the patronage' of Brunswick's Minister-President Dietrich Klagges – which she knew to be untrue – and noted that Gerstenhauer and Blume were still members.[98] Feistel-Rohmeder even sought to curry the favor of Walter Buch, the head of the Nazi Party Court (*Oberster Parteirichter*). Although she pretended to ask for his legal advice in the letter she wrote him, she clearly hoped that his German League membership and possible friendship with her father would help her cause.[99] Despite her best efforts, however, Feistel-Rohmeder did not win her case. In late February 1938, the court determined that Feistel-Rohmeder had not been insulted, only chastised for her *German Art Report* critique of the *Völkischer Beobachter*. The suit was dropped by the court.[100]

Until 1937, the German Art Society could sustain its belief that the Nazis would eventually recognize its members' cultural expertise. After the Great German Art Exhibition the organization continued to represent itself as a full participant in the cultural life of the Third Reich, but even its most ardent supporters realized that it was increasingly relegated to the sidelines. Subscriptions to *Das Bild* plummeted from 4,960 in April 1936 to 2,956 by June 1938. Even the Society's Second Traveling Exhibition revealed the members' sense of crisis. However, as long as *Das Bild* continued, the German Art Society would maintain a presence in the Third Reich.

For despite its small size, *Das Bild* and the Society served a useful function for the National Socialist regime. Steadfastly loyal, they pointed out the regime's enemies without ever challenging the party itself. *Das Bild* provided extensive coverage of art exhibitions throughout the Reich. It promoted contemporary artists, acceptable to the regime, and allied their art with the goals and values of the Third Reich. As a non-party organ, *Das Bild* lent some credence to the Nazi claim that their cultural policies reflected those of the public will. Particularly before 1937, Joseph Goebbels often claimed that Nazi cultural policy was to cultivate rather than regulate the arts. *Das Bild*, along with other non-party magazines and the National Socialist journal *Art in the Third Reich*, contributed to the regimentation of the arts all the while maintaining an illusion of a sort of cultural pluralism. The Society could thus continue its own mission, even as it served the interests of the Nazi state.

–6–

German and Nazi Art

Adolf Hitler's 1937 decision to abolish cultural modernism signaled a turning point for art in the Third Reich. However, it was a turn incompletely negotiated. The campaign to negate modernism had succeeded but the Nazis still lacked a positive program for the arts. In essence, they had answered only one part of the question 'what is German art?' Styles associated with modernism were to be avoided. The content would be accessible to the masses and avoid any negative social commentary. Beyond that, Nazi officials had no one aesthetic in mind. The Third Reich had an intricate, overlapping and often conflict-ridden cultural infrastructure, but it was quite uncertain just what kind of art their institutions were to foster.

The arts in the Third Reich operated on at least two interrelated levels. Policies, recommendations and outright bans were instituted from above; these directives were then interpreted into artistic practice from below.[1] The arts were a medium for political indoctrination. However, in the absence of a clear, positive program, artists and organizations could still pursue their own interests, within institutional and doctrinal limits.[2] The National Socialists' cultural apparatus regulated access to artistic professions and oversaw exhibitions, journals and galleries. The artists and art reporters disseminated the official cultural line and produced works of art which then filled the regime's exhibits, public buildings and art market. The creation of art for the Third Reich was thus an active process of constant renegotiation from above and below.

Thus the German Art Society continued to operate even after 1937. From the pages of *Das Bild*, the group repeated the official doctrine. But the Society also manipulated the official line in order to both justify its existence and integrate itself into the Third Reich. *Das Bild* and members' intense loyalty ensured that the German Art Society continued until 1944. The German Art Society's survival after 1937 illustrates how a non-party but pro-Nazi artists' group and journal disseminated the Third Reich's interpretation of culture, manipulated it for their own purposes and even criticized its results.

Despite a great deal of scholarship, 'Nazi art' remains problematic as a term to describe the arts in the Third Reich.[3] Certainly, paintings depicting Nazi leaders, the SA, SS, Hitler Youth and ideological themes ('the *Volk*', 'comradeship', 'young Germany', etc.) fall within the category, but such works never made up the majority of art produced. According to one estimate, for example, just over 3 percent of the works shown at the 1937 Great German Art Exhibition were of Nazi leaders, buildings or events. The vast majority of the works were landscapes (40 percent) followed by 'Womanhood and Manhood' (15.5 percent) and animals (10 percent).[4] Stylistically, too, it is difficult to identify one aesthetic that was unique to the period.[5] Monumental sculptures such as that by Arno Breker and Josef Thorak come closest, but these were considered exceptional even during the period.

Neither content nor style, then, offers much guidance to defining just what made art peculiarly 'Nazi'. Instead, the visual arts had to be transformed into expressions of National Socialist ideology through interpretation of the works in the media and of the exhibits, and by the artists' participation in the regime. 'Nazi art' was in fact a term rarely used. In seeking to define the type of art appropriate for the regime, artists and other experts struggled to identify 'German' art. To an extent, the arguments about German art that had been common in Germany since the turn of the century continued after 1937. The real difference was that now state organizations and Nazi Party offices played a decisive role in determining the institutional framework and the acceptable terms within which the debate could take place.

The interpretations which art reporters placed upon, for example, an innocuous yet well-executed landscape served as a Nazi gloss, like a supplemental layer of varnish that enabled the work to reflect an appropriately National Socialist light. Indeed, if the dominant interpretations that cast thematically 'non-Nazi' art into a suitably 'Nazi' mode are examined, the lack of a well-defined artistic program for the arts becomes even clearer. From 1937 until 1945, the National Socialist interpretation of German art went through three distinct phases, each with its own dominant theme. These were disseminated through speeches, the annual Great German Art shows and the Nazis' own art journal, *Art in the Third Reich* (*Die Kunst im Dritten Reich*).[6] Produced by Alfred Rosenberg's party agency, *Art in the Third Reich* was published from 1937 until April 1944. With a circulation of 25,000, it was the dominant Nazi organ for the visual arts.[7] As such, its articles signaled the main themes within which discussions about art in the Third Reich occurred and featured artists and works favored by the regime.

From 1937 until the start of the war, *Art in the Third Reich* consistently asserted that the visual arts were in a state of becoming.[8] Long slowed by the drag of modernism, painting and even sculpture, it was admitted, lagged behind architecture in terms of developing a wholly new direction. But after four years of National Socialism, cultural institutions had been freed from the modernist taint, and the cultural will of the *Volk* had been determined. As Alfred Rosenberg explained, 'the degenerate, the diseased, and the tortured' would no longer have pride of place; instead, the arts would be the purview of the 'strong, [and] the healthy, which pair the creative will with an inner power and an external character-building harmony'.[9] Like the new architecture, the new German art would be heroic and monumental. Its ideals would emanate from Nazi ideology and the character of the *Volk*, yet at the same time the visual arts would express the eternally German artistic sensibility.[10]

Just what such art looked like, however, remained an open question. To guide artists, *Art in the Third Reich* reproduced works by approved artists. Graphic works by Richard Klein, sculptures by Breker and Thorak and paintings by Adolf Ziegler, Wilhelm Petersen, Karl Storch, Adolf Wissel and others were featured in the special issue devoted to the first Great German Art Exhibition.[11] Most issues also included a section called 'Masterpieces of German Art'. Here, painters from earlier centuries were highlighted as artists whose works expressed the eternally Germanic sensibility. Albrecht Altdorfer, Albrecht Dürer, Lucas Cranach and Hans Holbein were models to be emulated.[12] Nineteenth-century artists appeared less regularly, but included Hans Thoma, Wilhelm Leibl and Ferdinand Georg Waldmüller.[13]

Overall, however, the National Socialist art journal was long on aesthetic pronouncements and short on contemporary artists who could qualify as true masters of German art. These shortcomings were recognized even by Nazi leaders. The Great German Art exhibitions held every summer in Munich were the penultimate venue for government-approved art and artists. Yet each year Hitler, Joseph Goebbels and other officials were dissatisfied with the submissions. Hitler was so incensed by the works chosen for the inaugural show that he selected many of the works himself.[14] Even after being approved by the Führer, however, Goebbels assessed the paintings' over all quality as 'quite catastrophic'.[15] Nor did the quality of submissions improve in subsequent years. In his last speech at a Great German Art Exhibition opening, in July 1939, Hitler acknowledged he was still awaiting a 'creative genius' who could do for painting what Thorak and Breker had done for sculpture: create a heroic art that gave form to the political and ideological truths of the Third Reich.[16] While pleased by architectural projects as designed by Albert Speer and others, Nazi art officials remained unimpressed by the 'new' painting and sculpture that were supposed to be created after 1937.

If the first phase evoked great expectations, the second can be characterized as one of certain victory. From the beginning of the Second World War until early 1943, German art joined the armed forces on their victorious conquest of the continent. Surely, crowed Nazi art reporters, the war would be the final spark that would set the culture of the Third Reich ablaze with glory. The victory of German culture abroad was especially emphasized. Remnants of German architecture in Danzig, Strassburg and elsewhere 'proved' those territories were rightfully German. Similarly, it was claimed German art exhibited in the newly conquered lands demonstrated the superiority of the German race. German artists who exhibited abroad or produced works on the battlefields were also mastering new cultural territory and, in so doing, they tied the new lands firmly to the growing Nazi empire.[17] The cultural imperialism of National Socialist culture was reflected in the title change of their official art journal in September 1939. No longer was it a journal about *Art in the Third Reich*; it was now a journal about *Art in the German Empire* (*Die Kunst im Deutschen Reich*).

Despite the racial impetus to cultural greatness which the Nazis assumed would accompany the war, however, officials remained skeptical about the actual results.[18] Part of the problem, of course, was that fighting the war was simply much more important than trying to win a new cultural form. The war absorbed the Nazis' interests and young men became soldiers, not artists. Although the Great German Art Exhibitions continued from 1940 through 1944, Hitler never again attended the opening ceremonies. Nor were the exhibits accompanied by a host of musical, theatrical and artistic events.[19] To the extent that Nazi elites remained interested in the arts, they expressed that enthusiasm in the looting of European masterpieces.[20] The new German masterpieces supposedly being produced at home could not compete with the cultural riches to be had in the occupied East and West.

The final phase of Nazi culture reinterpreted German art once again in the light of military events and was triggered by the devastating defeat at Stalingrad in January 1943. This last twist on art in the Third Reich transformed the Second World War into an epic cultural conflict between two rival powers: Europe and Bolshevism. German art was now extolled as the purest expression of European culture. Only the Third Reich and the Germans could defend the European artistic heritage from the barbaric Bolshevik assault. The war became a struggle between competing races whose culture expressed their values and ideals. At times the British and the Americans joined the Russians in an unwieldy amalgamation generally described as the Bolshevik-Anglo-American threat, but the emphasis was clearly on the Soviet Union.

The first clear indication of this final interpretation came in an *Art in the Third Reich* article entitled 'On the 30th of January 1943'.[21] Written by Rosenberg to commemorate the tenth anniversary of Hitler's accession to power, the piece proclaimed that more than ever the arts must not be abandoned, because they tied the soldier and the home front together. Fighting in the dark and cold on the Western and Eastern fronts, explained Rosenberg, the German soldier held in his mind's eye memories of home: 'the images of his cities and towns, the images of his forests and seas, the images of the German people itself in all of its branches'.[22] Paintings of home, and even of home's destruction, helped the soldiers face their duty on the battlefields. After the war, such artworks would attest to the sacrifice of the 'German nation [which fought] for the freedom of this old, venerable continent...'[23]

Even as art tied home and battlefield together, it also identified friend and foe. Robert Scholz, Rosenberg's art expert and managing editor for *Art in the Third Reich*, explained that:

> On the one side stand the imperialistic pretensions of Anglo-American and Bolshevik materialism; on the other, under the leadership of Germany, Europe, fighting to defend an outlook on life which sees in the production of culture the highest expression of the people's existence and which, quite simply, is the highest goal of human existence.[24]

Decades before, claimed the official art journal, all of Europe was crippled by the degeneracy of the skyscraper-style, jazz, Hollywood kitsch and every other kind of cultural Bolshevism. Then as now, Europe faced the 'combined forces' of the Americans, the British and the Soviets, all 'controlled' by the Jews. That the Anglo-American-Soviet coalition neither understood nor cared for culture was proven by their wanton destruction of 'European cities' and the terror of their bombs. The journal argued that art in all its manifestations demonstrated that in the battle against the American 'gangsters' and the 'Bolshevik subhumans', the 'genius of European culture stood beside the fighting soldiers' of Germany.[25] In this way, German art and its defenders became the standard-bearer of European culture.

In each of the three phases, the German Art Society's journal *Das Bild* adjusted its defense of the German style to conform to the Nazi interpretations. However, the journal did not simply follow the lead of *Art in the Third Reich*. While one might expect the content of both art magazines to be nearly identical, in fact there was virtually no overlap in terms of the articles, artists or art at all. Like the official party journal, *Das Bild* did cover Great German Art exhibitions, but even in those reviews *Das Bild* generally featured different artists and reproduced different works. For example, in September 1937, *Art in the Third Reich* highlighted the work of twenty-one artists exhibiting in the Great German Art show. Of those, only eight had works featured in *Das Bild* in all of 1937, and four (Thorak, Ferdinand Staeger, Oskar Graf and Max Zaeper) were featured either well before or well after the Great German Art exhibition reviews.[26] *Das Bild* did include excepts from Hitler's speeches at the openings of the 1937 and 1938 Munich shows. However, none of *Das Bild*'s reviews were mere repetitions of a prepared text. Articles by Bettina Feistel-Rohmeder, Edgar Schindler, Hans Adolf Bühler and others who had written for *Deutsche Bildkunst* were still characterized by the language and *völkisch* values they had used in the republic. And, as in the republic, the Society continued to criticize the art establishment.

The 1937 announcement that the arts would now embark on a new direction presented the German Art Society with its greatest challenge. Its journal did review the official shows in Munich each year; its editors repeated the claim that art could start anew and find new, young artistic talents for the Reich. Bühler praised the 1937 Great German Art Exhibition as a turning point in the arts. He grandly announced that 'The Third Reich is waiting for the great artistic deed' that would doubtless result from the awakening of the racial soul.[27] But the Society had difficulty embracing the supposedly new direction completely. Deep down, the Society refused to acknowledge that a new kind of German art was even a viable concept. After all, a new direction was really impossible according to the Society's understanding of German art. The German style was as eternal and unchangeable as the race from which it emanated. Even as Feistel-Rohmeder extolled the 'clear word and the visible deed of the Führer's exhibit' in Munich that 'brought victory for all that is *German* in the visual arts', she also had her reservations.[28] She and the others who wrote for *Das Bild* could not help but qualify the use of the word 'new' when used to describe the new direction in art. What was new was not the content or style of painting; it was that official agencies of the state now promoted only German art, just what the German Art Society had always advised.[29]

Das Bild reserved its most effusive praise of the Great German Art exhibitions not for the art shown there but for the role the Society had played in making it all possible. Feistel-Rohmeder and the other contributors constantly reminded readers that the Society and its journal had fought since 1920 for the very kind of genuine German art that the Führer had now acknowledged. *Das Bild* presented the 'brilliant Munich days' of 1937 as 'days of fulfillment', but for the Society, not the Nazis. Feistel-Rohmeder claimed that '*more than a quarter* of all the works exhibited in the House of German Art' were directly related to the Society's efforts.[30] Artists long promoted by the Society were widely exhibited and had seen their works purchased by Hitler and his closest colleagues. 'That which was our goal, what our Bühler, Heinsdorff, Broel, Widnmann, Gasch and still many others depict in their works, that had now been acknowledged: *the German style in painting!*', crowed Feistel-Rohmeder.[31]

Other than voicing its approval for the decision to finally eliminate modernist art, *Das Bild*'s contributors received the news that a new cultural direction would be sought rather coolly. *Das Bild* downplayed the 1937 Great German Exhibition, treating it not as a singular event but as just one of many exhibitions. Only five months after the exhibit opened was the show featured, and then in less than two pages.[32] The 1938 Great German Art Exhibition did not merit a review; *Das Bild* simply reproduced Hitler's opening speech and a few works from the show.[33] The 1939 show's reviews were extensive, but Feistel-Rohmeder's praise was limited. She complained that the show favored younger artists from Munich and Berlin over experienced artists from other parts of Germany. Feistel-Rohmeder wrote that 'it did not seem wrong to ask whether all German racial types and regions (*Stämme und Gaue*) of the Fatherland were equally represented' in the show.[34] Still, the only thing that really mattered was 'that the true face of German art of the present was revealed'; just why that was happening so slowly, she added, 'cannot be discussed here'.[35]

These criticisms point to the two of *Das Bild*'s more unique contributions to art in the Third Reich: regionalism and its emphasis upon contemporary artists. The German Art Society's definition of German art had always drawn upon the regional identities and traditions of its artists. Within the Great German Art exhibition reviews, *Das Bild* routinely noted the artists' hometowns or regions.[36] Even after 1937, every issue except January and the occasional special issue highlighted a particular region. Unlike *Art in the Third Reich*, *Das Bild* preserved regional identity and honored local artistic strengths and traditions. *Das Bild* also featured the work of far more contemporary German artists than the official journal ever did. Over the course of a year, *Art in the Third Reich* featured only a handful of living artists who demonstrated what the new German art would be. The Society's journal, however, treated the work of literally hundreds of artists. Walther Gasch, Siegfried Czerny, Richard Müller and a host of other Society members and non-members continued to be praised as practitioners of pure German art.[37] Unlike *Art in the Third Reich*, *Das Bild* did not need to look for new talent or work out a new direction. It had been promoting its German style and pure German artists since the republic.

This strength was, however, a drawback and Feistel-Rohmeder and Bühler recognized the Society's increasingly tenuous position within the Nazi cultural milieu. The group's membership remained relatively steady, with a total of 839 members in 1937.[38] But the circulation of *Das Bild* had plummeted from a high of 7,826 in 1934, to 3,373 in late 1937, to 2,435 in late 1939.[39] If the organization were to survive in the Third Reich, it had to shore up support for its art journal. And so the organization returned to a tactic it had used to such advantage before; it set out to forge contacts with powerful potential allies. One of the Society's most interesting searches for new allies involved an unlikely benefactor: Heinrich Himmler's *SS-Ahnenerbe* (roughly, Ancestors' Legacy).

The *SS-Ahnenerbe* was a cultural branch of the SS devoted to archeological, historical and racial investigations that 'proved' the connection between the modern German people and the ancient Germanic tribes.[40] In August 1938, Bühler wrote to Himmler and set in motion a series of events that led to a meeting between Bühler, Feistel-Rohmeder and an unnamed *SS-Ahnenerbe* official to discuss an alliance between the *Ahnenerbe* and *Das Bild*.[41] Two other contributors to *Das Bild*, SS officers Peter Paulsen and Heinrich Appel, may also have played a role in setting up the meeting. Both belonged to the *Ahnenerbe* and joined the staff of *Das Bild* in 1938, Appel assisting with matters related to folklore and Paulsen aiding with prehistory.[42]

On 17 March 1939, Bühler and Feistel-Rohmeder met with a representative of Himmler's *SS-Ahnenerbe*, hoping that it would sponsor *Das Bild* as the Karlsruhe art academy had in 1934.[43] During the meeting, they pointed out that like the *SS-Ahnenerbe* journal *Germanien*, *Das Bild* reported on archeological and artistic artifacts of ancient Germanic cultures. Perhaps, suggested Bühler and Feistel-Rohmeder, the SS could adopt the Society's journal, thereby profiting both *Das Bild* and the *Ahnenerbe*.

The report of this meeting provides insight into how *Das Bild* was regarded by at least some leading Nazis. Overall, the official presented a very negative assessment of the journal, Bühler and Feistel-Rohmeder. The main criticism tendered by the SS official was that the journal's editors continued to fight a battle that had already been won. While the *Das Bild*'s 'battle against alien culture' was 'certainly justified before 1933', it had since become 'outmoded' and a matter of general policy. The journal, the report continued, had failed to acknowledged the new cultural direction and had not provided itself with a new mission. As a result, *Das Bild* 'lack[ed] a clear direction, adhere[d] to secondary issues, and ignore[d] the essential'.[44]

For *Das Bild* to be of any value to the *SS-Ahnenerbe*, it would have to be completely reorganized. In particular, Bühler and Feistel-Rohmeder would have to be replaced by younger people who had greater ability and talent for political leadership. The clear implication was that Bühler, Feistel-Rohmeder and the others who worked on the journal were too old; to be of value, the elderly staff would have to step aside for the new, wholly National Socialist generation. If completely transformed, the official believed *Das Bild* could rise to a level comparable to that of the *Germanien*. Left to its own devices, however, *Das Bild* would slowly decline and eventually disappear. The official recommended that they 'wait for a while and let the journal swim in its old, familiar backwaters until new, capable powers in the field of art history' could be found 'to whom one could then transfer the leadership of the journal with the prospect of success'.[45] The complete reorganization of the journal was simply not worth the trouble, as was noted in the margins of the report. The officer's superiors took his advice; *Das Bild* was left alone.

This letter brings into sharp relief the crisis of mission that the new National Socialist cultural policy posed for the German Art Society. The annual Great German Art exhibitions, numerous art competitions and articles in *Art in the Third Reich* all appealed for artists to embark on a new path, to create a monumental and heroic art form that would unite the *Volk* and the Reich to the Führer.[46] Even Rosenberg recognized that it was not enough to look back at Germany's cultural achievements.[47] Artists now had to craft a new art that reflected the National Socialist ideology. The Nazis remained unclear as to what made art particularly 'German'. Yet there was a sense that the Reich's cultural direction had changed and was moving forward. Still, the German Art Society refused to budge.

However, the second phase of the National Socialist cultural evolution reinvigorated the German Art Society. The Society had always required an enemy against which it could contrast and hence define itself and propel its sense of mission. The war offered the Society the chance to march in step with the regime's interpretation of German culture. Building upon the new National Socialist line, Society members argued that the Second World War united the *Volk* in a higher purpose. Now more than ever, claimed the German Art Society, the Reich required the 'spiritual armament' that German art, and the Society, could provide.[48]

Das Bild echoed the National Socialists' cultural interpretation of the war and gave voice to the German Art Society's contribution. This was the beginning of the German age, trumpeted Bühler after the fall of France. The war and its triumphs would inspire Germany's artists as never before. The Führer united workers and generals and reawakened German spirit. The war, claimed Bühler, proved that the German *Volksgemeinschaft* had been realized. It was now the artists' duty to visually represent the new-found German unity.[49] In articles on the Germanic roots of Alsace, German art in Poland and artists' experiences at the front, the Society's journal painted a picture of German culture's triumphant march across Europe.[50]

Repeatedly the Society argued that German art united the home front to the war effort even as it visually represented the fighting German spirit on the battlefields.[51] The Society and the art it served thus became part of the war effort. Indeed, as the *German Art Report* explained, the Germans' struggle for their national existence only heightened the need for beauty and culture: 'While the outcome of the war is spoken in the language of iron, the home front will support the great struggle with all its means. The continuation of cultural life in its entirety is a part of this [home front support]...'[52] Art reflected the *Volk*'s 'soldierly greatness, willingness to sacrifice, and heroism' through which the personal was transformed into the national.[53] Art integrated the Germans into the nation and into the war effort.

It was in this light that the German Art Society reviewed the Great German Art exhibitions of 1940, 1941 and 1942.[54] When 'troops of art-seeking people (*Volksgenossen*)' streamed into the House of German Art, it became proof of yet another victory for the Führer.[55] And if art was important for the home front, it must also serve the soldiers. Nazi cultural administrations recognized the value of art at the front and organized exhibitions to be brought to the army in the field. The German Art Society joined in this effort. In early 1942, the Society donated over one hundred graphic works to a Culture Chamber program that sent art to army posts in the 'occupied East, occupied France, Belgium, Holland and Norway' as 'greetings from home'; some works were also sold to raise money for the war effort.[56]

However, as Society members followed German art's triumphant advance at home and abroad in the pages of *Das Bild*, they still felt ignored by the regime they supported. Even the Society's twentieth anniversary in 1940 offered more cause for complaint than celebration. In her comments before the assembled guests, Feistel-Rohmeder repeatedly emphasized that the group's accomplishments had come independently of the Third Reich and even predated it. The German Art Society, she reminded them, was the '*oldest*', and until the Combat League for German Culture's establishment 'the *only* art organization' that fought for what 'was *today* regarded as the National Socialist world view'.[57] The *Deutsche Bildkunst*, which continued as *Das Bild*, and the *German Art Correspondence*, which continued as the *German Art Report*, were among the '*first* pure *völkisch*' art publications. But now, no one seemed to remember that the 'first' pure German art exhibit was the Society's Lübeck show in 1929 or that 'the *first* large traveling exhibition' had been honored by Nazi leaders. Feistel-Rohmeder said that 'these are historical facts, which were then not unknown by the general public, but which today are rather forgotten'.[58] Even Great German Art exhibition reviews became opportunities for Feistel-Rohmeder to strike a rather superior attitude. After all, she noted in 1941, only 'we old fighters for German art' could really appreciate the victory and the triumph such exhibitions represented.[59]

However, the victory had not turned out to be as sweet as Feistel-Rohmeder had anticipated, back in the spring of 1933. Then, she had detailed just what the artists expected from the Third Reich.[60] Ironically, most of what she wanted had come true. Only, the Nazis had not positioned Society members as soldiers in the front ranks of the cultural war. Relegated to the periphery once more, German Art Society members were simply part of the rank and file of the regime's artists; only in the pages of *Das Bild* did they win any real prominence.

Overall, Feistel-Rohmeder was not pleased by the condition of the arts in the Third Reich and she used her review of the 1942 Great German Art exhibition to voice her concerns. Despite the flourishing of the arts under Hitler's care, she observed, there were growing complaints that the high prices art now commanded had led artists to cash in. They rapidly completed works and sold them 'right off the easel', as fast as they could. This meant lesser-quality works were produced and that potential art patrons were priced out of the market. Such an art boom (*'Hausse' von Kunstwerk*) had occurred once before, although that had been 'instigated by Jews'. Implying that such art profiteers were younger artists, 'whom we know quite well', she assured her readers that a speculative art market would not be allowed in the Third Reich.[61] However, in saying so, she drew attention to the fact that this was precisely the case. Feistel-Rohmeder also believed that art was beginning to stagnate. Artists needed to develop and grow; their art had to evolve and mature. But instead, artists were just producing works that depicted the same topics done in the same way, over and over again. This might get them into the Great German Art Exhibition, and it might help their sales, but such repetition retarded the growth of German art.[62]

It was the Nazis' final reinterpretation of art that offered the German Art Society its best opportunity to move closer to the center of the Third Reich's cultural life. When the Nazis proclaimed that the war offered the best defense against the destruction of German and European culture at the hands of the British, the Americans and the Russians, *Das Bild* dutifully picked up the new cultural line. Its contributing authors had no problem representing their beloved pure German art as being simultaneously 'European'. *Das Bild* portrayed the German people as heroic victims, fighting a war they never wanted, against an enemy bent on wholesale destruction. German art revealed the true character and desires of the *Volk*. 'Above all of the horror, above all of the ruins, remains our proud cultural will', claimed Feistel-Rohmeder.[63] Others agreed, explaining that the 1943 Great German Art Exhibition evoked in viewers triumphant joy as well as 'a deep sadness for the barbaric assault (*Attentat*) on German and European culture'.[64] That German art was the purest expression of European culture was demonstrated by the public's interest in art and the beauty of the works produced by artists. *Das Bild* noted that even as irreplaceable artworks were being 'frivolously destroyed' Germans continued to defend German and European art. Paintings, graphic works and sculptures created in the midst of war also reminded one of the promise that the arts would 'bloom anew' after the war was over.[65]

Das Bild also emphasized artists' contributions to restoring German culture in the East. The last two issues of *Das Bild* devoted a great deal of space to exhibitions held in the Wartheland and General Government. German artists, it was claimed, frequently visited Cracow, Warsaw and Lublin and depicted these 'now-German' cities in their works. Feistel-Rohmeder noted with approval that 'more than a dozen [artists] have already settled in the General Government'.[66] The Veit Stoss Prize, created by Hans Frank, head of the General Government, symbolized the continuation and the renewal of German art in the eastern territories.[67] Always eager to tie the Society with such ventures, Feistel-Rohmeder informed her readers that Erwin Puchinger, a Society member, had been awarded a Veit Stoss Prize in graphics. He and other artists who either worked in or drew inspiration from the East were winning 'new land for German art'.[68] Until the day of final victory, the Society and *Das Bild* would continue to celebrate such accomplishments and its defense of German art.

Indeed, the war opened up new possibilities for the Society. As the Nazis' cultural apparatus contracted, museums closed and even more artists were drafted, the German Art Society was able to regain some of its former position in the Third Reich. The best example of its move away from the periphery and toward the center was its Third Traveling Exhibition. It opened in Brunswick in January 1943, just days before the defeat of the Sixth Army at Stalingrad was announced to the German public and a few weeks before Goebbels gave his famous 'total war' speech.

The Society had planned to hold its third traveling art show in conjunction with its twentieth anniversary and as a counterpart to its 1937 exhibit. The second traveling Society show had featured artists from southern Germany and appeared primarily in south German towns. The third show was to focus on the north German artists and tour Hamburg, Berlin and the Ruhr. When war broke out, the show was postponed. Fearful that northern Germany would be targeted by the West, the Society decided to wait for the final victory and then celebrate with its exhibition.[69] However, when the third traveling exhibition was finally realized, it opened not in conjunction with a German victory as the Society had hoped, but in defiance of the Reich's enemies.

The exhibit's delay until late in the war actually helped the Society. While the second exhibition of 1937 had no support from leading Nazi officials, the third exhibition, like the Society's 1933 show, won the patronage of Dietrich Klagges, minister-president of Brunswick. He arranged for the exhibit to open in Brunswick's Herzog-Anton-Ulrich-Museum. The mayor and a German League official also attended the opening ceremony, held on 31 January 1943. The Society must have also found other backers for its exhibition, for the show appeared in Leipzig, from 20 June until the end of July 1943, and was scheduled to appear in Danzig and Dresden.[70] There was also enough support to publish a catalog.[71] Unlike the catalog to the Society's first traveling exhibit, there was no explanatory text, but it was still an improvement over the second show, which apparently did not warrant a catalog.

The Society's 'rehabilitation' was most likely due to the timing of its final exhibition. By 1943, the Nazis had largely set aside the attempt to craft a new kind of German art. The war was their main interest. Culture Chamber projects and personnel were being severely cut back, and those theaters and museums not yet bombed out were closing.[72] The Society's exhibition could offer the public a brief respite from their daily cares; after all, the war was all about culture, claimed the Nazis, so German cultural life had to continue despite the mounting death toll and domestic destruction. The Nazis thus welcomed the Society's support for the war effort.

The exhibition provided yet another venue for the Nazis to publicize their new interpretation of the war as a defensive battle for German/European culture. It also offered the Society the opportunity to take center stage and become a fully acknowledged participant in that battle. The opening speeches repeatedly emphasized the vital contribution that the German Art Society and its third art exhibition made to the war effort. More than ever, claimed Dietrich Klagges, Germans needed to be reminded that they were fighting for more than just territory; they were fighting to defend German and European culture:

> If, in light of the grave seriousness of our days, we still have the courage to dedicate ourselves to art ... then we do so not for pleasure's sake but in the realization that the difficult battle, which is being fought by our brave soldiers, side by side with our allies in the East and the South as well as on every ocean, preserves more than the naked existence of the German *Volk* ... this struggle has a higher purpose. [It] insures the

life of our people and at the same time European, yes, even world culture, a beautiful culture, created long ago by Nordic-Germanic peoples and whose leading proponent (*Hauptträger*) is the German *Volk*.[73]

Only Germany could defend Western civilization from certain destruction, claimed Klagges. He warmly acknowledged Feistel-Rohmeder and her leadership. Klagges also quoted the Society's statutes and remembered the group's Lübeck show in 1929 and the first traveling exhibition in 1933.[74]

In her review, Feistel-Rohmeder emphasized that the Society's third traveling art exhibition offered contemporaries proof as to just what the German Art Society had accomplished over its 23–year history. The show was to stir the memories of its members and document their cohesiveness, since many had been loyal supporters throughout the decades.[75] She also used her review to highlight Nazi support for the show. She noted that the central piece of the 'room of honor' was a portrait of Interior Minister Wilhelm Frick by Otto Wilhelm Pitthan. Feistel-Rohmeder alerted her readers that leading officials had played a vital role in providing the Society with this work. Frick had ensured that Pitthan could complete the portrait for its inclusion in the exhibit. Hitler himself had commissioned the portrait and his chancellery had to approve its showing in the exhibition, she reported. By placing the portrait between two landscapes by Otto Bloos – *Evening in South Thuringia* and *On the Westwall: Summer 1940* – the exhibit's room of honor emphasized the Society's support for the war and the debt it owed to Frick for his support for *Deutsche Bildkunst* in 1930.[76]

The work shown in the Society's 1943 exhibition also displayed just what the Society still maintained was the German style of art. Although it is difficult to tell exactly what was exhibited, several works were featured in both the show's catalog and in *Das Bild*.[77] As far as can be determined, most were landscapes done in the Romantic style. Michael Matthias Kiefer's *Swan Pair* evoked a sense of tranquility (Figure 6.1). The swans' bodies and reflections echo the ripples in the water that stretch out to a vaguely rendered horizon. In a painting by Albert Janesch, a fishing boat at dock quietly waits, with a still city behind it (Figure 6.2). In several instances some of the works, or works from the same series of prints, had been seen in *Das Bild* before. Although not shown in the catalog, Wilhelm Hempfing's *Self Portrait* was likely the same piece shown in the journal in 1936. Karl Hennemann exhibited woodcuts from the series of works also featured in 1936 and Klaus Wrage's woodcuts were from his series based on the *Edda* (Figure 6.3).[78] These works, like most of the others, completely ignored the contemporary situation. Only two portraits (of Frick and of Hitler) and two paintings made any direct reference to the Third Reich or the war.[79]

The exhibition showed, too, that the Society's members remained loyal and that the group could still attract non-member artists. At least forty-four, or just over

Figure 6.1 *Swan Pair* (*Schwanenpaar*) by Michael Matthias Kiefer. From *Das Bild*, January/February 1943, p. 10.

37 percent, of the total 118 exhibitors belonged to the Society.[80] Twenty of the 118 exhibitors (nearly 17 percent) had participated in the group's 1933 exhibition; six had exhibited in the 1929.[81] Indeed, until late in the war, the German Art Society continued to attract artists and other supporters. Table 6.1 details the membership figures available from 1928 through 1944.[82]

Table 6.1 German Art Society Membership, 1928–1944

Year	Individual Members	Corporate Members	Total
1928	65	1,450	1,515
1929	100	13,827	13,927
1936	281	450	731
1937	389	450	839
1940	400	500 (approx.)	900
1944	50 (approx.)	unavailable	unavailable

Society membership remained a relatively attractive option for a number of artists and organizations until at least 1940. A large complement of members had been with the organization since its earliest years. Unfortunately, there are no sources that indicate just how rapidly membership declined between 1940 and 1944, but there were still enough that the Society could launch its last exhibition

Figure 6.2 *Green Fishing Boat in Front of La Rochelle* (*Grünes Fischerboot vor La Rochelle*) by
Albert Janesch. From *Das Bild*, January/February 1943, p. 9.

in 1943. Although later sources do not identify the corporate members, earlier
materials indicated they included German League chapters in Darmstadt, Berlin,
Charlottenburg, Kassel and Kiel, the German School at Bad Berka, the Front
Soldiers' League of Visual Artists (*Frontkämpferbund Bildender Künstler*) of
Berlin, the Hans Thoma Society and the Munich artists of the *Bund*.[83]

That the Society continued to publish *Das Bild* also attests to the organization's
resiliency even late in the war. Over the ten years of publication, a total of 231
authors wrote for *Das Bild*, and most were not Society members.[84] Contributors to
Das Bild such as Franz Hofmann, Peter Paulsen, Walter Hotz and Edgar Schindler
continued to write for the journal even though they were serving in the army or the
SS.[85] Although fewer issues appeared in the war years, the number of contributors,

Figure 6.3 *Spring* (*Frühling*) by Karl Hennemann. From *Das Bild*, November 1936, p. 325.

articles and even images held relatively steady. In 1938, for example, 55 different authors contributed 117 articles to *Das Bild*. The number of contributors fell to a low of 29 in 1940, rose to 32 in 1942, then again to 36 in 1943. The number of articles declined but only gradually, from 72 in 1940, to 69 in 1942, to 63 in 1943.[86] Each issue was also still richly illustrated. In 1938, a total of 373 images appeared in *Das Bild*. Images declined in 1940, to 210, but rose again to 233 in 1942, and declining to 176 in 1943.[87] The final issue in January–March 1944 suggests that had the journal been able to continue, the number of authors and articles that made up *Das Bild* would have still been maintained; it comprised 16 articles by 10 different authors.[88]

Das Bild also did not have to rely on more female authors or artists to fill its pages. Because the male authors remained active, the number of female contributors did not increase significantly. Women generally comprised 6 to 10 percent of *Das Bild*'s contributors and accounted for 25 to 30 percent of the articles produced each year. More women did write for the journal in the war years, but even in 1943 they made up just one-sixth of the staff (6 of 36) and contributed just over one-third of the articles.[89] Female artists also did not receive greater attention during the war. Just four women were featured in articles in 1942, the largest number ever.

These strengths, however, could not belie the Society's weaknesses. Chairman Hermann Fecht in his speech at the opening bitterly noted the reluctance of some members to submit works for the group's final exhibit. Fecht attributed this largely to artists' greed; rather than supporting the Society, artists profited by selling their works on the open market.[90] The defensive attitude of the group also echoed in the pages of *Das Bild*. In her review of the show, Feistel-Rohmeder admitted that skeptics might wonder why the Society should continue its struggle. Her explanation justified the Society's continuation in part by criticizing Nazi cultural policy, although discreetly. Unlike some unnamed others, she wrote, the German Art Society had not abandoned its mission to identify and aid pure German artists who 'for whatever reasons' remained undiscovered.[91] Feistel-Rohmeder implied that because the few *völkisch* survivors in the Third Reich, like the German League and the Society, had been denied their role in promoting 'pure Germandom', one had to admit that 'this battle has not yet come to an end'.[92] The Society's third traveling art show thus redressed two failures of official policy: it offered talented, racially pure artists exhibition and sales opportunities, and honored *völkisch* old fighters.

Feistel-Rohmeder even claimed that the Third Reich had not successfully won the war against modernism. According to her, the modernists were simply in hiding, biding their time as they secretly plotted against brave Germans who were fighting for the salvation of their culture. Even as she evoked memories of the 1918 'stab-in-the-back myth', she warned that despite 'these negative forces' working in secret, the German Art Society

> has forgotten nothing, just as we have forgotten no deed and no name, and our day will come! For now we can only be certain that the quality of our members' work [as witnessed] in the traveling exhibit and in the pages of *Das Bild*, justifies our continuation (*Zusammenhaltes*): for the cultivation of pure Germandom, until the day of victory![93]

Even for Feistel-Rohmeder, this promise to settle accounts at some future date was unusually aggressive. The Society had to continue so that, after the war, it could maintain its vigil against the degenerates and prevent their return.

The defensive posture of both Feistel-Rohmeder and Fecht indicate that despite its ability to launch a third traveling exhibition, the twelfth Society exhibition overall, the organization was beginning to falter.[94] The advanced age of the membership and the war took their toll. Wartime issues of *Das Bild* were filled with features on artists who had reached a significant birthday or who had died. Ludwig Fahrenkrog and Alf Bachmann, who had both exhibited with the Society in 1929, 1933 and 1943, were now 76 and 80 years old respectively. Reinhold Rehm, Bühler and Wolfgangmüller were 66; Richard Müller was 69; Richard Guhr was 70; Paul Schultze-Naumburg was 74. Feistel-Rohmeder, who had officially become managing editor of *Das Bild* in 1941, was 70. Johann Vincent Cissarz, Ludwig Dill and Hermann Groeber were deceased.[95] Even Feistel-Rohmeder had to admit that those who had joined the Society's battle in its earliest years now had 'one foot in grave'.[96]

Although these older Society members remained active, the war made it extremely difficult to continue their efforts. Air raids destroyed artists' homes and studios.[97] Picture frames had been extremely hard to come by for works in the Third Traveling Exhibition.[98] The war also affected *Das Bild*. Ever smaller typeface was used to save on paper after 1942.[99] Paper shortages and other disruptions led to the journal's increasingly erratic publication. From late 1939 fewer issues made up a year's publication. Only nine issues appeared in 1941; in 1942, seven issues were produced; in 1943, five; and in 1944, just one.[100]

Even Feistel-Rohmeder began to falter. Shortly before her seventieth birthday in August 1943, she wrote her old *völkisch* ally, Paul Schultze-Naumburg, complaining bitterly that she was plagued by the pains of old age. She and her unemployed husband were living on the meager income of 300 RM per month. Her health was such that she feared she would soon be unable to continue working for *Das Bild* and for the German Art Society. As it was, she had to work from home because going out was too difficult. She also had no health insurance. However, she wrote Schultze-Naumburg, she had heard that there was help available from the Culture Chamber, if one had certain 'connections'. Although she did not ask him directly, Feistel-Rohmeder hoped that Schultze-Naumburg would intervene in her behalf.[101] He did just that and contacted his state propaganda office for help.

For the first time, Feistel-Rohmeder finally received the recognition from the Nazi authorities she had so long desired. Moved by the plight of an old fighter, both the propaganda ministry and the Culture Chamber offered Feistel-Rohmeder their assistance. Using funds from the Visual Arts Chamber's *Künstlerdank Spende* (roughly, artists recognition fund), they awarded her an honorary stipend of 1,000 RM on the occasion of her seventieth birthday. Much to her delight, Feistel-Rohmeder also received a birthday telegram from Goebbels. In her thank-you letter to him, she vowed that as long as God gave her the power to do so, she would continue to serve the cause of German art.[102] Even more exciting for her, Hitler approved a monthly stipend (*monatlicher Ehrensold*) 'in recognition of service to the German art movement'. Frick acknowledged her long battle by granting her a 'considerable honorarium' (*namhafte Ehrengabe*).[103] The *Völkischer*

Beobachter printed in honor of her birthday an article praising Feistel-Rohmeder's accomplishments.[104] At long last, Nazi leaders recognized Feistel-Rohmeder's contribution to the Third Reich and the cause of German art. As rewarding as such personal recognition was, more gratifying for Feistel-Rohmeder was her belief that these honors also symbolized official acknowledgement of her German Art Society.

However, because the German Art Society had allied itself with the Third Reich, its battle came to an end with the regime it served. The last issued of *Das Bild* appeared in January–March 1944, not because the authorities ordered its closure but because of the war. In April, air raids destroyed Feistel-Rohmeder's home; in October, *Das Bild*'s publishing house, C. F. Müller, was also bombed. Finally in December, Hermann Fecht, chairman of the Society and owner of the publishing house, reluctantly laid off his staff, including Feistel-Rohmeder.[105] Feistel-Rohmeder, however, refused to admit defeat. She applied for and received funds from the National German Press Association so she could rebuild her destroyed library. She also repeatedly requested that the press agency provide her with the necessary materials so she could keep informed of the regime's art policies.[106]

There was, however, little to be informed about. Although the public appetite for cultural diversions remained strong, even the Culture Chamber was forced to reduce its staff and productions. In August 1944, Goebbels finally ordered the Culture Chamber to mobilize for the total war effort, effectively shutting down Germany's cultural life. 'In the visual arts, all competitions and exhibitions were prohibited and all instructional facilities were closed.'[107] Musical, theater and cabaret productions closed; only film and radio continued to offer some entertainment.

With the cessation of *Das Bild* in early 1944, the German Art Society ceased to exist. Feistel-Rohmeder and her husband lived for a time with the Fecht family outside Karlsruhe.[108] Just what her experiences were in the last days of the Third Reich or in the German recovery remain unknown. At some point, she and her husband moved into a state home for the elderly in Karlsruhe. But despite her losses Feistel-Rohmeder remained defiant to the end. She even attempted to revive the German Art Society as the German Art Community (*Deutsche Kunstgemeinschaft*) in 1951. This organization was to continue the Society's battle, for according to Feistel-Rohmeder, German art in the 1950s required the same protection it had in the 1920s and 1930s. Although nothing seems to have come of this effort, it underscores her fervent belief for the necessity to protect German art.[109] Her family even acknowledged this in Feistel-Rohmeder's obituary. When she died at the age of seventy-nine on 3 February 1953, her family honored 'her selfless battle for "pure German art", for the German character and German values' in the 'first half of this century'.[110] There was no mention made of her Nazi past, of course.

The German Art Society and *Das Bild* connected art in the Third Reich with its *völkisch* heritage. Although even during the republic the National Socialists sought to distance themselves from the older, right-wing racialist movement, the art and culture that ended up being associated with their Third Reich owed a debt to groups like the Society. Looking over the German Art Society's experiences especially after 1937, three contributions to art in the Third Reich stand out: the Society and its journal disseminated the Nazi interpretation of culture; their exhibitions and reviews provided venues within which the appropriate German style of art could be worked out; and finally, they further integrated artists into the Third Reich. However, the Society never simply followed orders imposed from above. It shaped those orders to suit its own interests and even ensure the group's survival.

Between 1933 and 1937, the German Art Society helped shape the eventual decision to eliminate most modernist art. The quest for a new style after 1937 did present the Society with difficulty, but it continued to offer positive examples of art appropriate for the Third Reich. During the war, *Das Bild* enthusiastically tied its art to the war effort and transformed its German style of art into the purest evocation of Western, European, civilization. Adopting the Nazis' cultural interpretations required no ideological adjustment; the Society had always believed that cultural productions necessarily reflected the artists' race and the primary task was to connect the *Volk* to their racial heritage. Although members were critical of the regime's policies at times, the Society remained a reliable, loyal proponent of the Nazis' main cultural themes.

This does not, however, mean that the pages of *Das Bild* were filled with images of National Socialism. However, *Das Bild* does suggest that art supportive of the Third Reich was less an aesthetic and more a rhetorical practice. Because of its own policies and purges, the Third Reich had no choice but to rely on a stylistically realistic, occasionally monumental, mode of representation. This nineteenth-century-like style was instrumentalized to promote a National Socialist interpretation of culture. Neither style nor content of paintings but their interpretation in reviews, speeches and media made art 'Nazi'. Thus, the regime needed artists capable of producing acceptable works and interpreting even non-Nazi topics in suitably National Socialist tones.

'Literal' depictions of National Socialism were extremely rare in *Das Bild*, as in *Art in the Third Reich* and the Great German Art exhibitions. For example, a visual inspection of *Das Bild's* content in 1936 reveals just 2.6 percent of images (9 of 346) had overtly Nazi content. These included portraits of Nazi leaders and drawings of Hitler's rooms in the Landsberg prison by Richard Müller (Figure 6.4). Another 2.6 percent were of war. Most were depictions of the First World War, like Bühler's highly romanticized *Homecoming*. As the young idealized soldier wearily lays his head in a young woman's lap, her hands appear to give him a kind

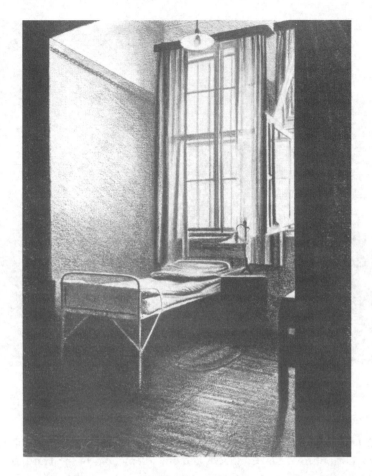

Figure 6.4 *Adolf Hitler's Cell in the Fortress Prison in Landsberg on Lech* (*Die Zelle Adolf Hitlers im der Festungs-Anstalt in Landsberg am Lech*) by Richard Müller. From *Das Bild*, October 1936, p. 309.

of blessing as she absorbs his sacrifice (Figure 6.5). But there is nothing that marks the soldier as a Nazi. Even if the eighteen Nazi/war images are combined with the six works that referenced the Berlin Olympics (plates, coins, plaques), just under 7 percent of the images bore any overt connection to National Socialism visually.

The lack of both Nazi and war themes in 1936 was typical for *Das Bild*. Works depicting Hitler were surprisingly rare; the first appeared in 1936 and in all there were only eight. Images of Goebbels, Goering and others did increase after the war, but in ten years of publication there were only twenty-seven depictions of Third Reich officials. In 1942, just over 2 percent of the images emphasized National Socialism; in 1943, this increased but to just 4 percent. As would be expected, military themes became more common after 1939, but even in 1942,

Figure 6.5 *Homecoming* (*Heimkehr*) by Hans Adolf Bühler. From *Das Bild*, February 1936, p. 57.

just 12.4 percent of the images referenced war; this declined to just over 7 percent in 1943. Portraits of officials, SS, SA and other depictions of the Third Reich did play an important role in tying the journal and its readers to the regime. However it is possible that precisely because they were so readily identified as propaganda, their value as 'art' was reduced. SD (*Sicherheitsdienst*) reports in 1943 noted that works with contemporary topics such as the war or National Socialism found few buyers. The SD also reported that the public responded to paintings of war not as examples of high art, but as documentation of the war effort, an extension of war reports that appeared in the press and in films.[111] Hans Stadelmann's *Tank Assault*, one of two war images in the May 1941 issue of *Das Bild*, illustrates the SD's point. A solid yet unimaginative depiction of tanks attacking on a *Blitzkrieg* battlefield, it was hardly the kind of thing the typical German would want in the living room (Figure 6.6).

In their reports, the SD observed that the artists responded to the market; since the public did not buy propagandistic works, the artists produced landscapes, still lifes and genre scenes that sold well.[112] It was these kinds of works that filled the pages of *Das Bild*. In 1936, landscapes were the most popular topic, comprising

Figure 6.6 *Tank Assault* (*Kampfwagenangriff*) by Hans Stadelmann. From *Das Bild*, May 1941, p. 79.

nearly 20 percent of the works. Photographs of traditional German architecture such as city halls, fortresses and churches made up 15.8 percent; early, medieval and Gothic 'artifacts', 15 percent; paintings of peasants, 11.2 percent. Other topics included portraits of non-party officials (5.7 percent), women and girls (4.6 percent), animals (4 percent) and mothers with children (1.4 percent).

These non-Nazi topics were transformed into artwork supportive of the Third Reich through their interpretation in the party-approved context of the German Art Society's journal. Thus landscapes became representations of the beloved home of the *Volk*; peasants embodied racially pure constancy; even still lifes became celebrations of the Germanic love of beauty. In these landscapes, genre scenes, still lifes and portraits, time stood still and permanence and the status quo, at times real but more often imagined, were emphasized. Such stability was equated with the thousand-year Reich and the eternal vitality of the *Volk*. A vase of flowers, a lovely woman or a small child took on even greater significance during the war. Through reviews, they became reminders of life's small pleasures, signifiers of what the soldiers were fighting for and of 'the invincibility of German art'.[113] Genre paintings became portraits that captured the inner experiences of the *Volk*.[114] *Das Bild*'s reviews situated these non-political subjects within a racialized context, in essence 'Nazifying' them.

Even those works that can be read as Nazi art operated on multiple levels. Consider Wilhelm Sauter's *Heroes' Shrine*, featured in a two-page spread in 1936. The pages' only text, 'To the Heroes' Day of Remembrance, 8 March 1936', and the four-panel piece effectively reinterpreted the First World War in a Nazi mode (Figure 6.7). Sauter depicted SA men as frontline soldiers. In the center panel, a wounded soldier, the swastika visible on the remnants of his torn shirt, is supported by comrades who resemble SA members. The men on the far left and right of this group look to the two flanking panels depicting soldiers before and after battle. The base of the assemblage is a grave which recognizes no difference between fallen soldiers and dead Nazis. The text above it, too, makes no such distinction and reads 'Do not forget them. They gave their best for Germany'. Readers of *Das Bild* in 1936 would likely have placed Sauter's work within the broader context of the day, too. The Third Reich had rearmed, retaken the Rhineland and the Saar. The shame of the Versailles Treaty had been erased; the sacrifices of the last war had not been in vain. The Nazis had brought the war dead a kind of redemption, as Sauter suggested in his painting. Readers familiar with the avant-garde of the republic would also have been struck by Sauter's rejection here of works like Otto Dix's *War Cripples* or his painting of rotting dead soldiers in the trenches. The German Art Society had rejected such works in its 1929 letter to Hindenburg and then saw them defamed as 'war sabotage' in the degenerate art show of 1937. A

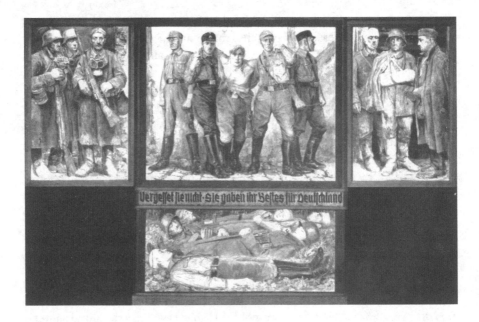

Figure 6.7 *Heroes' Shrine* (*Heldenschrein*) by Wilhelm Sauter. From *Das Bild*, March 1936, p. 90.

later review of Sauter's work would make exactly these connections.[115] Thus, Nazi art continued to be defined by what it was not, as well as what it was.

Such paintings of fighting SA men reminded readers of the years of struggle while honoring the rank and file who made the Third Reich possible. Depictions of the war tied the homefront to the battlefields. All such overtly Nazi images clearly served as propaganda for the regime. The non-Nazi images that appeared beside them took on the same role by association. Within *Das Bild*, these images underscored the journal's service to the Third Reich and integrated its artists into the Nazi cultural milieu.

The German Art Society and its journal incorporated hundreds of artists and authors into the Third Reich. Certainly, this was achieved primarily through the Culture Chamber. But the Society and *Das Bild* offered artists a more intimate counterpart to the Chamber. As a member of the Culture Chamber, an artist was one of literally thousands. But the Society members always regarded themselves as a select elite. Through Society meetings and the pages of *Das Bild*, members could keep track of each other, share in each other's accomplishments and maintain their belief that they were special.[116]

The Nazis' art journal, *Art in the Third Reich*, also offered little hope for many painters or sculptors to win recognition. Most issues consisted of only three or four articles and very few living artists won the privilege of being featured in its pages. *Das Bild*, by contrast, highlighted artists' participation in important exhibitions and routinely offered features on individual members. It provided art journalists and artists the opportunity to publish articles and reproduced works by hundreds of artists. The German Art Society thus offered both sociability and attention that the Culture Chamber simply could not offer. Thus, the German Art Society complemented the Nazis' cultural program in important ways. It carried out the regime's directives, promoted the careers of loyal artists and integrated artists and readers further into the Third Reich. And at the same time, the Society was able to continue its original mission to defend pure German art.

Finally, the German Art Society offered the Third Reich positive examples of art 'cleansed' of all racial and aesthetic 'degeneracy' and a cadre of experienced artists. First in the pages of *Deutsche Bildkunst* and the *German Art Correspondence*, and then in *Das Bild*, the Society consistently promoted what it called the German style of art for over twenty-three years. This 'style' became the first tangible example of the kind of art the regime would support. Just as the Society's 1933 exhibition had been one of the first pure German art exhibitions of the Third Reich, its final traveling art show of 1943 was one of the last. In between those years, the German Art Society critiqued the slow pace of reforms and the government's unwillingness to recognize its art experts as the rightful leaders in the cultural realm, but it also supported the regime's ideological and political goals. Indeed, the Society had helped popularize those goals even in the republic. Although never entrusted with the kind of authority it anticipated, the German Art Society helped to shape art in the Third Reich from below. Its members served as combatants in the battle against modern art and then worked to win recognition of its German style as the official artistic style of the Third Reich. To the extent that there was really no difference between the Society's pure German art and 'Nazi art', the German Art Society did succeed.

Notes

Introduction

1. For example, P. O. Rave, *Kunstdiktatur im Dritten Reich*, U. M. Schneede (ed.) (Argon, 1988); H. Lehmann-Haupt, *Art under a Dictatorship* (Oxford University Press, 1954); F. Roh, *'Entartete' Kunst: Kunstbarbarei im Dritten Reich* (Fackelträger Verlag, 1962); J. Wulf, *Die bildenden Künste im Dritten Reich: Eine Dokumentation* (Siegbert Mohn Verlag, 1963); M. Koch, 'Kulturkampf in Karlsruhe: Zur Ausstellung Regierungskunst 1919–1933', in *Kunst in Karlsruhe 1900–1950* (C. F. Müller Verlag, 1981), pp. 102–28; W. Rössling, 'Kunst in Karlsruhe 1933–1945', in ibid., pp. 129–33; C. Zuschlag, *'Entartete Kunst': Ausstellungsstrategien im Nazi-Deutschland* (Wernersche Verlagsgesellschaft, 1995), pp. 32, 33, 36.
2. H. Brenner, *Die Kunstpolitik des Nationalsozialismus* (Rowohlt Taschenbuch Verlag, 1963).
3. B. Hinz, *Art in the Third Reich*, R. and R. Kimber, trans (Pantheon, 1979).
4. A. E. Steinweis, 'Weimar Culture and the Rise of National Socialism: The *Kampfbund für deutsche Kultur*', *Central European History* 24 (1991), pp. 402–23; idem, *Art, Ideology, and Economics in Nazi Germany: The Reich Chambers of Music, Theater, and the Visual Arts* (University of North Carolina Press, 1993); J. Petropoulos, *Art as Politics in the Third Reich* (University of North Carolina Press, 1996); idem, 'A Guide through the Visual Arts Administration of the Third Reich', in G. R. Cuomo (ed.), *National Socialist Cultural Policy* (St. Martin's Press, 1995), pp. 121–53.
5. See for example, A. Kaes et al. (eds), *The Weimar Republic Sourcebook* (University of California Press, 1994); G. Stark, *Entrepreneurs of Ideology: Neoconservative Publishers in Germany, 1890–1933* (University of North Carolina Press, 1981); J. Hermand and F. Trommler, *Die Kultur der Weimarer Republik* (Nymphenburger Verlagshandlung, 1978); J. H. Ulbricht, 'Kulturrevolution von rechts: Das völkische Netzwerk 1900–1930', in D. Heiden and G. Mai (eds), *Nationalsozialismus in Thüringen* (Böhlau Verlag, 1995), pp. 29–48.
6. U. Puschner et al. (eds), *Handbuch zur 'Völkischen Bewegung' 1871–1914* (K. G. Saur, 1996).

7. H. Mittig, 'Art and Oppression in Fascist Germany', in I. Rogoff (ed.), *The Divided Heritage: Themes and Problems in German Modernism* (Cambridge University Press, 1991), p. 211.

8. P. Paret, *The Berlin Secession: Modernism and Its Enemies in Imperial Germany* (The Belknap Press of Harvard University, 1980); B. I. Lewis, *Art For All? The Collision of Modern Art and the Public in Late Nineteenth-century Germany* (Princeton University Press, 2003).

Chapter 1

1. Paul Ortwin Rave highlighted Feistel-Rohmeder's anti-modernist campaign but credited Bühler with the Society's first traveling exhibition. For a new edition of his 1949 work see P. O. Rave, *Kunstdiktatur im Dritten Reich*, ed. U. M. Schneede (Argon, 1988). The other and best treatment of the Society fails to mention Feistel-Rohmeder in the text: H. Brenner, *Die Kunstpolitik des Nationalsozialismus* (Rowohlt Taschenbuch Verlag, 1963). Bühler continues to get more attention in recent literature. M. Koch, 'Kulturkampf in Karlsruhe: Zur Ausstellung Regierungskunst 1919–1933', in *Kunst in Karlsruhe 1900–1950* (C. F. Müller Verlag, 1981), pp. 102–28, and W. Rössling, 'Kunst in Karlsruhe 1933–1945', in ibid., pp. 129–33. Those who have recognized Feistel-Rohmeder's role, but only for before 1933, include R. Merker, *Die bildenden Künste im Nationalsozialismus: Kulturideologie, Kulturpolitik, Kulturproduktion* (DuMont Buchverlag, 1983); O. Thomae, *Die Propaganda-Maschinerie: Bildende Kunst und Öffentlichkeitsarbeit im Dritten Reich* (Gebrüder Mann, 1978); H. Lehmann-Haupt, *Art under a Dictatorship* (Oxford University Press, 1954); F. Roh, *'Entartete' Kunst: Kunstbarbarei im Dritten Reich* (Fackelträger-Verlag, 1962); J. Wulf, *Die bildenden Künste im Dritten Reich: Eine Dokumentation* (Siegbert Mohn Verlag, 1963).

2. B. Feistel-Rohmeder, *Im Terror des Kunstbolschewismus: Urkundungsammlung des 'Deutschen Kunstberichtes' aus den Jahren 1927–1933* (C. F. Müller Verlag, 1938), pp. 3–6, 211–17.

3. E. Schindler, 'Der "Ehrenbeamtin der Deutschen Kunst": Zum 65. Geburtstag von Frau Bettina Feistel-Rohmeder am 24. August 1938', *Das Bild*, August 1938, pp. 229, 233; H. A. Bühler, 'An Bettina Feistel-Rohmeder zum 65. Geburtstag', *Das Bild*, August 1938, p. 229.

4. See the correspondence between Feistel-Rohmeder and the Reichsverband der deutschen Presse, BA R103/19.

5. Rohmeder (1843–1930) married Johanna Barfus in 1867. I have found no record of Johanna's death so the idea that she died before Rohmeder remarried is admittedly an assumption. B. Feistel-Rohmeder, 'Zum 8. Juni 1943, dem 100. Geburtstag Wilhelm Rohmeders', *Das Bild*, April–June 1943, p. 70; 'Rohmeder, Johann Wilhelm, Dr.', *Wer ist's?* 6th edn (Verlag von H. A. Ludwig Degener, 1912), p. 1322.

6. U. Loham, *Völkischer Radikalismus: Die Geschichte des Deutsch-völkischen Schutz- und Trutzbundes 1919–1923* (Leibnitz-Verlag, 1970), pp. 293, 297, note 43 p. 343, note 16, pp. 431–2; Feistel-Rohmeder, 'Zum 8. Juni 1943'.

7. 'Rohmeder, Johann Wilhelm, Dr', p. 1322; ibid., *Wer ist's?* 8th edn (Verlag von H. A. Ludwig Degener, 1922), p. 1287.

8. H. Fecht, 'Zur Eröffnung der 2.Wanderausstellung der Deutschen Kunstgesellschaft', *Das Bild*, October 1937, p. 319; Feistel-Rohmeder, 'Zum 8. Juni 1943'.

9. Ibid., and her portrait of Rohmeder on p. 71 there. See the dedication page in B. Feistel-Rohmeder, *Das Frauenbildnis in der venezianischen Renaissance*, 3rd edn (Friedrich Rothbarth, GmbH, 1905).

10. 'Rohmeder, Johann Wilhelm, Dr ', p. 1322 does not include his second wife's birth date, but she was probably much younger than Wilhelm (who was 56 when he remarried). Their sons were born in 1902 and 1906, and their daughter in 1908. I have not found a birthdate for Feistel-Rohmeder's daughter, but she was probably born around these years.

11. Rohmeder joined the NSDAP before 1923. Feistel-Rohmeder, 'Zum 8. Juni 1943'; Loham, *Völkicher Radikalismus*, p. 302. Feistel-Rohmeder belonged to the woman's section of the German League; she joined the Nazis in 1929 and her party number was 152225. BDC, Feistel-Rohmeder file.

12. The only record regarding her daughter is Feistel-Rohmeder's obituary, *Badische Neuste Nachrichten*, 14 February 1953, p. 16; there her name is listed as Charlotte Matting-Sammler.

13. *Adressbuch der Stadt Karlsruhe, 1935/36*, located in Stadt Karlsruhe, Stadtbibliothek, Archiv, Sammlungen. There he is identified as 'Hch. Feistel'. In Feistel-Rohmeder's obituary he identified himself as 'Hch. Arthur Feistel'. *Badische Neuste Nachrichten*, 14 February 1953, p. 16. Feistel was not a member of the Nazi Party.

14. 'Feistel-Rohmeder, Bettina', *Allgemeines Lexikon der bildenden Künstler, Von Antike bis zur Gegenwart* (Verlag E. A. Seemann, 1915), vol. 11, pp. 359–60; Schindler, 'Der "Ehrenbeamtin der deutschen Kunst"'; C. Zuschlag, *'Entartete Kunst': Ausstellungsstrategien im Nazi-Deutschland* (Wernersche Verlagsgesellschaft, 1995), p. 370.

15. B. Feistel-Rohmeder, 'Einiges über Raumkunst', *Offizielle Ausstellungszeitung der Internationalen Kunst- und Gartenbau-Ausstellung Mannheim 1907*, Nr 26, 26 May 1907.

16. She displays familiarity with Italian in Feistel-Rohmeder, *Das Frauenbildnis*. She owned works in English (by Ruskin and Houston Stewart Chamberlain) and in French (by Huysman). Her library also contained numerous works by Goethe, Schiller, Lessing, Kleist and Gottfried Keller, and art histories by Wölfflin, Meier-Graefe and Justi. Fachbibliothek Bettina Feistel-Rohmeder, attachment to Bettina Feistel-Rohmeder to the Landesverband Baden-Westmark im Reichsverband der deutschen Presse, 22 November 1944, BA R103/19.

17. She wrote for the *Heidelberger Tagblatt* and the *Heidelberger Zeitung*; 'Feistel-Rohmeder, Bettina', p. 360.

18. The quotation is from ibid. The workshop is also mentioned in Schindler, 'Der "Ehrenbeamtin der Deutschen Kunst"', p. 233. However no listing for the workshop could be found in the Mannheim directories.

19. The heavy damage sustained in Mannheim and Dresden has made the reconstruction of Feistel-Rohmeder's early life extremely difficult. Because she founded the German Art Society in her Dresden home in November 1920, that is the most certain date of her presence there. She moved to Karlsruhe in November 1933; see *Deutscher Kunstbericht*, November 1933, GLA 235/40093.

20. B. Feistel-Rohmeder, 'Was zu Heidelberg began...', *Das Bild*, March 1934, pp. 95–101; E. Schindler, 'Nochmals: "Was zu Heidelberg began..."', *Das Bild*, March 1936, pp. 97–100.

21. Thode was responding to recent publications by Julius Meier-Graefe. For a more extended treatment of his lectures, see P. Paret, *The Berlin Secession: Modernism and Its Enemies in Imperial Germany* (The Belknap Press of Harvard University, 1980), pp. 170–7. The lectures were published in H. Thode, *Böcklin und Thoma: Acht Vorträge über neudeutsche Malerei* (Carl Winters Universitätsbuchhandlung, 1905).

22. Ibid., p. 154.

23. Ibid., p. 18.

24. Ibid., p. 164.

25. Ibid., p. 154.

26. Ibid., pp. 2–5.

27. R. Lenman, 'Painters, Patronage and the Art Market in Germany 1850–1914', *Past and Present*, No. 123 (1989), pp. 107–40; idem, 'A Community in Transition: Painters in Munich, 1886–1914', *Central European History* 6 (1982), pp. 3–33.

28. Paret, *The Berlin Secession*; B. I. Lewis, *Art For All? The Collision of Modern Art and the Public in Late Nineteenth-century Germany* (Princeton University Press, 2003).

29. O. Kallscheuer and C. Leggewie, 'Deutsche Kulturnation versus französische Staatsnation? Eine ideengeschichtliche Stichprobe', in H. Berding (ed.),

Nationales Bewusstsein und kollektive Identität (Suhrkamp, 1994), pp. 112–62; D. Langewiesche, 'Kulturelle Nationsbildung im Deutschland des 19 Jahrhunderts', in M. Hettling and P. Nolte (eds), *Nation und Gesellschaft in Deutschland: Historische Essays* (Verlag C. H. Beck, 1996), pp. 46–64; J. J. Sheehan, 'Nation und Staat: Deutschland als "imaginerte Gemeinschaft"', in ibid., pp. 33–45; R. Lenman, *Die Kunst, die Macht und das Geld: Zur Kulturgeschichte des kaiserlichen Deutschland 1871–1918* (Campus Verlag, 1994).

30. Paret, *The Berlin Secession.*
31. Feistel-Rohmeder, 'Was zu Heidelberg begann...'.
32. Schindler, 'Nochmals: "Was zu Heidelberg begann..."', p. 97.
33. Ibid.
34. P. U. Hein, 'Volkische Kunstkritik', in U. Puschner et al. (eds), *Handbuch zur 'Völkischen Bewegung'* (K. G. Saur, 1996), pp. 613–33; Lewis, *Art For All?*
35. L. Dupeux, 'La version "volkisch" de l'alternative, 1830–1933', *Revue d'Allemagne* 22 (1990), pp. 381–9; R. Hering, '"Des deutschen Volkes Wiedergeburt": Völkischer Nationalismus und politische Erneuerungspläne', *Zeitschrift für Geschichtswissenschaft* 42 (1994), pp. 1079–84; G. Hartung, 'Völkische Ideologie', in U. Puschner et al. (eds), *Handbuch zur 'Völkischen Bewegung'* (K. G. Saur, 1996), pp. 22–41.
36. R. Chickering, *We Men Who Feel Most German: A Cultural Study of the Pan-German League, 1886–1914* (George Allen & Unwin, 1984), pp. 234–6.
37. Ibid., p. 236; Loham, *Völkischer Radikalismus*, p. 34.
38. M. R. Gerstenhauer, *Der völkische Gedanke in Vergangenheit und Zukunft* (Armanen-Verlag, 1933), pp. 42–6; D. Fricke, 'Der "Deutschbund"', in U. Puschner et al. (eds), *Handbuch zur 'Völkischen Bewegung'* (K. G. Saur, 1996), pp. 329–32.
39. Aufruf, Entwurf von Schulrat Dr Rohmeder beraten in der DDB, Gem Mchn [Deutschbund Gemeinde München], 1916, attached to the letter Bettina Feistel-Rohmeder to Walter Buch, 8 December 1937, BDC, Feistel-Rohmeder file.
40. All quotes from ibid.; emphasis in the original.
41. Ibid.
42. Other members did credit Rohmeder. See H. Fecht, 'Zur Eröffnung der 2. Wanderausstelung der Deutschen Kunstgesellschaft', *Das Bild*, October 1937, pp. 319–20.
43. For example B. Feistel-Rohmeder, 'Elsa Munscheid', *Deutsche Bildkunst*, September 1929, pp. 31–2; idem, 'Aus dem Leben einer niederrheinischen Kirchenmalerin', *Das Bild*, September 1934, pp. 289–99; idem, 'Zwei thüringisch-sächsische Malerinnen: Katharina Krabbes-Dresden und Paula Henneberg-Weimar', *Das Bild*, July 1942, pp. 107–10.

44. A. Todorow, 'Frauen im Journalismus der Weimarer Republik', *Internationales Archiv für Sozialgeschichte der deutschen Literatur* 16 (1991), p. 90.
45. Ibid., p. 93.
46. Ibid., p. 101.
47. K. Bruns, 'Völkische und deutschnationale Frauenvereine im "zweiten Reich"', in U. Puschner et al. (eds), *Handbuch zur 'Völkischen Bewegung' 1871–1918* (K. G. Saur, 1996), pp. 379–80; see also L. J. Rupp, 'Mother of the *Volk*: The Image of Women in Nazi Ideology', *Signs* 3 (1977), pp. 362–79.
48. Bruns, 'Völkische und deutschnationale Frauenvereine', p. 380.
49. Ibid., p. 382.
50. G. T. Kaplan and C. E. Adams, 'Early Women Supporters of National Socialism', in J. Milfull (ed.), *The Attractions of Fascism: Social Psychology and Aesthetics of the 'Triumph of the Right'* (Berg, 1990), p. 194. For the 'Weimar' new woman, see for example M. Meskimmon and S. West (eds), *Visions of the 'Neue Frau': Women and the Visual Arts in Weimar Germany* (Scolar, 1995); K. von Ankum (ed.), *Women in the Metropolis: Gender and Modernity in Weimar Culture* (University of California Press, 1997); A. Grossman, 'The New Woman and the Rationalization of Sexuality in Weimar Germany', in A. Snitow et al. (eds), *Powers of Desire: The Politics of Sexuality* (Monthly Review Press, 1984), pp. 153–71.
51. Kaplan and Adams, 'Early Women Supporters of National Socialism', p. 195; C. Koonz, *Mothers in the Fatherland: Women, the Family, and Nazi Politics* (St. Martin's Press, 1987); idem, 'Nazi Women before 1933: Rebels against Emancipation', *Social Science Quarterly* 56 (1976), pp. 553–63; Rupp, 'Mother of the *Volk*'.
52. Feistel-Rohmeder, *Das Frauenbildnis*, and idem, 'Rassische Selbsterkenntnis', *Deutsche Bildkunst*, January/February 1933, pp. 29–31.
53. Feistel-Rohmeder, *Das Frauenbildnis*, p. 32. Women's willingness to bear pain for others echoes throughout the book.
54. That the greatest contributors to the Renaissance were Aryan was accepted within German racialist circles. See for example H. S. Chamberlain, *Foundations of the Nineteenth Century* (Howard Fertig, 1968), vol. 2, pp. 187–96. For a good sample of such theories see Roh, *'Entartete' Kunst*.
55. Feistel-Rohmeder, *Das Frauenbildnis*, pp. 56–7.
56. Ibid., p. 72.
57. Ibid., pp. 54–5, 72.
58. Ibid., p. 66.
59. Ibid., p. 17.
60. Ibid., p. 68.
61. Ibid.

62. Feistel-Rohmeder, 'Rassische Selbsterkenntnis', pp. 29–31.

63. Ibid., p. 29.

64. Ibid.

65. Emphasis in the original; ibid., p. 29.

66. Ibid. Although she does not cite a specific book, the dates referred to suggest she had in mind H. F. K. Günther, *Rassenkunde des Deutschen Volkes* (J. F. Lehmann, 1922). Günther was an honorary member of the German Art Society.

67. Feistel-Rohmeder, 'Rassische Selbsterkenntnis', p. 29.

68. Ibid.

69. Ibid. There she cites L. F. Clauss, *Die nordische Seele* (Verlag Max Niemeyer, 1923).

70. Feistel-Rohmeder, 'Rassische Selbsterkenntnis', p. 29. F. W. Prinz zur Lippe, *Angewandte Rassenseelenkunde* (Adolf Klein Verlag, 1931).

71. Feistel-Rohmeder, 'Rassische Selbsterkenntnis'.

72. P. Schultze-Naumburg, *Kunst und Rasse* (J. F. Lehmanns Verlag, 1928), pp. 92–3, for example.

73. Emphasis in the original; B. Feistel-Rohmeder, 'Woran sollen wir erkennen, ob ein Kunstwerk Deutsch ist?' in idem, *Im Terror des Kunstbolschewismus*, p. 150.

74. Feistel-Rohmeder, 'Woran sollen wir erkennen, ob ein Kunstwerk Deutsch ist?'

75. Feistel-Rohmeder, 'Rassische Selbsterkenntnis'; Schultze-Naumburg, *Kunst und Rasse*.

76. Feistel-Rohmeder, 'Rassische Selbsterkenntnis', p. 30.

77. Ibid.

78. Friedrich Hopf, a public health official in Dresden, was a leading member of the Pan-German League. He sponsored the founding of the German-*völkisch* Defense League in 1911. See G. Eley, *Reshaping the German Right: Radical Nationalism and Political Change after Bismarck* (Yale University Press, 1980), pp. 139, 159, 259, note 95, p. 282.

79. Heinrich Blume joined the SA in 1923 and the NSDAP in 1924. He represented the Nazi Party as a member of the *Völkisch-Sozialer Block* in the 1924 Reichstag. A teacher in Melsungen, he also belonged to the *NS-Lehrerbund*. 'Personalakten betreffend Rektor Heinrich Blume', NHStAH, Hann. 180 Hannover E 8 Acc. 15/89 Nr. 48; 'Entnazifizierungsakte Heinrich Blume', NHStAH, Nds. 171 Hannover Nr. 20260.

80. Based on my reconstruction of the German Art Society's membership, roughly 5 percent of the Society's members were female (10 out of 182 identified members who belonged between 1920 and 1944).

Chapter 2

1. For just a few of the best works, see S. West, *The Visual Arts in Germany 1890–1937: Utopia and Despair* (Rutgers University Press, 2001); B. Schraeder and J. Schebera, *The 'Golden' Twenties: Art and Literature in the Weimar Republic*, K. Vanovich, trans (Yale University Press, 1988); E. Kolb, *Die Weimarer Republik*, 2nd edn (R. Oldenbourg Verlag, 1988).
2. P. Paret, *The Berlin Secession: Modernism and Its Enemies in Imperial Germany* (The Belknap Press of Harvard University, 1980).
3. P. Gay, *Weimar Culture: The Outsider as Insider* (Harper and Row, 1968); W. Laqueur, *Weimar: A Cultural History, 1918–1933* (Putnam, 1974).
4. B. Feistel-Rohmeder, *Im Terror des Kunstbolschewismus: Urkundensammlung des 'Deutschen Kunstberichtes' aus den Jahren 1927–1933* (C. F. Müller Verlag, 1938); idem, 'Von Deutscher Malerei und Graphik in Dresden', *Das Bild*, July 1934, pp. 229–34; L. Meiners, 'Richard Müller: Zu seinem 65. Geburtstag', *Das Bild*, July 1939, pp. 206–8.
5. Feistel-Rohmeder, *Im Terror des Kunstbolschewismus*, pp. 3–6, 211–17; Deutsche Kunstgesellschaft, *Satzungen* (A. Bernecker, nd [c.1929]) in ThHStAW, ThVBM/C 933, Bl 160–1.
6. Feistel-Rohmeder, *Im Terror des Kunstbolschewismus*, p. 211.
7. Ibid.; A. L. Müller, 'Richard Guhr', *Das Bild*, July 1934, pp. 224–9. Hardly ignored, Guhr was a successful artist who among other projects designed in 1912 the huge Hercules figure that still stands atop the Dresden *Rathaus*.
8. Feistel-Rohmeder, *Im Terror des Kunstbolschewismus*, p. 211.
9. L. Fritzsching, 'Die wirtschaftliche Lage der bildenden Künstler seit Kriegsende', *Annalen des Deutschen Reichs für Gesetzgebung, Verwaltung und Volkswirtschaft, Jahrgang 1921 und 1922* (J. Schweitzer Verlag, 1923), pp. 146–8; G. D. Feldman, *The Great Disorder: Politics, Economics, and Society in the German Inflation, 1914–1924* (Oxford University Press, 1993), pp. 539–41.
10. Fritzsching, 'Die wirtschaftliche Lage'; F. Hellwag, 'Die derzeitige wirtschaftliche Lage der bildenden Künstler', in L. Sinzheimer (ed.), *Die geistige Arbeiter*, erster Teil, *Freies Schriftstellertum und Literaturverlag* (Verlag von Duncker and Humblot, 1922), pp. 145–75; G. Schreiber, *Die Not der deutschen Wissenschaft und der geistigen Arbeiter: Geschehnisse und Gedanken zur Kulturpolitik des Deutsche Reiches* (Verlag von Quelle und Meyer, 1923).
11. J. V. Rühn, 'Die Kunst und die Revolution', undated (*c.*1919) manuscript located in BA Berlin, R32/482, Bl 23–45; the quote is from Bl 26.
12. Fritzsching, 'Die wirtschaftliche Lage', p. 156.

13. Both quotes are from Hellwag, 'Die derzeitige wirtschaftliche Lage', p. 161.

14. These figures are based on data represented in slightly different form in ibid., pp. 157–9.

15. Ibid., p. 150.

16. Ibid.

17. Ibid., pp. 150–60.

18. Fritzsching, 'Die wirtschaftliche Lage'. Hellwag, 'Die derzeitige wirtschaftliche Lage der bildenden Künstler,' pp. 148–50.

19. Fritzsching, 'Die wirtschaftliche Lage', p. 184.

20. For example, 'Zur Preisbildung der Kunstwerk', *Kunst und Wirtschaft* 2 (1 August 1922). p. 2; 'Bericht des Reichswirtschaftsverbandes', *Kunst und Wirtschaft* 4 (1 October 1923), p. 2; 'Bericht des Reichswirtschaftsverbandes', *Kunst und Wirtschaft* 4 (1 September 1923), p. 2.

21. 'Bericht des Reichswirtschaftsverbandes', *Kunst und Wirtschaft* 4 (1 March 1923), p. 1; 'Luxussteuer und moderne Graphik', ibid., p. 2, and continued in *Kunst und Wirtschaft 4* (16 April 1921), pp. 1–2; 'Bericht des Reichswirtschaftsverbandes', *Kunst und Wirtschaft* 4 (16 May 1923), p. 1. See also Feldman, *The Great Disorder*, p. 537.

22. See the correspondence between Erwin Redslob and numerous artist associations and newspaper articles on artists' pleas for help, in BA Berlin, R32/117 and R32/470.

23. O. Marcus, 'Notgemeinschaft der deutschen Kunst', *Kunst und Wirtschaft* 4 (1 June 1923), p. 1; idem, 'Die Notgemeinschaft der deutschen Kunst', *Kunst und Wirtschaft* 4 (1 July 1923), pp. 1–2.

24. A. Weber, *Die Not der geistigen Arbeiter* (Duncker und Humblot, 1923); K. Jarausch, *The Unfree Professions* (Oxford University Press, 1990); Feldman, *The Great Disorder*, especially pp. 527–55.

25. Schreiber, *Die Not der deutschen Wissenschaft und der geistigen Arbeiter*, K. Jarausch, 'Die Not der geistigen Arbeiter: Akademiker in der Berufskrise 1918–1933', in W. Abelshauser (ed.), *Die Weimarer Republik als Wohlfahrtsstaat* (Stuttgart, 1987), pp. 280–300; A. Kaes, 'Die ökonomische Dimension der Literatur: Zum Strukturwandel der Institution Literatur in der Inflationszeit (1918–1923)', in G. D. Feldman et al. (eds), *Konsequenzen der Inflation/Consequences of Inflation* (Colloquium Verlag, 1988), pp. 307–29; B. Widdig, *Culture and Inflation in Weimar Germany* (University of California Press, 2001).

26. Fritzsching, 'Die wirtschaftliche Lage', p. 153; Schreiber, *Die Not der deutschen Wissenschaft und der geistigen Arbeiter*, p. 130.

27. Fritzsching, 'Die wirtschaftliche Lage', pp. 154–5.

28. Feistel-Rohmeder, *Im Terror des Kunstbolschewismus*.

29. Ibid.; W. Willrich, *Die Säuberung des Kunsttempels: Eine kunstpolitische Kampfschrift zur Gesundung deutscher Kunst im Geiste nordischer Art* (J. F. Lehmanns Verlag, 1937).

30. Deutsche Kunstgesellschaft, *Satzungen*.

31. Feistel-Rohmeder, *Im Terror des Kunstbolschewismus*, p. 212. For Krause's first name, see U. Loham, *Völkischer Radikalismus: Die Geschichte des Deutschvölkischen Schutz- und Trutzbundes 1919–1923* (Leibnitz-Verlag, 1970), p. 273.

32. G. Eley, *Reshaping the German Right: Radical Nationalism and Political Change after Bismarck* (Yale University Press, 1980), pp. 139, 159, 259, note 95, p. 282; Feistel-Rohmeder, *Im Terror des Kunstbolschewismus*, pp. 211–14.

33. Ibid.

34. Feistel-Rohmeder, *Im Terror des Kunstbolschewismus*, p. 213; E. Schindler, 'Der "Ehrenbeamtin der Deutschen Kunst": Zum 65. Geburtstag von Frau Bettina Feistel-Rohmeder am 24. August 1938', *Das Bild*, August 1938, p. 229; B. Feistel-Rohmeder, 'Rückblick und Ausblick', in 'Aus der Deutschen Kunstgesellschaft', *Das Bild*, November, 1935, unpaginated.

35. Feistel-Rohmeder, *Im Terror des Kunstbolschewismus*, p. 213; idem, 'Rückblick und Ausblick'.

36. B. Feistel-Rohmeder, 'Julius Widnmann', *Das Bild*, January/February 1940, p. 29; Feistel-Rohmeder, *Im Terror des Kunstbolschewismus*, p. 213.

37. Ibid., and Feistel-Rohmeder, 'Rückblick und Ausblick'.

38. Feistel-Rohmeder, *Im Terror des Kunstbolschewismus*, p. 214.

39. Deutsche Kunstgesellschaft, *Satzungen*.

40. Feistel-Rohmeder, *Im Terror des Kunstbolschewismus*, pp. 213–14; idem, 'Julius Widnmann', p. 29; idem, 'Rückblick und Ausblick'; idem, 'München 1941', *Das Bild*, July/August 1941, p. 125.

41. For details on the organization, press reaction and sales of the exhibition see SHStAD, Ministerium für Volksbildung, Nr. 14923, Internationale Kunstausstellung Dresden 1926.

42. That modernist art and artists were young and new, and thus favored by the republic, were constant themes in Feistel-Rohmeder, *Im Terror des Kunstbolschewismus*.

43. N. Pevsner, 'Internationale Kunstausstellung: Die ältere deutsche Malerei', *Dresdner Anzeiger*, 7 August 1926, in SHStAD, Ministerium für Volksbildung, Nr. 14923, Internationale Kunstausstellung Dresden 1926.

44. 'Internationale Kunstausstellung Dresden 1926 (2)', *Sächsisches Staatszeitung*, Nr. 167, 21 July 1926; 'Kunst und Wissenschaft. Internationale Kunstausstellung (1)', *Sächsisches Staatszeitung*, 20 July 1926; 'Internationale Kunstausstellung Dresden 1926 (3)', *Sächsisches Staatszeitung*,

24 July 1926; Pevsner, 'Internationale Kunstausstellung', all in SHStAD, Nr. 14923, Internationale Kunstausstellung Dresden 1926.

45. These tactics can be seen in Bettina Feistel-Rohmeder to Walter Buch, 8 December 1937, BDC, Feistel-Rohmeder file, and in the 1932 correspondence between Feistel-Rohmeder and Dietrich Klagges in NStAW, Braunschweigisches Staatsministerium, Akten betr Deutsche Kunstgesellschaft, Bd 1, 1932, 12 A Neu 13/18763.

46. H. Blume, 'Der Kampf geht weiter!' *Deutschbund-Nachrichten* November 1939, pp. 25–6. Blume also belonged to the SA and the NSDAP in the 1920s. For more, see NHStAH, 'Personalakten betreffend Rektor Heinrich Blume', Hann. 180 Hannover E 8 Acc. 15/89 Nr. 48, Bd 2, and NHStAH, 'Entnazifizierungsakte Heinrich Blume', Nds 171 Hannover Nr. 20260.

47. Loham, *Völkischer Radikalismus*, p. 34.

48. For the League's support of the *Bartelsbund* and the *Heimatschule Bad Berka*, see *Deutschbund Blätter*, April 1929.

49. Two issues of the *Deutsche Bildkunst* – September 1929 and April 1930 – can be found in ThHStAW, ThVBM/C 933, Bl 171–81. Two double issues – August/September 1932 and January/February 1933 – are in the library of the Staatliche Kunsthalle Karlsruhe.

50. Buchorn's *Parsifals Heimkehr* can be found in *Deutsche Bildkunst*, April 1930, p. 39; Rehm's *Verlorenes Land: Burg Persen* is in ibid., September 1929, p. 30.

51. Feistel-Rohmeder, *Im Terror des Kunstbolschewismus*, p. 214; 'Jahresbericht der Deutschen Kunstgesellschaft', *Deutsche Bildkunst*, September 1929, p. 32.

52. Feistel-Rohmeder, *Im Terror des Kunstbolschewismus*, pp. 3–4, 7.

53. *Mitteilungen des Kampfbundes für deutsche Kultur*, February 1929, p. 31.

54. See the material in *Kunst in Karlsruhe 1900–1950* (C. F. Müller Verlag, 1981); J. Heusinger von Waldegg, *Die Hochschule der bildenden Künste Karlsruhe im Dritten Reich* (Staatliche Akademie der Bildenden Künste Karlsruhe, 1987).

55. *German Art Correspondence* material in BDC, Feistel-Rohmeder file. For citation of *Die Sonne*, see 'Aus der Deutschen Kunstgesellschaft', *Deutsche Kunstkorrespondenz*, April 1930, p. 3, in ThHStAW, ThVBM/C 933, Bl 164. For examples of the reciprocal relationship between the Society and the Combat League, see Feistel-Rohmeder, *Im Terror des Kunstbolschewismus*, p. 36; 'Die Zeichen der Zeit: Ein Briefwechsel', *Mitteilungen des Kampfbundes für deutsche Kultur*, February 1929, pp. 26–7; 'Die Deutsche Kunstgesellschaft', *Mitteilungen des Kampfbundes für deutsche Kultur*, September/ October 1929, pp. 20–1; 'Von der "Deutschen Kunstgesellschaft"...', *Mitteilungen des Kampfbundes für deutsche Kultur*, April/May 1930, p. 13.

56. Feistel-Rohmeder, *Im Terror des Kunstbolschewismus*, pp. 8–9, 30, 39, 46, 56–7, 164–8.

57. 'Märchen', *Deutsche Kunstkorrespondenz*, December 1931, in Feistel-Rohmeder, *Im Terror des Kunstbolschewismus*, p. 152.

58. 'Solche und Solche', *Deutsche Kunstkorrespondenz*, May 1928, in Feistel-Rohmeder, *Im Terror des Kunstbolschewismus*, pp. 31–2.

59. Paul Ortwin Rave, an assistant to Ludwig Justi at the Berlin National Gallery, believed the *Correspondence* was an influential source against modernist art. P. O. Rave, *Kunstdiktatur im Dritten Reich*, ed. U. M. Schneede (Argon, 1988), pp. 26, 30, 37, 40. See also H. Brenner, *Die Kunstpolitik des National-sozialismus* (Rowohlt Taschenbuch Verlag, 1963), p. 19; O. Thomae, *Die Propaganda-Maschinerie: Bildende Kunst und Öffentlichkeitsarbeit im Dritten Reich* (Gebrüder Mann, 1978).

60. See the schedule of the League congress and the advertisements for the show in *Deutschbund Blätter*, April 1929.

61. 'Jahresbericht der Deutschen Kunstgesellschaft'. Kirdorf's donation earned him an honorary membership in the Society. For more on him see H. A. Turner, Jr., 'Hitler's Secret Pamphlet for Industrialists, 1927', *Journal of Modern History* 40 (1968), pp. 349–74.

62. Deutsche Kunstgesellschaft, *Satzungen*.

63. Most of the exhibitors are named in Feistel-Rohmeder, 'Frühlingsfahrt', *Deutsche Bildkunst*, September 1929, p. 29.

64. Ibid.

65. See A. B. Enns' critique of the exhibition in *Lübeckische Blätter*, 1929, 404ff, cited in Brenner, *Die Kunstpolitik des Nationalsozialismus*, note 5, p. 255.

66. 'Reinhold Rehm', *Deutsche Bildkunst*, September 1929, p. 30.

67. The quotes and hints at other renderings of a similar theme are from E. Kühn, 'Richard Guhr vollendet am 30. September 1943 sein 70. Lebensjahr', *Das Bild*, July 1943, p. 84; for the image, see *Deutsche Bildkunst*, September 1932, p. 23.

68. Feistel-Rohmeder, 'Frühlingsfahrt', p. 29; see also Feistel-Rohmeder, *Im Terror des Kunstbolschewismus*, p. 215.

69. 'Kunstausstellung der Deutschen Kunstgesellschaft in Lübeck', *Melsungen Tagblatt*, Nr. 134, 11 June 1929.

70. Ibid.; Feistel-Rohmeder, 'Frühlingsfahrt', p. 29.

71. 'Kunstausstellung der Deutschen Kunstgesellschaft in Lübeck', *Melsungen Tagblatt*, Nr. 134, 11 June 1929; *Deutsche Zeitung*, 18 June 1929; *Deutsch-bund Blätter*, April 1929, pp. 22, 24; 'Die Deutsche Kunstgesellschaft', *Mitteilungen des Kampfbundes für deutsche Kultur*, September-October 1929, pp. 20–1; 'Die Kunstausstellung der Deutschen Kunstgesellschaft in Lübeck', *Deutsche Kunstkorrespondenz*, June 1929, in Feistel-Rohmeder, *Im Terror des Kunstbolschewismus*, p. 58; and ibid., p. 215.

72. Feistel-Rohmeder, 'Frühlingsfahrt', p. 29.

73. Ibid.

74. Ibid., and Feistel-Rohmeder, *Im Terror des Kunstbolschewismus*, p. 215.

75. For part of Enns' review see Brenner, *Die Kunstpolitik des Nationalsozialismus*, note 5, p. 255. See also Feistel-Rohmeder, 'Die Kunstausstellung der Deutschen Kunstgesellschaft in Dresden', and idem, 'Frühlingsfahrt', p. 29.

76. 'Jahresbericht der Deutschen Kunstgesellschaft'.

77. Ibid.; Feistel-Rohmeder, *Im Terror des Kunstbolschewismus*, pp. 211–14. See also the sources listed for my reconstructed membership list below.

78. 'Jahresbericht der Deutschen Kunstgesellschaft'.

79. These 100 members are not the same 100 (unidentified) members mentioned in the 1929 annual report. Rather, these are men and women whose membership could be verified. The sources for the reconstruction of the membership and the data in the following tables are *Deutsche Bildkunst*, September 1929, April 1930, August/September 1932, January/February 1933; *Das Bild*, January–December 1934 (which mentioned members' earlier affiliations with the Society); Deutsche Kunstgesellschaft, *I. Wanderausstellung Deutscher Kunst* (np, nd [1933]); *Mitteilungen des Kampfbundes für deutsche Kultur*, 1929–31; and Feistel-Rohmeder, *Im Terror des Kunstbolschewismus*.

80. The Munich members were Hans Geyer, Hermann Groeber and Ernst Emil Heinsdorff; in Karlsruhe, Hans Adolf Bühler, August Gebhard, Hermann Binz and Hermann Kupferschmid; in Dresden, Georg Beutel, Walther Gasch, Johannes Eckert, Eugen Friedrich Hopf and Wolfgang Willrich.

81. To avoid counting the same member twice when more than one occupation was given, I placed him or her in the occupational category which carried the most prestige. For example, an artist who was also a professor is listed here under 'professor'.

82. Feistel-Rohmeder, *Im Terror des Kunstbolschewismus*, p. 213.

83. This is a constant refrain in Feistel-Rohmeder, *Im Terror des Kunstbolschewismus*.

84. This was already a problem in the Wilhelmine Empire. See for example, P. Drey, *Die wirtschaftlichen Grundlagen der Malkunst: Versuch einer Kunstökonomie* (J. G. Cotta'sche Buchhandlung Nachfolger, 1910); P. Paret, *The Berlin Secession: Modernism and Its Enemies in Imperial Germany* (The Belknap Press of Harvard University, 1980).

85. Wirtschaftlicher Verband bildender Künstler Südwestdeutschlands E.V., 'Jahresbericht 1926', GLA 235/5839.

86. Ibid., and Wirtschaftlicher Verband bildender Künstler Südwestdeutschlands E.V., 'Jahresbericht 1927', in GLA 235/5839. See also R. Bosselt, 'Sterbende Berufe? Versuch einer Betrachtung unserer Lage ohne Selbsttäuschung', *Kunst und Wirtschaft*, 1 September 1927, pp. 209–14.

87. Ibid., p. 212; A. Segal, 'Vom Schicksal der bildenden Künstler', *Kunst und Wirtschaft*, 1 September 1927, pp. 214–15.

88. See M. F. Deshmukh, 'Max Liebermann: Observations on the Politics of Painting in Imperial Germany, 1870–1914', *German Studies Review* 3 (1980), pp. 171–206; Paret, *The Berlin Secession*.

89. Of the 68 core members whose birthdates have been found, 59 were born before 1889; most were born before 1880.

90. *German Art Correspondence* articles bitterly noted the awards and positions won by modernist artists. See for example Feistel-Rohmeder, *Im Terror des Kunstbolschewismus*, pp. 31, 162.

91. For example, H. Ursprung, 'Alois Brunner', *Deutsche Bildkunst*, February 1933, p. 22; 'Georg Liebhart erzählt sein Leben', ibid., p. 25; J. A. Beringer, 'Deutsche Kunst im Norden', *Deutsche Bildkunst*, January 1933, pp. 3–8; the sense of persecution also resonates throughout Feistel-Rohmeder, *Im Terror des Kunstbolschewismus*.

92. T. Butz, 'Die Ausstellung "Entartete Kunst" im Kunstverein Karlsruhe, September 1933', GLA 235/40090.

93. See the purchase list for the exhibit located in the SHStAD, Ministerium für Volksbildung, Nr. 14923. By way of comparison, the Expressionist artist Conrad Felixmüller received 3,500 marks for a painting sold from the same exhibit.

94. Paret, *The Berlin Secession*; *Kunst in Karlsruhe 1900–1950*.

95. Feistel-Rohmeder, *Im Terror des Kunstbolschewismus*, p. 206. She never mentioned that Guhr was Dix's teacher.

96. This fear was not unique to the Society. For example, the Prussian Academy of Fine Arts debated the place of modernists in its ranks. W. Mittenzwei, *Der Untergang einer Akademie oder die Mentalität des ewigen Deutschen: Der Einfluss der nationalkonservativen Dichter an der Preussischen Akademie der Künste, 1919–1947* (Aufbau-Verlag, 1992), chapter 1.

97. See the footnote beneath 'Solche und Solche', *Deutsche Kunstkorrespondenz*, May 1928, in Feistel-Rohmeder, *Im Terror des Kunstbolschewismus*, p. 31.

98. J. H. Ulbricht, 'Kulturrevolution von rechts: Das völkische Netzwerk 1900–1930', in D. Heiden and G. Mai (eds), *Nationalsozialismus in Thüringen* (Böhlau Verlag, 1995), pp. 36–8. For more on anti-republican authors and publishers, see G. D. Stark, *Entrepreneurs of Ideology: Neoconservative Publishers in Germany, 1890–1933* (University of North Carolina Press, 1981).

99. B. Feistel-Rohmeder, 'Die Münchner Künstlergruppe "Der Bund"', *Deutsche Bildkunst*, February 1933, pp. 27–8.

100. J. A. Beringer, 'Über Zeichner und Graphiker aus Süddeutschland', *Deutsche Bildkunst*, August 1932, p. 9; 'Die "Deutsche Kunstgesellschaft, Sitz

Dresden", und der Kampf um die Deutsche Kunst', in Feistel-Rohmeder, *Im Terror des Kunstbolschewismus*, pp. 190–1.

101. Feistel-Rohmeder claimed that because Berlin was a haven for degenerates there were relatively few Society members in Berlin. B. Feistel-Rohmeder, 'Zur weiteren Übersicht über das Deutsche Schaffen in Berlin', *Deutsche Bildkunst*, January 1933, p. 14.

102. Ulbricht, 'Kuturrevolution von rechts', pp. 36–7; idem, 'Die "Deutsche Heimatschule" in Bad Berka: Ein vergessenes Kapitel regionaler Schulgeschichte', *Heimat Thüringen: Kulturlandschaft, Lebensraum, Umwelt* 3 (1996), p. 23. Note that Bartels is not in the core membership list.

103. Academy affiliations and student-teacher relationships were determined in part by the artists' biographical entries in *Allgemeines Lexikon der bildenden Künstler: Von Antike bis zur Gegenwart* (Verlag E. A. Seemann, 1915, etc.).

Chapter 3

1. B. Feistel-Rohmeder, 'In eigener Sache der Deutschen Bildkunst', *Deutsche Bildkunst*, September 1932, p. 32.

2. There was a constant tension between *völkisch* organizations and the NSDAP. See for example, M. Broszat, 'Die völkische Ideologie und der Nationalsozialismus', *Deutsche Rundschau* 84 (1958), pp. 53–68; L. Dupeux, 'La version "volkisch" de l'alternative, 1830–1933', *Revue d'Allemagne* 22 (1990), pp. 381–9; R. Hering, '"Des deutschen Volkes Wiedergeburt": Völkischer Nationalismus und politische Erneuerungspläne', *Zeitschrift für Geschichtswissenschaft* 42 (1994), pp. 1079–84; J. Hermand, *Old Dreams of a New Reich: Völkisch Utopias and National Socialism*, P. Levesque, trans, in collaboration with S. Soldovieri (Indiana University Press, 1992).

3. These were pro-modernist shows only in the sense that they accepted all styles of art. 'Ein Briefwechsel', *Deutsche Kunstkorrespondenz*, January 1929, in B. Feistel-Rohmeder, *Im Terror des Kunstbolschewismus: Urkundensammlung des 'Deutschen Kunstberichtes' aus den Jahren 1927–1933* (C. F. Müller Verlag, 1938), pp. 47–8.

4. Ibid., p. 48.

5. Ibid., p. 47.

6. Ibid. P. Schultze-Naumburg, *Kunst und Rasse* (J. F. Lehmanns Verlag, 1928).

7. 'Ein Briefwechsel', pp. 47–8.
8. Ibid., p. 48.
9. Ibid.
10. See also 'Die Zeichen der Zeit: Ein Briefwechsel', *Mitteilungen des Kampfbundes für deutsche Kultur*, February 1929, pp. 10–11.
11. Not March 1930 as Feistel-Rohmeder remembered in *Im Terror des Kunstbolschewismus*, p. 214. Because Brenner had only this source, she dated the founding of the Council as March 1930, as have subsequent historians. H. Brenner, *Die Kunstpolitik des Nationalsozialismus* (Rowohlt Taschenbuch Verlag, 1963), p. 19. For the correction, see 'Bericht über die Zusammenkunft der Vertreter gleichgerichteter Kunst- und Kulturverbände in Weimar am 10. Lenzings [March], Gasthof Kaiserin Augusta', *Deutschbund-Blätter*, April 1929, pp. 37–8, in ThHStAW, ThVBM/C 933, Bl 169ff. Hereafter this document will be cited as 'Bericht über die Zusammenkunft ... [des Führerrates]', 10 March 1929.
12. Point 3, Satzungen [des Führerrates], attached to the letter Bettina Feistel-Rohmeder and Heinrich Blume to Education and Interior Minister Dietrich Klagges, 27 September 1932, NStAW, Braunschweigisches Staatsministerium, Akten betr. Deutsche Kunstgesellschaft, Bd 1, 1932, 12 A Neu 13/18763.
13. Brenner, *Die Kunstpolitik des Nationalsozialismus*, pp. 19, 37; B. Hinz, *Art in the Third Reich*, R. and R. Kimber, trans (Pantheon, 1979), pp. 26–7.
14. 'Bericht über die Zusammenkunft ... [des Führerrates]', 10 March 1929; 'Jahresbericht der Deutschen Kunstgesellschaft', *Deutsche Bildkunst*, September 1929, p. 32.
15. 'Bericht über die Zusammenkunft ... [des Führerrates]', 10 March 1929; Satzungen [des Führerrates]. Compare to the Society's exhibition guidelines and statutes in Feistel-Rohmeder, *Im Terror des Kunstbolschewismus*, pp. 212–13, and Deutsche Kunstgesellschaft, *Satzungen* (A. Bernecker, nd [*c*.1929]), ThHStAW, ThVBM/C 933, Bl 160–1.
16. Führerrat der vereinigten Deutschen Kunst- und Kulturverbände, Geschäftsordnung, attached to the letter Feistel-Rohmeder and Blume to Klagges, 27 September 1932.
17. Führerrat der vereinigten Deutschen Kunst- und Kulturverbände, Geschäftsordnung, point G.
18. Ibid., point C.
19. 'Bericht über die Zusammenkunft ... [des Führerrates]', 10 March 1929.
20. 'Der Führerrat der vereinigten Deutschen Kunst- und Kulturverbände und die Deutsche Kunstgesellschaft', *Deutsche Bildkunst*, April 1930, p. 41.
21. Führerrat der vereinigten Deutschen Kunst- und Kulturverbände, Geschäftsordnung, point B.

22. 'Bericht über die Zusammenkunft ... [des Führerrates]', 10 March 1929. For Hugenberg's group see 'An unsere Mitglieder und Freunde: Der "Schutzverein für die geistigen Güter Deutschlands"', *Mitteilungen des Kampfbundes für deutsche Kultur*, February 1929, pp. 13–14.

23. J. H. Ulbricht, 'Die "Deutsche Heimatschule" in Bad Berka: Ein vergessenes Kapitel regionaler Schulgeschichte', *Heimat Thüringen: Kulturlandschaft, Lebensraum, Umwelt* 3 (1996), pp. 22–3.

24. 'Bericht über die Zusammenkunft ... [des Führerrates]', 10 March 1929; 'Der Führerrat der vereinigten Deutschen Kunst- und Kulturverbände und die Deutsche Kunstgesellschaft'; and Feistel-Rohmeder, *Im Terror des Kunstbolschewismus*, p. 214.

25. Feistel-Rohmeder, *Im Terror des Kunstbolschewismus*, p. 124.

26. P. D. Stachura, 'Der kritische Wendepunkt? Die NSDAP und die Reichstagwahlen vom 20. Mai 1928', *Vierteljahrshefte für Zeitgeschichte* 26 (1978), p. 84.

27. Ibid., and p. 91. See also T. Childers, *The Nazi Voter: The Social Foundations of Fascism in Germany, 1919–1933* (University of North Carolina Press, 1983), chapter 3; L. E. Jones, *German Liberalism and the Dissolution of the Weimar Party System, 1918–1933* (University of North Carolina Press, 1988).

28. B. Feistel-Rohmeder, 'Die Geister sammeln sich', *Deutsche Kunstkorrespondenz*, August/September 1928, in Feistel-Rohmeder, *Im Terror des Kunstbolschewismus*, pp. 34–7.

29. Both quotes are from Stachura, 'Der kritische Wendepunkt?' pp. 91, 93.

30. Ibid., pp. 95–6.

31. A. E. Steinweis, 'Weimar Culture and the Rise of National Socialism: The *Kampfbund für deutsche Kultur*', *Central European History* 24 (1991), p. 407.

32. 'Die Geisteswende', *Mitteilungen des Kampfbundes für deutsche Kultur*, January 1929, cited in Steinweis, 'Weimar Culture and the Rise of National Socialism', p. 405.

33. Ibid., pp. 402–23; R. Bollmus, *Das Amt Rosenberg und seine Gegner: Studium zum Machtkampf im nationalsozialistischen Herrschaftssytem* (Deutsche Verlags-Anstalt, 1970), chapters 1 and 2.

34. *Mitteilungen des Kampfbundes für deutsche Kultur*, February 1929, p. 15; *Mitteilungen des Kampfbundes für deutsche Kultur*, June–August 1930, p. 15.

35. 'Bericht über die Zusammenkunft ... [des 'Führerrates]', 10 March 1929; Niederschrift der Arbeitssitzung des Führerrates am 28.12.29 zu Dresden, ThHStAW, ThVBM/C 933, Bl 173–4; Bettina Feistel-Rohmeder to Wilhelm Frick, 15 April 1930, ThHStAW, ThVBM/C 933, Bl 146–8. For more on

Gasch, see M. Seydewitz, *Dresden: Musen und Menschen. Ein Beitrag zur Geschichte der Stadt, ihrer Kunst und Kultur* (Buchverlag Morgen, 1973), pp. 175, 179–81.

36. See the list of congress participants in *Mitteilungen des Kampfbundes für deutsche Kultur*, June–August 1930, pp. 13–14.

37. Steinweis, 'Weimar Culture and the Rise of National Socialism'.

38. A. E. Steinweis, *Art, Ideology, and Economics in Nazi Germany: The Reich Chambers of Music, Theater, and the Visual Arts* (University of North Carolina Press, 1993), chapter 1.

39. Ibid., p. 16. For examples of artists demanding financial support see the material in GLA 235/5839.

40. Steinweis, *Art, Ideology, and Economics in Nazi Germany*, p. 14.

41. 'Die Kunstgelahrten [*sic*]', *Deutsche Kunstkorrespondenz*, January 1931, in Feistel-Rohmeder, *Im Terror des Kunstbolschewismus*, p. 117.

42. 'Der Kampf um den "Neuen Stil" in der bildenden Kunst', February 1931, in Feistel-Rohmeder, *Im Terror des Kunstbolschewismus*, pp. 121–3; 'Der Streit um die "Deutsche Kunstgemeinschaft"', *Deutsche Kunstkorrespondenz*, April 1931, in ibid., pp. 132–3.

43. 'Merkwürdige Kunstausstellung in Dresden', *Deutsche Kunstkorrespondenz*, December 1931, in ibid., p. 155.

44. 'Bilderpreise', *Deutscher Kunstbericht*, March 1932, in ibid., pp. 163–4. The National Association of Germany's Visual Artists also protested against the purchase of the van Gogh; Reichsverband bild. Künstler an den Herrn Reichskanzler, 18 April 1932, GLA 235/5839.

45. 'Kunst und Wirtschaft', *Deutsche Kunstbericht*, September 1932, in Feistel-Rohmeder, *Im Terror des Kunstbolschewismus*, p. 173.

46. Emphasis in the original. 'Bericht über die Zusammenkunft … [des Führerrates]', 10 March 1929.

47. Ibid.

48. Satzungen [des Führerrates].

49. Ibid.

50. 'Bericht über die Zusammenkunft … [des Führerrates]', 10 March 1929; Niederschrift der Arbeitssitzung des 'Führerrates' am 28.12.29 zu Dresden.

51. Niederschrift der Arbeitssitzung des 'Führerrates' am 28.12.29 zu Dresden.

52. 'Bericht über die Zusammenkunft … [des Führerrates]', 10 March 1929; Feistel-Rohmeder's estimate is in Niederschrift der Arbeitssitzung des 'Führerrates' am 28.12.29 zu Dresden.

53. Niederschrift der Arbeitssitzung des 'Führerrates' am 28.12.29 zu Dresden; of the potential Dresden sponsors, only a Dr von Mayenburg was identified.

54. 'Jahresbericht der Deutschen Kunstgesellschaft'.

55. 'Kunstgemeinschaften', *Deutsche Bildkunst*, September 1929, p. 32.

56. Ibid. The December issue of *Deutsche Bildkunst* has not been located, although it does appear to have been published. See Niederschrift der Arbeitssitzung des 'Führerrates' am 28.12.29 zu Dresden. This issue seems to have been the only visual record of the Lübeck show; no catalog has been located.

57. 'Jahresbericht der Deutschen Kunstgesellschaft'. Only a painting by Julius Widnmann was specifically mentioned as being sold. See Niederschrift der Arbeitssitzung des 'Führerrates' am 28.12.29 zu Dresden.

58. 'Jahresbericht der Deutschen Kunstgesellschaft'.

59. Niederschrift der Arbeitssitzung des 'Führerrates' am 28.12.29 zu Dresden.

60. Ibid.; *Deutsche Kunstkorrespondenz*, April 1930, ThHStAW, ThVBM/C 933, Bl 163; 'An die Mitglieder des Deutschbundes und der Deutschen Kunstgesellschaft', *Deutsche Bildkunst*, April 1930, unpaginated [appears between pp. 39 and 40]; 'Der Führerrat der vereinigten Deutschen Kunst- und Kulturverbände und die Deutsche Kunstgesellschaft', ibid., p. 41; 'Eine Deutsche Kunstzeitschrift!' (possibly from a late 1929/early 1930 *Deutsche Bildkunst*), ThHStAW, ThVBM/C 933, Bl 175–6; 'Von der "Deutschen Kunstgesellschaft"', *Mitteilungen des Kampfbundes für deutsche Kultur*, April/May 1930, p. 13.

61. Feistel-Rohmeder, 'In eigener Sache der Deutschen Bildkunst', p. 32.

62. Even the Combat League expressed reservations regarding the efficacy of establishing an art journal because of the expense. 'Von der "Deutschen Kunstgesellschaft"'.

63. Niederschrift der Arbeitssitzung des 'Führerrates' am 28.12.29 zu Dresden. The departure of the *Block* is mentioned in passing in the letter Feistel-Rohmeder to Frick, 15 April 1930. The same letter also lists fourteen members of the Council, including the *Bund Deutsche Schrift*, not mentioned in other sources.

64. See Feistel-Rohmeder's exasperation regarding the number of art organizations that divided scarce resources in her *Im Terror des Kunstbolschewismus*, pp. 117–18, 178–9.

65. Plan der Ausstellung (dated 23 October 1932), sent to the cultural ministry in Thuringia, 6 April 1933, ThHStAW, ThVBM/C 936, Bl 4.

66. Brenner, *Die Kunstpolitik des Nationalsozialismus*, pp. 22–5, 169–70; B. M. Lane, *Architecture and Politics in Germany, 1918–1945* (Harvard University Press, 1968), pp. 156–7.

67. Brenner, *Die Kunstpolitik des Nationalsozialismus*, p. 23; Hinz, *Art in the Third Reich*, pp. 25–6.

68. Lane, *Architecture and Politics in Germany, 1918–1945*, pp. 157–60; P. Schultze-Naumburg, *Kampf um die Kunst* (Verlag Frz. Eher Nachf., GmbH, 1932).

69. See the *Reichsverband bildender Künstler* publication *Kunst und Wirtschaft*, 14 April 1930, for its censure of Frick; 'Der Reichsverband bildender Künstler und Dr Frick' and 'Der Kampf um die Kunst', in Feistel-Rohmeder, *Im Terror des Kunstbolschewismus*, pp. 87–8, 123–6.

70. 'Der Kampf um den "Neuen Stil" in der bildenden Kunst', pp. 122–3.

71. Ibid.

72. Feistel-Rohmeder to Frick, 15 April 1930. For her attacks on 'Negro culture', see Feistel-Rohmeder, *Im Terror des Kunstbolschewismus*, pp. 9, 80.

73. Feistel-Rohmeder to Frick, 15 April 1930; see the reverse of Bl 148 for Schultze-Naumburg's handwritten recommendation, dated 9 September 1930.

74. Feistel-Rohmeder and Blume to Klagges, 27 September 1932. Here the exhibit is represented as a Society venture dating back to a decision made at the Society's 1931 meeting in Detmold. However, the exhibition plan presented the show as a joint Society/Combat League endeavor. See Plan der I. Wanderausstellung Rein Deutscher Bildender Kunst, attached to the letter Bettina Feistel-Rohmeder to Education and Interior Minister Dietrich Klagges, 15 October 1932. All are in NStAW, Braunschweigisches Staatsministerium, Akten betr. Deutsche Kunstgesellschaft, Bd 1, 1932, 12 A Neu 13/18763.

75. Feistel-Rohmeder and Blume to Klagges, 27 September 1932.

76. The Society's cooperation with the Combat League for the exhibition was with local Combat League chapters rather than with its central office in Munich. Plan der I. Wanderausstellung Rein Deutscher Bildender Kunst.

77. Feistel-Rohmeder and Blume to Klagges, 27 September 1932.

78. What appears to be a rough draft of a letter never sent apologetically rejects the Society's request. Dietrich Klagges to the German Art Society, 14 October 1932. Within a week, Klagges changed his mind and agreed to support the exhibition. Dietrich Klagges to the German Art Society, 21 October 1932. Both documents are in NStAW, Braunschweigisches Staatsministerium, Akten betr. Deutsche Kunstgesellschaft, Bd 1, 1932, 12 A Neu 13/18763.

79. Klagges to the German Art Society, 21 October 1932.

Chapter 4

1. B. Feistel-Rohmeder, *Im Terror des Kunstbolschewismus: Urkundensammlung des 'Deutschen Kunstberichtes' aus den Jahren 1927–1933* (C. F. Müller Verlag, 1938). For a good treatment of the Nazis' use of modernism in the arts see S. West, *The Visual Arts in Germany 1890–1937: Utopia and Despair* (Rutgers University Press, 2001), chapter 8.

2. The literature on the inconsistencies in and power struggles over art in the Third Reich is vast, but some of the best include: H. Brenner, 'Die Kunst im politischen Machtkampf, 1933–1934', *Vierteljahrshefte für Zeitgeschichte* 10 (1962), pp. 17–42; idem, *Die Kunstpolitik des Nationalsozialismus* (Rowohlt Taschenbuch Verlag, 1963); R. Bollmus, *Das Amt Rosenberg und seine Gegner: Studium*
   zum Machtkampf im nationalsozialistischen Herrschaftssystem (Deutsche Verlags-Anstalt, 1970); A. E. Steinweis, *Art, Ideology, and Economics in Nazi Germany: The Reich Chambers of Music, Theater, and the Visual Arts* (University of North Carolina Press, 1993); and J. Petropoulos, *Art as Politics in the Third Reich* (University of North Carolina Press, 1996).
3. Brenner, *Die Kunstpolitik des Nationalsozialismus*, p. 36.
4. Ibid.; Brenner, 'Die Kunst im politischen Machtkampf, 1933–1934'. This process also occurred in state and local governments. For example, see J. H. Grill, *The Nazi Movement in Baden, 1920–1945* (University of North Carolina Press, 1983).
5. Deutsche Kunstgesellschaft, *Satzungen* (A. Bernecker, nd [1929]), ThHStAW, ThVBM/C 933, Bl 160–1. For the board members, see Deutsche Kunstgesellschaft, *I. Wanderausstellung Deutscher Kunst* (np, nd [1933]), p. 3.
6. The Executive Council disbanded because the Cartel of Visual Artists, precursor to the Chamber of Culture, was 'the only umbrella organization of the visual arts recognized by the NSDAP'. Steinweis, *Art, Ideology, and Economics in Nazi Germany*, p. 37. See also 'Zusammenschluss der bildenden Künstler', *Kunst und Wirtschaft*, 1 July 1933; Feistel-Rohmeder, *Im Terror des Kunstbolschewismus*, p. 216.
7. Plan der I. Wanderausstellung Rein Deutscher Bildender Kunst, 15 October 1932, NStAW, Braunschweigisches Staatsministerium, Akten betr. Deutsche Kunstgesellschaft, Bd 1, 1932, 12 A Neu 13/18763.
8. See the list of exhibition committees in *I. Wanderausstellung Deutscher Kunst*, pp. 2–3.
9. *Deutscher Kunstbericht*, November 1933, GLA 235/40090; 'Aus dem "Deutschen Kunstbericht 9"', *Das Bild*, May 1934, unpaginated.
10. Plan der I. Wanderausstellung Rein Deutscher Bildender Kunst.
11. For Brunswick's German League chapter, see the brief mention in J. Dürkop, 'Die Deutsche Seele in der Malerei', *Braunschweigische Landeszeitung*, 30 April 1933, p. 10 in ThHStAW, ThVBM/C 936, Bl 9. For the German League congress and the Frankfurt station, see 'Aus dem "Deutschen Kunstbericht 9"'. Feistel-Rohmeder hoped the exhibit would be hosted in Weimar as part of an art week held at the *Deutsche Heimatschule Bad Berka*, but these plans were never realized. See Bettina Feistel-Rohmeder an dem Thüringischen Volksbildungsministerium, 13 May 1933, ThHStAW, ThVBM/C 936, Bl 6–8.

12. Plan der I. Wanderausstellung Rein Deutscher Bildender Kunst, and the correspondence between the Society and Klagges, NStAW, Braunschweigisches Staatsministerium, Akten betr. Deutsche Kunstgesellschaft, Bd 1, 1932, 12 A Neu 13/18763. See also the letters between the Society and the Thuringia Education Ministry, dated 6 April, 10 May, and 13 May 1933, in ThHStAW, ThVBM/C 936, Bl 3–8.

13. Heinrich Blume an dem Thüringischen Volksbildungsministerium, 6 April 1933, ThHStAW, ThVBM/C 936, Bl 3.

14. 'Eröffnung der Wanderausstellung "Deutsche Kunst"', *Braunschweigische Landeszeitung*, 1 May 1933, p. 7, ThHStAW, ThVBM/C 936, Bl 10.

15. Ibid.

16. Ibid.

17. Ibid.

18. See the works reproduced in *I. Wanderausstellung Deutscher Kunst*.

19. Artists affiliated with the German Art Society regularly exhibited in the Great German Art exhibitions held between 1937 and 1944. Out of the 77 artists who exhibited in the Society's 1933 exhibition, 17 exhibited in the first Great German Art show. Compare *I. Wanderausstellung Deutscher Kunst* and *Grosse Deutsche Kunstausstellung 1937* (Verlag Knorr & Hirth GmbH, 1937).

20. Dürkop, 'Die Deutsche Seele in der Malerei'.

21. Ibid.

22. The catalog identified members by listing 'DKG' (*Deutsche Kunstgesellschaft*) after their names; *I. Wanderausstellung Deutscher Kunst*. Other members not listed there were determined by my reconstructed membership list. For the Lübeck exhibitors, see B. Feistel-Rohmeder, 'Frühlingsfahrt', *Deutsche Bildkunst*, April 1929, p. 29.

23. Dates and locations are from Feistel-Rohmeder, *Im Terror des Kunstbolschewismus*, pp. 195–6, 215; *I. Wanderausstellung Deutscher Kunst*, front cover; *Deutscher Kunstbericht*, November 1933; 'Aus dem "Deutschen Kunstbericht 9"'; M. Koch, 'Kulturkampf in Karlsruhe: Zur Ausstellung Regierungskunst 1919–1933', in *Kunst in Karlsruhe 1900–1950* (C. F. Müller Verlag, 1981), p. 127 note 119. 'Ausstellungen – Darmstadt', *Kunst und Wirtschaft*, July 1933, p. 129, dates the Darmstadt showing from 1 August to 15 September; Koch dates the Karlsruhe show as being from 9 September to 15 October. I have been unable to reconcile this apparent overlap. There were plans for the show to travel to Weimar and Berlin, but lack of space (in Weimar) and lack of desire (in Berlin) worked against the exhibition's appearance there. For a brief account of Ludwig Justi's refusal of the show, see P. O. Rave, *Kunstdiktatur im Dritten Reich*, ed. U. M. Schneede (Argon, 1988), pp. 46–7.

24. See the materials in 'Grenzlandkundgebung im Herbst 1933...', GLA 235/7012.

25. *Deutscher Kunstbericht*, November 1933. Philipp, Prince of Hesse, later served as an art agent for Hitler and other Nazi elites. He was an early member of the Nazi Party, SA-*Obergruppenführer* and head of Hitler's project to create a museum of plundered art in his hometown of Linz. Petropoulos, *Art as Politics in the Third Reich*, pp. 301–3, 319.

26. 'Aus dem "Deutschen Kunstbericht 9"'.

27. The most complete treatment of the early degenerate shows are C. Zuschlag, '"Es handelt sich um eine Schulungsausstellung": Die Vorläufer und die Stationen der Ausstellung "Entartete Kunst"', in S. Barron (ed.), *'Entartete Kunst': Das Schicksal der Avantgarde im Nazi-Deutschland* (Hirmer Verlag, 1992), pp. 83–103; and C. Zuschlag, *'Entartete Kunst': Austellungsstrategien im Nazi-Deutschland* (Wernersche Verlagsgesellschaft, 1995).

28. 'Was die Deutschen Künstler von der neuen Regierung erwarten!' *Deutscher Kunstbericht*, March 1933, in Feistel-Rohmeder, *Im Terror des Kunstbolschewismus*, pp. 181–4.

29. B. Hinz, *Art in the Third Reich*, R. and R. Kimber, trans (Pantheon Books, 1979), p. 27.

30. 'Was die Deutschen Künstler von der neuen Regierung erwarten!' p. 181. All emphasis appeared in the original.

31. Ibid., p. 182. In 1938, this last prediction was partially realized when Goebbels ordered the incineration of art taken from Germany's museums. It remains unclear just how much art was actually destroyed. See Rave, *Kunstdiktatur im Dritten Reich*, pp. 124–6; Brenner, *Die Kunstpolitik des Nationalsozialismus*, p. 110; R. Müller-Mehlis, *Die Kunst im Dritten Reich*, 2nd edn (Wilhelm Heyne Verlag, 1976).

32. All quotes from 'Was die Deutschen Künstler von der neuen Regierung erwarten!' pp. 182–3.

33. Ibid., pp. 181, 184.

34. Rave, *Kunstdiktatur im Dritten Reich*, pp. 43–4; Hinz, *Art in the Third Reich*, pp. 26–8; Bollmus, *Das Amt Rosenberg*, pp. 27–9; Koch, 'Kulturkampf in Karlsruhe', p. 103; Brenner, *Die Kunstpolitik des Nationalsozialismus*, p. 37.

35. Ibid., pp. 36–7.

36. For a detailed account of Gasch's actions as art commissioner, see ibid., pp. 173–5.

37. 'Was die Deutschen Künstler von der neuen Regierung erwarten!' p. 181.

38. Wacker was repeatedly fined and arrested for his party activities during the republic; he was also one of the few Nazi officials who held a doctorate. Otto Wacker, Lebenslauf, 17 April 1934, GLA 235/37452, Bl 7; E. O. Bräunche, 'Die Entwicklung der NSDAP in Baden bis 1932/33', *Zeitschrift für die Geschichte des Oberrheins*, NF 86 (1977), pp. 331–75; Grill, *The Nazi Movement in Baden, 1920–1945*, pp. 275–6.

39. W. Rössling, 'Kunst in Karlsruhe 1933–1945', in *Kunst und Karlsruhe 1900–1950* (C. F. Müller Verlag, 1981), pp. 130–2, and Bühler's personnel file, GLA 66/6094.

40. Koch, 'Kulturkampf in Karlsruhe', pp. 102–28; Rössling, 'Kunst in Karlsruhe 1933–1945'.

41. Koch, 'Kulturkampf in Karlsruhe', p. 107.

42. Ibid., pp. 102–28; Rössling, 'Kunst in Karlsruhe 1933–1945', pp. 129–33.

43. F. Wilkendorf, 'Regierungskunst 1919 bis 1933: Der gesammelte Kultur-bolschewismus der Bevölkerung zum vernichtenden Urteil übergeben', *Der Führer*, 8 April 1933; A. Gebhard, 'Die Ausstellung "Regierungskunst 1918 bis 1933" in der Badischen Kunsthalle', *Der Führer*, 23 April 1933; Koch, 'Kulturkampf in Karlsruhe'; and J. Heusinger von Waldegg, *Die Hochschule der bildenden Künste Karlsruhe im Dritten Reich* (Staatliche Akademie der Bildenden Künste Karlsruhe, 1987), pp. 10–11.

44. In the past it was claimed that the Karlsruhe degenerate show was the first such exhibit. See for example Rave, *Kunstdiktatur im Dritten Reich*, p. 45; Brenner, *Die Kunstpolitik des Nationalsozialismus*, p. 37; and Hinz, *Art in the Third Reich*, p. 28. However, the Mannheim show opened four days before the Karlsruhe one. For the corrective, see Koch, 'Kulturkampf in Karlsruhe', p. 118, and Zuschlag, '"Es handelt sich um eine Schulungsausstellung"', p. 99.

45. See 'Tabelle 1: Vorläufer der Ausstellung "Entartete Kunst" 1937 in München', in Zuschlag, '"Es handelt sich um eine Schulungsausstellung"', pp. 99–103.

46. Zuschlag, '"Es handelt sich um eine Schulungsausstellung"', p. 83.

47. Rave, *Kunstdiktatur im Dritten Reich*, pp. 44–6; Brenner, *Die Kunstpolitik des Nationalsozialismus*, pp. 35–7; Bollmus, *Das Amt Rosenberg*, pp. 27–9; these sources argue the shows were organized by a combination of Combat League, Society and Executive Council members. Zuschlag, '"Es handelt sich um eine Schulungsausstellung"', p. 83, argues the shows, while sharing similar methods and ideas, were 'organizationally and personally independent of each other'. He also believes that the Society did not play a significant role. See Zuschlag, '*Entartete Kunst*', p. 37.

48. Rave, *Kunstdiktatur im Dritten Reich*, p. 46 mentions Beringer; Zuschlag, '"Es handelt sich um eine Schulungsausstellung"', p. 99, lists von Waldstein as the organizer. Beringer also contributed to the Society's art journal. See for example J. A. Beringer, 'Allemannische Malerei', *Das Bild*, February 1934, p. 53; idem, 'Romantische Graphik', *Das Bild*, March 1936, p. 75.

49. Zuschlag, 'Tabelle 1', in '"Es handelt sich um eine Schulungsausstellung"', p. 99.

50. 'Regierungskunst 1918 bis 1933', *Deutscher Kunstbericht*, April/May 1933, in Feistel-Rohmeder, *Im Terror des Kunstbolschewismus*, p. 185; 'Die

"Deutsche Kunstgesellschaft, Sitz Dresden", und der Kampf um die Deutsche Kunst', *Deutscher Kunstbericht*, June 1933, in ibid., p. 189.

51. 'Regierungskunst 1918 bis 1933', p. 185.

52. Rave, *Kunstdiktatur im Dritten Reich*, pp. 53–4; Zuschlag, 'Tabelle 1', in '"Es handelt sich um eine Schulungsausstellung"', p. 101; 'Die Stadt Dresden zeigt ihre entartete Kunst', *Deutscher Kunstbericht*, September/October 1933, in Feistel-Rohmeder, *Im Terror des Kunstbolschewismus*, pp. 204–7; R. Müller, 'Spiegelbilder des Verfalls in der Kunst', *Dresdener Anzeiger*, 23 September 1933, in Brenner, *Die Kunstpolitik des Nationalsozialismus*, pp. 175–7.

53. F. Walter, *Schicksal einer deutschen Stadt: Geschichte Mannheims 1907– 1945*, vol. 1 (Fritz Knapp Verlag, 1949); Brenner, *Die Kunstpolitik des Nationalsozialismus*, pp. 174–5.

54. *Kölnische Illustrierte Zeitung*, 17 August 1935; the Dresden show became the central core of the larger, national 'Degenerate Art' exhibition of 1937. Zuschlag, '"Es handelt sich um eine Schulungsausstellung"', p. 85.

55. This is based on information in ibid., especially pp. 99–103. Zuschlag's reconstruction of the local degenerate shows is invaluable, but note he does not believe the Society played a role in the degenerate shows. Zuschlag, *'Entartete Kunst'* , p. 37. For Society reviews of some of these shows, see B. Feistel-Rohmeder, 'Zur Ausstellung "Entartete Kunst" im Kunst- und Gewerbeverein Regensburg E.V.', in 'Aus dem Deutschen Kunstbericht', *Das Bild*, February 1936, unpaginated; 'Zur Ausstellung "Entartete Kunst" in Ingolstadt', in 'Aus dem Deutschen Kunstbericht', *Das Bild*, June 1936, unpaginated.

56. Badischer Kunstverein, 'Protokoll der Generalversammlung am Freitag, dem 31. März 1933' and 'Sitzung des Gesamtvorstandes am Montag, dem 22. May 1933', in *Kunst in Karlsruhe*, pp. 100–1; and Koch, 'Kulturkampf in Karlsruhe', p. 119. Kupferschmid's name occasionally appears as Kupfer-schmied.

57. See the documents in 'Personalakten betr. August Gebhard', GLA 235/1415 and 'Personalakten betr. Hans Adolf Bühler', GLA 466/6094.

58. Rössling, 'Kunst in Karlsruhe 1933–1945', p. 130; Koch, 'Kulturkampf in Karlsruhe', pp. 84–101.

59. The quote is from Rössling, 'Kunst in Karlsruhe 1933–1945', p. 130, and see note 25, p. 133; Heusinger von Waldegg, *Die Hochschule der bildenden Künste Karlsruhe im Dritten Reich*, p. 40; *Deutscher Kunstbericht*, November 1933, p. 3.

60. Ibid.; 'Aus der Deutschen Kunstgesellschaft', in 'Aus dem "Deutschen Kunstbericht 9"'.

61. Both quotes are from G. Bussmann, '"Degenerate Art" – A Look at a Useful Myth', in C. Joachimides (ed.), *German Art in the Twentieth Century: Painting and Sculpture, 1905–1985* (Prestel-Verlag, 1985), pp. 116–17; for a

more complete account of the students' protest, see Brenner, *Die Kunstpolitik des Nationalsozialismus*; and idem, 'Die Kunst im politischen Machtkampf 1933/34', pp. 21–4.

62. Ibid.

63. I. Klein, *Vom kosmogonischen zum völkischen Eros: Eine sozialgeschichtliche Analyse bürgerlich-liberaler Kunstkritik in der Zeit von 1917 bis 1936* (tuduv, 1991), pp. 257, 261, 266, and 267–77; K. Baumann, 'Kunstzeitschriften in Deutschland 1927–1939: Auf der Suche nach der "deutschen Kunst"', in L. Ehrlich et al. (eds), *Das Dritte Weimar: Klassik und Kultur im Nationalsozialismus* (Böhlau Verlag, 1999), pp. 133–48; A. Hüneke, 'Der Versuch der Ehrenrettung des Expressionismus als "deutscher Kunst" 1933', in *Zwischen Widerstand und Anpassung: Kunst im Deutschland, 1933–1945* (Akademie der Künste, 1980), pp. 51–3.

64. For good examples of these ideas see O. Reidrich, 'Nationale und Internationale Kunst', *Die Kunst für Alle* 48 (February 1933), pp. 136, 151; B. E. Werner, 'Der grosse Pendelschlag: Zur Frage "Was ist deutsche Kunst?"' *Die Kunst für Alle* 49 (October 1933), pp. 12–15; U. Christoffel, 'Wo stehen wir heute in der Kunst?' *Die Kunst für Alle* 49 (June 1934), pp. 229–38.

65. K. Backes, *Hitler und die bildenden Künste: Kulturverständnis und Kunstpolitik im Dritten Reich* (DuMont Verlag, 1988).

66. See for example Petropoulos, *Art as Politics in the Third Reich*; Steinweis, *Art, Ideology, and Economics in Nazi Germany*; Brenner, *Die Kunstpolitik des Nationalsozialismus*; R. Merker, *Die bildenden Künste im Nationalsozialismus: Kulturideologie, Kulturpolitik, Kulturproduktion* (DuMont Buchverlag, 1983).

67. The most complete treatment of the Culture Chamber is Steinweis, *Art, Ideology, and Economics in Nazi Germany*.

68. E. Fröhlich, 'Die kulturpolitische Pressekonferenz des Reichspropaganda ministeriums', *Vierteljahrshefte für Zeitgeschichte* 22 (1974), pp. 347–81; Brenner, 'Die Kunst im politischen Machtkampf 1933/34', and idem, *Die Kunstpolitik des Nationalsozialismus*.

69. Fröhlich, 'Die kulturpolitische Pressekonferenz des Reichspropaganda-ministeriums'; Brenner, 'Die Kunst im politischen Machtkampf 1933/34', and idem, *Die Kunstpolitik des Nationalsozialismus*; Bollmus, *Das Amt Rosenberg und seine Gegner*, chapter 2; Klein, *Vom kosmogonischen zum völkischen Eros*. For Feistel-Rohmeder's critique of Goebbels' involvement, see B. Feistel-Rohmeder, 'Kunst der Nation', in 'Aus dem "Deutschen Kunst-bericht 5–7"', *Das Bild*, March 1934, unpaginated.

70. A. Rosenberg, 'Revolution in der bildenden Kunst?' *Völkischer Beobachter*, 6 July 1933; idem, 'Revolutionäre an sich!' *Völkischer Beobachter*, 14 July 1933; Brenner, 'Die Kunst im politischen Machtkampf 1933/34'.

71. Hitler at the 1933 cultural conference of the *Reichsparteitag* in Nuremberg, September 1933, quoted in A. Hüneke, 'Spurensuche – Moderne Kunst aus deutschem Museumsbesitz', in S. Barron (ed.), *'Entartete Kunst': Das Schicksal der Avantgarde im Nazi-Deutschland* (Hirmer Verlag, 1992), p. 122.
72. For a sample of such statements, see J. Wulf, *Die bildenden Künste im Dritten Reich: Eine Dokumentation* (Siegbert Mohn Verlag, 1963).
73. Feistel-Rohmeder, *Im Terror des Kunstbolschewismus*, pp. 187–204; the quote is from p. 187.
74. Ibid., p. 198.
75. Ibid., p. 187.
76. Both quotes are from ibid., p. 190.
77. Ibid., pp. 187–208.
78. Ibid., p. 195.
79. For other examples of the Society's defense of its mission and assault on the pro-modernist forces, see ibid., pp. 199–208.
80. T. Butz an den Herrn Minister des Kultus und Unterrichts, Staatliche Kunstpflege betr., 25 November 1933; Th. Butz, 'Zur Ausstellung "Deutsche Kunst" im Kunstverein Karlsruhe, September 1933' (this is his review of the Society's traveling exhibition and a response to a speech by Gebhard at the art academy), both in GLA 235/40090. Some of the strongest protests concerned Bühler's inclusion of Alexander Kanoldt in the Karlsruhe degenerate art show; these even reached Rust's ministry in Berlin. See Koch, 'Kulturkampf in Karlsruhe', pp. 120–1 and the accompanying notes; Rössling, 'Kunst in Karlsruhe 1933–1945', p. 130.
81. Butz, 'Zur Ausstellung "Deutsche Kunst"'. Butz's background and even his full name remain unknown. See Rössling, 'Kunst in Karlsruhe, 1933–1945', pp. 130, 132 note 15.
82. Butz, 'Zur Ausstellung "Deutsche Kunst"'.
83. Ibid.

Chapter 5

1. H. Brenner, *Die Kunstpolitik des Nationalsozialismus* (Rowohlt Taschenbuch Verlag, 1963).
2. Der Minister des Kultus, des Unterrichts und der Justiz, 'Nr. A 287, Bekanntmaching, Kunstzeitschrift "Das Bild"', *Amtsblatt des Ministeriums*

des Kultus, des Unterrichts und der Justiz, Nr. 28 (31 December 1933), pp. 207–8.

3. 'Mitteilung an die beschickten Schriftleitungen', *Deutscher Kunstbericht*, November 1933, p. 1, GLA 235/40090.

4. 'Grenzlandkundgebung im Herbst 1933...', GLA 235/7012.

5. Der Minister des Kultus, des Unterrichts und der Justiz, 'Nr. A 287, Bekanntmaching, Kunstzeitschrift "Das Bild"', pp. 207–8.

6. Ibid.

7. Ibid., p. 207.

8. C. F. Müller Verlag to the Minister of Culture, Education and Justice, 25 January 1934, and the undated summary of the journal's distribution to the schools, GLA 235/6569.

9. In their letters to the ministry, teachers often described their use of the journal, GLA 235/6569. Teachers often referred to *Das Bild* as either a publication of the NSDAP or as a National Socialist journal. See for example the letter from three Durlach teachers, Karl Mauer, Alfred Rudi and Otto Merkle, to the Ministry of Education and Culture, 23 September 1934, GLA 235/6570.

10. O. Wacker, 'Geisteshaltung und Stil', *Das Bild*, January 1934, pp. 9–10, 12, 16–17.

11. The exact timing is uncertain. *Das Bild*'s masthead no longer listed the academy in August 1934. However, in 1935, Feistel-Rohmeder claimed that the journal was published by the Society in June 1934. B. Feistel-Rohmeder, 'Rückblick und Ausblick', in 'Aus dem Deutschen Kunstbericht', *Das Bild*, November 1935, unpaginated.

12. The loss of the ministry's subsidy is implied in correspondence between the schools and the ministry. School and teacher subscriptions steadily declined, especially after 1935 when subscriptions needed to be renewed. Many of the cancellation notices refer to 'Erlass Nr. A 14243' (undated) and 'Erlass Nr. E 288', 19 September 1934. These have not been located but may have announced the loss of the subsidy. See the correspondence in GLA 235/6570.

13. See Bühler's resignation letter and Minister des Kultus und Unterrichts, Aktenvermerk, 23 December 1935, GLA 235/40092.

14. Color reproductions were rare, but see Ernst Moritz Geyger, *Viehfütterung* (1885), *Das Bild*, February 1936, between pp. 32 and 33, and Hitler's *Klosterruine von Messines*, *Das Bild*, December 1936, between pp. 356 and 357.

15. The *German Art Report* was printed on slightly smaller, thinner paper and generally appeared as unnumbered pages at the beginning and end of *Das Bild*. For some reason, when a year's issues were bound, the *German Art Report* pages tended to be removed before binding. The collections of *Das Bild* located at the University of Wisconsin, Madison, and the New York Public Library have a number of these pages intact.

16. The C. F. Müller archives were destroyed in the war, but subsidies are implied in the annual reports of the German Art Society. See the combined 1935 and 1936 annual reports from 6 June 1936 in 'Aus dem Deutschen Kunstbericht', *Das Bild*, June 1936, unnpaginated; 'Aus der Deutschen Kunstgesellschaft (1937 annual report)', *Deutscher Kunstbericht*, June (?) 1937, BDC, Feistel-Rohmeder file.

17. Ibid.

18. C. F. Müller has no publication records for the journal. However, what appear to be circulation figures (as opposed to the total number of issues printed) were recorded quarterly but they are often difficult to locate within *Das Bild*. The figures, recorded for example as 'D.A.4.Vj.1937', were listed within the fine print of publishing information and usually appeared on the last, unnumbered page of the *German Art Report*. Because the *Report* was typically removed before binding a year's issues, these pages are often missing; thus the gaps in the table provided. See *Das Bild*, February 1934, March 1934, May 1934, and April 1936, bottom of the last (unnumbered) pages of *Deutscher Kunstbericht*; *Das Bild*, October 1937, p. 320; January 1938, p. 32; March 1938, p. 100; June 1938, p. 196; June 1939, p. 192; and October-December 1939, p. 308. After 1939, no figures were published.

19. M. Mallmann, *'Das Innere Reich': Analyse einer konservativen Kulturzeitschrift im Dritten Reich* (Bouvier Verlag Herbert Grundmann, 1978); H. Denkler, 'Janusköpfig: Zur ideologischen Physiognomie der Zeitschrift "Das Innere Reich" (1934–1944)', in H. Denkler and K. Prümm (eds), *Die deutsche Literatur im Dritten Reich: Themen–Traditionen–Wirkungen* (Philipp Reclam jun, 1976), pp. 382–405.

20. Mallmann, *'Das Innere Reich'*, pp. 67–8.

21. Information is based on the tables of content and lists of contributors in *Das Bild*, 1934 and 1938.

22. Kircher is briefly mentioned in documents located in GLA 235/40254. See also the request by Bühler for Kircher to evaluate the holdings, 27 March 1933, and Gerda Kircher, Bericht über die im ganz befindl. Bestandsaufnahme der Gemälde der Bad. Kunsthalle, 22 June 1933, both in GLA 235/40248.

23. For a sample of articles on *Das Bild* favorites, see F. Wilkendorf, 'Georg Siebert, ein Maler des Volkes', *Das Bild*, March 1936, p. 92; A. Vollmar, 'Emil Ernst Heinsdorff', *Das Bild*, May 1937, p. 149 (note that Heinsdorff's name sometimes appears as Ernst Emil as well); W. Hansen, 'Wolfgang Willrich', *Das Bild*, November 1936, p. 332; H. Meyer, 'Walther Gasch', *Das Bild*, August 1938, p. 247; E. Frobenius and H. Richter, 'Die Tierbildhauerin Etha Richter-Dresden', *Das Bild*, August 1938, p. 251; F. Wilkendorf, 'Siegfried Czerny, der Bildnissmaler und Maltechniker', *Das Bild*, March 1939, p. 78.

24. For her paintings, see *Auf Berg Persen*, *Das Bild*, May 1935, p. 141, and *Bildnisstudie*, *Das Bild*, April–June 1943, p. 71; for poems and articles see

H. A. Bühler, 'An Bettina Feistel-Rohmeder zum 65. Geburtstag', *Das Bild*, August 1938, p. 229; E. Schindler, 'Der "Ehrenbeamtin der Deutschen Kunst": Zum 65. Geburtstag von Frau Bettina Feistel-Rohmeder am 24. August 1938', *Das Bild*, August 1938, p. 229; and E. Schindler, 'Zum "Magischen Recht" der bildenden Kunst: Bettina Feistel-Rohmeder zum 70. Geburtstag', *Das Bild*, October–December 1943, pp. 139–40.

25. For example, E. Schindler, 'Albin Egger-Lienz', *Das Bild*, May 1935, pp. 142–5; idem, 'Zu Thoraks Reitfiguren', *Das Bild*, November 1940, p. 173.

26. For example, 'Dürer als Schöpfer des Selbstbildnisses', *Das Bild*, April 1935, p. 109; K. Luther, 'Die Nationalgalerie erwarb vier unbekannte Werke von C. D. Friedrich', *Das Bild*, July 1937, p. 199; H. A. Bühler, 'Hans Thoma zum 100.Geburtstag', *Das Bild*, January/February, 1940, p. 1.

27. 'Ankundigung', *Das Bild*, January 1934, just after the table of contents.

28. Ibid.; Wacker, 'Geisteshaltung und Stil'; H. A. Bühler, 'Zum Geleit', *Das Bild*, January 1934, pp. 1–5.

29. Point 5 of the combined 1935 and 1936 Society annual reports, 6 June 1936.

30. See for example, A. Babel, 'Deutsche Kunst', *Das Bild*, October 1935, pp. 297–8; H. Bastanier, 'Deutsche Kunst Goslar 1935', *Das Bild*, October 1935, pp. 311–18.

31. F. Behn, 'Zwei Meisterwerke frühgermanischen Kunstgewerbes aus dem Mittelalter', *Das Bild*, March 1934, p. 69; H. A. Bühler, 'Germanischer Schmuck der Völkerwanderungszeit', *Das Bild*, January 1935, pp. 5–7.

32. B. Feistel-Rohmeder, 'Die Wandbilder in Kohren von Walther Gasch', *Das Bild*, July/August 1941, p. 116.

33. A. L. Müller, 'Richard Guhr', *Das Bild*, July 1934, p. 228.

34. For example, F. Wilkendorf, 'Wilhelm Sauter', *Das Bild*, March 1939, pp. 74–7.

35. L. Meiners, 'Richard Miller: Zu seinem 65. Geburtstag', *Das Bild*, July 1939, p. 207.

36. B. Feistel-Rohmeder, 'Von Deutscher Malerei und Graphik in Dresden', *Das Bild*, July 1939, pp. 229–34; Meyer, 'Walther Gasch'.

37. G. Brüns, 'Das Sauerland in der bildenden Kunst', *Das Bild*, September 1939, p. 261.

38. For example, W. Zimmermann, 'Von saarländischen Kunstwerken', *Das Bild*, March 1935, pp. 65–9; B. Feistel-Rohmeder, 'Öberrheinische Maler', *Das Bild*, February 1936, pp. 52–7.

39. Brenner, *Die Kunstpolitik des Nationalsozialismus*.

40. E. Schindler, 'Alfred Rosenberg als Kämpfer für Deutsche Kunst', *Das Bild*, January 1941, p. 13; O. Biedermann, 'Idee und Tat: Zehn Jahre Kampf und Arbeit der Dienststelle Rosenberg', *Das Bild*, January–March 1944, p. 32.

41. B. Feistel-Rohmeder, *Im Terror des Kunstbolschewismus: Urkundensammlung des 'Deutschen Kunstberichtes' aus den Jahren 1927–1933* (C. F. Müller Verlag, 1938), p. 214.

42. The combined 1935 and 1936 German Art Society annual report, 6 June 1936; 'Aus der Deutschen Kunstgesellschaft, (1937 annual report)'.

43. K. Luther, 'Kollektiv-Ausstellung der NS-Kulturgemeinde Berlin', *Das Bild*, April 1935, pp. 122–8; E. Schindler, 'Blut und Boden: Die Herbstkunstausstellung der Gaudienststelle München-Oberbayern der NS-Kulturgemeinde', *Das Bild*, November 1935, pp. 369–72; idem, 'Heroische Kunst: Zur Ausstellung des NS-Kulturgemeinde in München', *Das Bild*, July 1936, p. 219.

44. K. Luther, 'Die Ausstellung "Der Wald" der NS-Kulturgemeinde Berlin', *Das Bild*, June 1936, p. 196.

45. 'Aus der "Deutschen Kunstgesellschaft", Sitz Karlsruhe i. B.', *Das Bild*, January 1935, p. 32.

46. Ibid., and 'An den Reichsleiter des Kulturamtes für Kunstpflege Herrn Alfred Rosenberg, Berlin', *Das Bild*, January 1935, p. 32.

47. Ibid.

48. Ibid.

49. Ibid. Only Society chairman Bruno Goldschmitt was specifically identified; the others were simply listed as '61 signatories'.

50. It is, of course, possible that Rosenberg corresponded with the organization. However, there is no record of this in the *Amt Rosenberg* files (NS 8) of the Bundesarchiv. Moreover, Feistel-Rohmeder and the Society leadership never made any claims that Rosenberg favored the organization, something they surely would have done if they could.

51. For example, 'Aus dem "Deutschen Kunstbericht 9"', *Das Bild*, May 1934, unpaginated; 'Aus dem Deutschen Kunstbericht', *Das Bild*, September 1937, after p. 288.

52. See the full-page ad in *Das Bild*, February 1936, between pages of the *German Art Report* supplement.

53. See the combined 1935 and 1936 German Art Society annual reports, 6 June 1936. Goldschmitt (sometimes spelled Goldschmidt) held the title of *Oberstudiendirektor* and may have taught at the Munich art academy. He served as chair after Blume's retirement from 1934 until June 1936. Although the Munich chapter did become more active in the leadership, Karlsruhe remained headquarters for the Society.

54. B. Feistel-Rohmeder, 'Kunst der Nation', in 'Aus dem "Deutschen Kunstbericht 5–7"', *Das Bild*, March 1934, unpaginated. O. Troebes, 'Verklungene Malerei'; idem, 'Nolde Ausstellung'; and B. Feistel-Rohmeder, 'Wahres Geschichten', all in 'Aus dem "Deutschen Kunstbericht 9"', *Das*

Bild, May 1934, unpaginated. See also the articles in 'Aus dem Deutschen Kunstbericht', *Das Bild*, November 1935, unpaginated.

55. The celebration was described and excerpts from Hofmann's lecture reproduced in 'Die Deutsche Kunstgesellschaft', in 'Aus dem Deutschen Kunstbericht', *Das Bild*, November 1935, unpaginated.

56. Ibid.

57. Ibid.

58. Ibid. Emphasis in the original.

59. 'Sorge um den Weg der Deutschen Kunst', in 'Aus dem Deutschen Kunstbericht', *Das Bild*, June 1936, unpaginated; 'In eigener Sache', *Das Bild*, April 1936, p. 132; 'Noch einmal in eigener Sache', *Das Bild*, May 1936, p. 164.

60. 'Sorge um den Weg der Deutschen Kunst'.

61. J. Petropoulos, *Art as Politics in the Third Reich* (University of North Carolina Press, 1996), p. 45.

62. A. E. Steinweis, *Art, Ideology, and Economics in Nazi Germany: The Reich Chambers of Music, Theater, and the Visual Arts* (University of North Carolina Press, 1993).

63. E. Fröhlich, 'Die kulturpolitische Pressenkonferenz des Reichspropagandaministeriums', *Vierteljahrshefte für Zeitgeschichte* 22 (1974), pp. 363–72.

64. Ibid.; Steinweis, *Art, Ideology, and Economics in Nazi Germany*, pp. 53–62.

65. Excerpt from Hitler's opening speech at the Great German Art Exhibition, cited in A. Dresler, *Deutsche Kunst und entartete 'Kunst': Kunstwerk und Zerrbild als Spiegel der Weltanschauung* (Deutscher Volksverlag, 1938), p. 31.

66. Ibid.

67. See for example, B. E. Werner, 'Der grosse Pendalschlag: Zur Frage "Was ist deutsche Kunst?"' *Die Kunst für Alle* 49 (October 1933), pp. 12–15; B. Kroll, 'Zum "Tag der Deutschen Kunst"', *Die Kunst für Alle* 49 (November 1933), pp. 63–7; J. Wackerle, 'Nachklang zum Fest der Deutschen Kunst', *Die Kunst für Alle* 49 (December 1933), pp. 79–85.

68. Both exhibitions have been treated in detail elsewhere. See for example, S. Barron (ed.), *'Entartete Kunst': Das Schicksal der Avantgarde im Nazi-Deutschland* (Hirmer Verlag, 1992); G. Bussmann, '"Degenerate Art" – A Look at a Useful Myth', in C. Joachimides (ed.), *German Art in the Twentieth Century: Painting and Sculpture, 1905–1985* (Prestel-Verlag, 1985), pp. 113–24; Brenner, *Die Kunstpolitik des Nationalsozialismus*; R. Merker, *Die bildenden Künste im Nationalsozialismus: Kulturideologie, Kulturpolitik, Kulturproduktion* (DuMont Buchverlag, 1983); C. Zuschlag, *'Entartete Kunst': Ausstellungsstrategien im Nazi-Deutschland* (Wernersche Verlagsgesellschaft, 1995).

69. See the September 1937 issue of *Die Kunst im Dritten Reich* which was devoted to the Great German Art Exhibition and the 'new' direction in the arts.
70. Feistel-Rohmeder, *Im Terror des Kunstbolschewismus*, p. 217.
71. B. Feistel-Rohmeder, 'Ausstellungs-Bildberichte', *Das Bild*, October 1937, pp. 310–11; idem, 'Zum Abschluss der Ausstellungs- und Ausstellungs-bildberichte des Jahres 1937', *Das Bild*, January 1938, pp. 31–2. No catalog for this show has been located.
72. Feistel-Rohmeder, 'Ausstellungs-Bildberichte (October)', p. 310. The Society's second exhibit opened in Munich on 3 October 1937 and then probably traveled to Stuttgart. The exhibit came to Karlsruhe in January 1938 and closed soon after in Heilbronn. See Feistel-Rohmeder, 'Zum Abschluss der Ausstellungs- und Ausstellungsbildberichte des Jahres 1937', p. 32.
73. Feistel-Rohmeder, 'Ausstellungs-Bildberichte (October)', pp. 310–11; idem, 'Ausstellungs-Bildbericht', *Das Bild*, November 1937, pp. 344–8; idem, 'Zum Abschluss der Ausstellungs- und Ausstellungsbildberichte des Jahres 1937', pp. 31–2; idem, 'Wir stellen aus in Paris', *Das Bild*, November 1937, pp. 342–4.
74. Feistel-Rohmeder, 'Ausstellungs-Bildberichte (October)', pp. 310–12; idem, 'Zum Abschluss der Ausstellungs- und Ausstellungsbildberichte des Jahres 1937', pp. 31–2.
75. Ibid., p. 31.
76. Compare Deutsche Kunstgesellschaft, *I. Wanderausstellung Deutscher Kunst* (np, nd [1933]) and *Grosse Deutsche Kunstausstellung 1937* (Verlag Knorr & Hirth GmbH, 1937).
77. Feistel-Rohmeder, *Im Terror des Kunstbolschewismus*, pp. 211–17. This theme is a constant refrain in articles for both the *German Art Report* and *Das Bild*.
78. H. Fecht, 'Zur Eröffnung der 2. Wanderausstellung der Deutschen Kunst-gesellschaft', *Das Bild*, October 1937, p. 314.
79. Ibid., p. 319.
80. Ibid., p. 320.
81. Ibid.
82. Feistel-Rohmeder, *Im Terror des Kunstbolshevismus*, p. 6.
83. 'In eigener Sache' and 'Noch einmal in eigener Sache'.
84. For the earlier attacks, Feistel-Rohmeder, *Im Terror des Kunstbolschewismus*, pp. 40–1, 46, 121–3, 145–8, 154–5, 164–9, 200–2, 204–7. For the Nazi-era criticisms, see 'Gleichschaltung', *Deutscher Kunstbericht*, May 1934, and 'Verständnislose Zeitgenossen', *Deutscher Kunstbericht*, December 1934, both located in suit materials marked 'Abschriften. III. Der Deutsche Kunstbericht über die Galerie Arnold', BDC, Feistel-Rohmeder file.

85. B. Feistel-Rohmeder, 'Ein alter Bekannter des Deutschen Kunstberichtes', *Deutscher Kunstbericht*, June (?) 1937, BDC, Feistel-Rohmeder file. By Gutbier's 'activity abroad', Feistel-Rohmeder was referring to exhibits of German modernists which he had arranged in the US and other countries.

86. *Völkischer Beobachter* an die Schriftleitung der Kunstzeitschrift '*Das Bild*', 28 October 1937, BDC, Feistel-Rohmeder file.

87. Ibid.

88. Berchtold (the first-name initial is difficult to decipher) was an SA *Gruppenführer* and an old fighter. Apparently because the lawsuit involved a member of the SA, it was moved from a lower court to the high party court. See Berchtold an Herrn Dr Egger, Leiter der Geschäftsstelle des Kreisgerichtes München der NSDAP, 9 February 1938; Egger an das Gaugericht München, 15 February 1938; Gaugericht München-Oberbayern (Lebeau) an das Oberste Parteigericht I. Kammer, 17 February 1938, all in BDC, Feistel-Rohmeder file. For the workings on the Nazi Party Court, see Donald M. McKale, *The Nazi Party Courts: Hitler's Management of Conflict in his Movement, 1921–1945* (University Press of Kansas, 1974).

89. See the materials entitled 'Abschriften. III. Der Deutsche Kunstbericht über die Galerie Arnold' and 'Abschriften. II. Die Presse und sonstige Stimmen über die "Galerie Arnold" u. ihre Künstler', BDC, Feistel-Rohmeder file.

90. See p. 3 of the section entitled 'III. Die Beleidigung' in materials marked 'I. Der Vorgang selbst', BDC, Feistel-Rohmeder file.

91. Ibid., pp. 1–4.

92. Ibid., p. 1.

93. Ibid., p. 2.

94. Ibid. She included the letter NSDAP Hauptarchiv/Dr. Uetrecht to Bettina Feistel-Rohmeder, 7 August 1937 in 'Abschriften, III', BDC, Feistel-Rohmeder file.

95. 'III. Die Beleidigung', p. 2.

96. Ibid., p. 3; she listed five articles, all published in the *Völkischer Beobachter* in 1930.

97. See point B, 'I. Der Vorgang selbst'.

98. 'III. Die Beleidigung', p. 3.

99. Bettina Feistel-Rohmeder an den Obersten Parteirichter Walter Buch, 8 December 1937, BDC, Feistel-Rohmeder file.

100. Knop (an official in the Obersten Parteigericht, München-Oberbayern) to Bettina Feistel-Rohmeder, 25 February 1938, BDC, Feistel-Rohmeder file.

Chapter 6

1. A. E. Steinweis, *Art, Ideology, and Economics in Nazi Germany: The Reich Chambers of Music, Theater, and the Visual Arts* (University of North Carolina Press, 1993), p. 132.

2. U. Ketelsen, 'Kulturpolitik des III. Reichs und Ansätze zu ihrer Interpretation', *Text und Kontext* 8 (1980), p. 232.

3. See K. Baumann, 'Kunstzeitschriften in Deutschland 1927–1939: Auf der Suche nach der "deutschen Kunst"', in L. Ehrlich et al. (eds), *Das Dritte Weimar: Klassik und Kultur im Nationalsozialismus* (Böhlau Verlag, 1999), pp. 133–48; B. Hinz, *Art in the Third Reich*, R. and R. Kimber, trans (Pantheon, 1979).

4. Ibid., p. 16, citing H. Brenner, *Die Kunstpolitik des Nationalsozialismus* (Rowohlt Taschenbuch Verlag), pp. 112f.

5. The best analysis of Nazi aesthetics remains Hinz, *Art in the Third Reich*.

6. The title *Die Kunst im Dritten Reich* was changed to *Die Kunst im Deutschen Reich* in September 1939. I have chosen to refer simply to the journal's first title in the text. All articles are from the edition of the journal that focused on painting, not the architectural edition. Hereafter the journal will be cited as *KiDR*.

7. Rosenberg's agency was the *Amt Rosenberg* which he held from 1934; the circulation figures are from J. Petropoulos, *Art as Politics in the Third Reich* (University of North Carolina Press, 1996), p. 66.

8. H. Kiener, 'Vom Werden des neuen Stils', *KiDR*, January 1937, pp. 8–10; P. Rosner, 'Der Führer und Wir', *KiDR*, January 1937, p. 4; 'Die Rede des Führers zur Eröffnung der "Grosse Deutsche Kunstausstellung 1938"', *KiDR*, July 1938, pp. 229–32; R. Scholz, 'Besinnung im Malerischen: Gedanken zur Ausstellung im Haus der Deutschen Kunst', *KiDR*, July 1938, pp. 236–42.

9. A. Rosenberg, 'Wege deutscher Kunstpolitik', *KiDR*, January 1938, p. 4.

10. A. Heilmeyer, 'Die Kunst im Dritten Reich', *KiDR*, January 1937, p. 6; A. H. [*sic*], 'Wege zur Monumentalmalerei', *KiDR*, April 1937, pp. 128–32; W. Horn, 'Stil aus Zucht und Innerlichkeit: Zur Frühausstellung der Preussischen Akademie der Künste', *KiDR*, April 1939, pp. 118–25.

11. See the July/August and September 1937 issues of *KiDR*.

12. Cranach was featured in the September 1938 issue of *KiDR*; Altdorfer in the August 1938 and the February 1939 issues; Holbein in March 1939; Dürer in May and December 1939.

13. Thoma's 100th birthday was celebrated in the October issue of *KiDR*. Leibl was featured in January 1940; Waldmüller in March 1940.

14. Petropoulos, *Art as Politics in the Third Reich*, pp. 58–9.

15. J. Petropoulos, 'A Guide through the Visual Arts Administration of the Third Reich', in G. R. Cuomo (ed.), *National Socialist Cultural Policy* (St. Martin's Press, 1995), p. 146 note 42. See also Brenner, *Die Kunstpolitik des Nationalsozialismus*, pp. 116–18; E. Fröhlich, 'Die kulturpolitische Pressekonferenz des Reichspropagandaministeriums', *Vierteljahrshefte für Zeitgeschichte* 22 (1974), pp. 347–81.

16. 'Die Rede des Führers zur Eröffnung der "Grossen Deutschen Kunstausstellung 1939" im Haus der Deutschen Kunst in München', *KiDR*, August 1939, pp. 240–2. These sentiments were echoed in R. Scholz, 'Tradition und Zeitauftrag: Zu den Gemälden in der "Grossen Deutschen Kunstausstellung 1939"', *KiDR*, August 1939, pp. 245–57.

17. W. Rittich, 'Deutsche Kunst im Ausland: Zur Ausstellung "Deutsche Graphik der Gegenwart" in Athen', *KiDR*, December 1939, pp. 380–9; W. Horn, 'Symbole der Tat: Zur Ausstellung "Polenfeldzug in Bildern und Bildnissen"', *KiDR*, February 1940, pp. 37–53.

18. Entry for 28 July 1940 in E. Fröhlich (ed.), *Die Tagebücher von Joseph Goebbels: Sämtliche Fragmente*, Part 1, *Aufzeichnungen 1924–1941*, vol. 4 (K. G. Saur, 1987), p. 256.

19. For Hitler's absence at these ceremonies after 1939 and the more limited cultural fare offered, compare 'Das Fest des schöpferischen Geistes. Sonderbeilage des Völkischer Beobachters zum Tage der Deutschen Kunst 1938', *Völkischer Beobachter*, 8 July 1938, with 'Vom Stellvertreter des Führers eröffnet. Die "Grosse Deutsche Kunstausstellung 1940"', *Völkischer Beobachter*, 28 July 1940; 'Im Kampf um die Sinngebung deutscher Kulturgeschichte. Neue Bewährungsprobe deutscher Kunst in geschichtlichen Stunde', *Völkischer Beobachter*, 27 July 1941.

20. Petropoulos, *Art as Politics in the Third Reich*.

21. A. Rosenberg, 'Zum 30. Januar 1943', *KiDR*, January 1943, p. 6. German art had been described as the highest form of European culture much earlier, but in an offensive, not defensive, posture. For example, the plans for the Führer Museum in Linz, which dated back to 1938, saw European masterpieces as Germanic in content or inspiration.

22. Rosenberg, 'Zum 30. Januar 1943', p. 6.

23. Ibid.

24. R. Scholz, 'Die Kunst im Europäischen Schicksalskampf: Zur Grossen Deutschen Kunstausstellung in München 1943', *KiDR*, July/August 1943, p. 140.

25. All quotes from ibid., p. 143. See also R. Scholz, 'Heroische Sinnbilder', *KiDR*, February 1943, p. 28; idem, 'Die Malerei in der Grossen Deutschen Kunstausstellung 1943', *KiDR*, July/August 1943, pp. 145–56; W. Horn, 'Malerei als Formausdruck der Zeit', *KiDR*, April 1944, pp. 76–8.

26. Compare July–December 1937 issues of *KiDR* with those of *Das Bild*.
27. H. A. Bühler, 'Die bildende Kunst im Dritten Reich', *Das Bild*, July 1937, p. 198.
28. B. Feistel-Rohmeder, 'Ausstellungs-Bildberichte,' *Das Bild*, October 1937, p. 310; emphasis in the original.
29. Ibid. See also Bühler, 'Die bildende Kunst im Dritten Reich', *Das Bild*, May 1937, pp. 130–1, continued in July, p. 198.
30. All quotes from B. Feistel-Rohmeder, 'Zum Abschluss der Ausstellungs- und Ausstellungsbildberichte des Jahres 1937', *Das Bild*, January 1938, p. 31; emphasis in original.
31. Ibid., pp. 31–2, emphasis in original.
32. B. Feistel-Rohmeder, 'Ausstellungsbildberichte der "Grossen Kunstaus-stellung im Haus der Deutschen Kunst zu München"', *Das Bild*, December 1937, pp. 369–70. The 1937 Great German Art show was mentioned in passing in Feistel-Rohmeder, 'Ausstellungs-Bildberichte (October 1937)', pp. 310–11; and idem, 'Zum Abschluss der Ausstellungs- und Ausstellungsbild-berichte des Jahres 1937', pp. 31–2.
33. 'Der Führer spricht', *Das Bild*, July 1938, pp. 197–202.
34. B. Feistel-Rohmeder, 'Die Grosse Deutsche Kunstausstellung 1939 im Haus der Deutschen Kunst zu München', *Das Bild*, August 1939, p. 227.
35. Ibid., p. 228.
36. B. Feistel-Rohmeder, 'Die Grosse Deutsche Kunstausstellung 1939 im Haus der Deutschen Kunst zu München: III', *Das Bild*, October–December 1939, pp. 292–6. See also K. E. Hirt, 'Einige Tiroler Künstler', *Das Bild*, May 1939, pp. 146–7; A. Schäfer, 'Ein Maler der Heimat', *Das Bild*, September 1939, pp. 267–8.
37. H. Meyer, 'Walther Gasch', *Das Bild*, August 1938, pp. 247–9; F. Wilkendorf, 'Siegfried Czerny, der Bildnissmeister und Maltechniker', *Das Bild*, March 1939, pp. 78–81; L. Meiners, 'Richard Müller: Zu seinem 65. Geburtstag', *Das Bild*, July 1939, pp. 206–9.
38. There were 389 individual and 450 corporate members. 'Die Deutsche Kunstgesellschaft...', *Deutscher Kunstbericht*, June (?) 1937, BDC, Feistel-Rohmeder file.
39. *Das Bild*, March 1934, May 1934, bottom of the last (unnumbered) pages of *Deutscher Kunstbericht*; *Das Bild*, October 1937, p. 320 and October–December 1939, p. 308.
40. M. Kater, *Das 'Ahnenerbe' der SS 1935–1945: Ein Beitrag zur Kulturpolitik des Dritten Reiches* (Deutsche Verlags-Anstalt, 1974).
41. Bühler to Himmler, 8 August 1938, BDC, Bühler file, detailed elaborate plans for a project he hoped Himmler would support; this may have led to the meeting about *Das Bild*.

42. This appears to be the same Peter Paulsen responsible for looting thousands of artworks from Poland, including the Veit Stoss altarpiece. From 1938 until 1943, he wrote a total of nine articles for *Das Bild*. Paulsen is discussed in Petropoulos, *Art as Politics in the Third Reich*, pp. 102–3.

43. The meeting was reported in a letter to Reichsführer SS, Persönlicher Stab, z Hd v SS-Hauptsturmführer Dr R. Brandt, *c*.19 June 1939, BDC, Bühler file. The author, an *SS-Obersturmbannführer*, signed only with his initials, which appear to be 'WW'.

44. All quotes from ibid.

45. Ibid.

46. 'Die Rede des Führers zur Eröffnung der "Grosse Deutsche Kunstausstellung 1938"', *KiDR*, July 1938, pp. 229–32; and Scholz, 'Besinnung im Malerischen', pp. 236–42.

47. Rosenberg, 'Wege deutscher Kunstpolitik', p. 4.

48. 'An unsere Leser', *Das Bild*, September 1939, p. 257.

49. H. A. Bühler, 'Das Deutsche Zeitalter', *Das Bild,* June 1940, p. 81, continued in July 1940, p. 97.

50. B. Feistel-Rohmeder, 'Kunstschaffen im Deutschen Danzig', *Das Bild*, October–December 1939, p. 306; B. Ebhardt, 'Grusss an das Elsass!' *Das Bild*, July 1940, pp. 98–100. The journal's April 1940 issue was dedicated to German art in Poland. See especially K. Trost, 'Deutscher Anteil an Krakau', *Das Bild*, April 1940, pp. 50–5; E. Schindler, 'Der Polenfeldzug im künstlerischen Zeugnis', *Das Bild*, April 1940, p. 60.

51. H. T. Wüst, 'Die Kunst muss im Volke stehen', *Das Bild*, March 1940, p. 49; B. Feistel-Rohmeder, 'Vom Bildwerk im Volksglauben: Heilige Nächte', *Das Bild*, December 1940, 185–90; H. Schwarze, 'Heldengedenktag 1941: Donon', *Das Bild*, March 1941, p. 37; H. T. Wüst, 'Krieg und künstlerisches Ingenium', *Das Bild*, February/March 1942, pp. 33–5.

52. 'An die bildenden Künstler Grossdeutschlands!' in 'Deutscher Kunstbericht', *Das Bild*, January 1942, unpaginated.

53. Wüst, 'Krieg und künstlerisches Ingenium', p. 33.

54. B. Feistel-Rohmeder, 'München 1940', *Das Bild*, July 1940, p. 101, and August 1940, pp. 114–22; idem, 'München 1941', *Das Bild*, August 1941, pp. 125–36; idem, 'München 1942', *Das Bild*, July/August 1942, pp. 117–23.

55. Feistel-Rohmeder, 'München 1941', p. 125.

56. B. Feistel-Rohmeder, 'Sammlung der Deutschen Kunstgesellschaft: "Graphik für die Wehrmacht"', *Das Bild*, April 1942, pp. 60–1.

57. Emphasis in the original; B. Feistel-Rohmeder, 'Die Deutsche Kunstgesellschaft E.V., Sitz Karlsruhe (B)', in 'Aus der Deutschen Kunstgesellschaft', *Das Bild*, October 1940, unpaginated (below October's table of contents).

58. Ibid.

59. Feistel-Rohmeder, 'München 1941', p. 125.

60. B. Feistel-Rohmeder, *Im Terror des Kunstbolschewismus: Urkundensammlung des 'Deutschen Kunstberichtes' aus den Jahren 1927–1933* (C. F. Müller Verlag, 1938), pp. 181–4.

61. Feistel-Rohmeder, 'München 1942', p. 117. These fears appear to have been common; see also Steinweis, *Art, Ideology, and Economics in Nazi Germany*, pp. 150–1.

62. Feistel-Rohmeder, 'München 1942', p. 118.

63. B. Feistel-Rohmeder, 'Von älteren und neuen Berliner Freunden', *Das Bild*, October–December 1943, p. 138.

64. H. T. Wüst, 'Plastik und Malerei in München 1943', *Das Bild*, August 1943, p. 90.

65. Ibid., p. 99.

66. The quote is from B. Feistel-Rohmeder, 'Deutsche Künstler sehen das Generalgouvernement', *Das Bild*, January–March 1944, pp. 9–10. See also idem, 'Die ersten Ausstellungen deutscher Kunst im Generalgouvernement', *Das Bild*, October–December 1943, p. 146; idem, 'Maler im Wartheland', *Das Bild*, October–December 1943, p. 152; W. Nowak, 'Altar des Ostens', *Das Bild*, October–December 1943, pp. 148–50.

67. Veit Stoss was a 15th-century artist from Nuremberg, famous for his altarpiece. The Veit Stoss Prize was to inspire artists to restore German creativity to the new Reich and occupied territories.

68. Feistel-Rohmeder, 'Deutsche Künstler sehen das Generalgouvernement', p. 9.

69. Feistel-Rohmeder, 'Die Deutsche Kunstgesellschaft E.V., Sitz Karlsruhe (B.)'.

70. 'Deutscher Kunstbericht', *Das Bild*, January/February 1943, unpaginated; B. Feistel-Rohmeder, 'Zur Ausstellung im Leipziger Kunstverein in Museum der bildenden Künste der 3. Wanderausstellung der Deutschen Kunstgesellschaft', *Das Bild*, April–June 1943, p. 62. The show was scheduled for Dresden from 5 September to 3 October; 'Ausstellungskalender', *Deutscher Kunstbericht, Das Bild*, July–September 1943.

71. *III. Wanderausstellung Deutscher Kunst der Deutschen Kunstgesellschaft E. V. Sitz Karlsruhe* (C. F. Müller Verlag, 1943); a copy is in the library of the Herzog-Anton-Ulrich-Museum in Brunswick.

72. For effects of the war on Nazi cultural institutions see Brenner, *Die Kunstpolitik des Nationalsozialismus*; Steinweis, *Art, Ideology, and Economics in Nazi Germany*; Petropoulos, *Art as Politics in the Third Reich*.

73. This translation is a rough approximation of the German, which consists of one very long sentence. See 'Rede des Herrn Ministerpräsidenten Klagges anlässlich der III. Wanderausstellung der Deutschen Kunstgesellschaft', *Das Bild*, January/February 1943, p. II [*sic*].

74. Ibid., p. I.
75. B. Feistel-Rohmeder, 'Ausstellungsbericht', *Das Bild*, January/February 1943, p. 17.
76. Ibid., p. 18.
77. Titles of works in the catalog do not always match those reproduced there or the works illustrated in the special exhibit issue of *Das Bild*, January/February 1943.
78. The earlier depictions of these works can be found in the 1936 volume of *Das Bild*. See pp. 323 (Hempfing's portrait), 329 (Hennemann's woodcut), and 287 (Wrage's woodcut).
79. *III. Wanderausstellung Deutscher Kunst.*
80. Ibid. The catalog did not identify members but I have identified 43.
81. Compare the list of artists in ibid. to those in Deutschen Kunstgesellschaft, *I. Wanderausstelluung Deutscher Kunst* (np, nd [1933]), and B. Feistel-Rohmeder, 'Frühlingsfahrt', *Deutsche Bildkunst*, September 1929, p. 29.
82. 'Jahresbericht der Deutschen Kunstgesellschaft ... 1929', in 'Aus dem Deutschen Kunstbericht', *Deutsche Bildkunst*, September 1929, p. 32; 'Aus dem Deutschen Kunstbericht', *Das Bild*, June 1936, unpaginated; *Deutscher Kunstbericht*, June (?) 1937, BDC, Feistel-Rohmeder file; 'Aus dem Deutschen Kunstbericht', *Das Bild*, September 1940, unpaginated; and a passing comment in 'Mitteilung der Schriftleitung', *Das Bild*, March 1944, p. 40.
83. 'Aus der Deutschen Kunstgesellschaft', in 'Deutscher Kunstbericht', *Das Bild*, May 1935, unpaginated; see also the 1937 annual report in *Deutscher Kunstbericht*, June (?) 1937; 'Die Münchner Künstlergruppe "Der Bund"...', in 'Aus dem Deutschen Kunstbericht', *Das Bild*, February 1936, unpaginated.
84. See the indexed list of authors for *Das Bild*, 1934–44. Only 27 of the 231 appear to have been members.
85. For example, 'Aus der Mitarbeiterliste', *Das Bild*, January/February 1943, above the table of contents.
86. Numbers are based on the tables of content and the indexed list of contributors for *Das Bild*, 1938, 1940, 1942 and 1943.
87. See the indexed list of images in *Das Bild,* 1936, 1940, 1942 and 1943.
88. See the table of contents, *Das Bild*, January–March 1944.
89. Numbers are based on the tables of contents and the indexed list of contributors for *Das Bild*, 1934–44.
90. 'Begrüssungsansprache des Vorsitzenden der Deutschen Kunstgesellschaft', *Das Bild*, January/February 1943, pp. I–II [*sic*].
91. B. Feistel-Rohmeder, 'Die III. Wanderausstellung der Deutschen Kunstgesellschaft', *Das Bild*, January/February 1943, p. 1.

92. Ibid.

93. Ibid.

94. Ibid.

95. For a sample see, H. T. Wüst, 'Zum Tode von Johann Vincenz Cissarz', *Das Bild*, January 1943, p. 22; E. Kühn, 'Richard Guhr vollendet am 8. September sein 70. Lebensjahr', *Das Bild*, April–June, 1943; Feistel-Rohmeder, 'Von älteren und neuen Berliner Freunden', p. 146.

96. B. Feistel-Rohmeder, 'Mittwinternacht-religio: Urbild, Bild, Sinnbild', *Das Bild*, October–December 1943, p. 159.

97. Bühler resigned from *Das Bild* because his home was heavily damaged. The destruction of Willy ter Hell's studio is mentioned in Feistel-Rohmeder, 'Von älteren und neuen Berliner Freunden', p. 138.

98. 'Begrüssungsansprache des Vorsitzenden der Deutschen Kunstgesell-schaft', p. I.

99. Compare for example the fonts used in H. A. Bühler, 'Hans Thoma zum 100. Geburtstag', *Das Bild*, January/February 1940, p. 1, and O. Biedermann, 'Idee und Tat: 10 Jahre Kampf und Arbeit der Dienststelle Rosenberg', *Das Bild*, January–March 1944, p. 32.

100. *Das Bild* officially became a quarterly publication in 1943. 'Mitteilung an unsere Bezieher', *Das Bild*, February/March 1943, table of contents page.

101. An excerpt of Feistel-Rohmeder's letter to Schultze-Naumburg is included in Reichspropagandaamt Thüringen an das Reichspropagandaamt Baden, 10 August 1943, in BDC, Feistel-Rohmeder file.

102. Feistel-Rohmeder to Goebbels, 30 August 1943, BDC, Feistel-Rohmeder file.

103. F. W., 'Zum 70. Geburtstag der Hauptschriftleiterin Bettina Feistel-Rohmeder', in BDC, Feistel-Rohmeder file. See also Landesleiter der Reichskammer der bildenen Künste an das Reichsministerium für Volks-saufklärung und Propaganda, 12 October 1943, in ibid.

104. K. Trost, 'Eine völkische Vorkämpferin feiert Geburtstag. Hauptschriftleiterin Bettina Feistel-Rohmeder 70 Jahre alt', *Völkischer Beobachter*, 15 August 1943. An excerpt can be found in BDC, Feistel-Rohmeder file. See also F. W., 'Zum 70. Geburtstag der Hauptschriftleiterin Bettina Feistel-Rohmeder'.

105. Bettina Feistel-Rohmeder an den Landesverband Baden-Westmark im Reichsverband der deutschen Presse, 22 November 1944, and An alle Betriebsangehörigen der Firma C.F. Müller, 2 December 1944, both in BA R103/19.

106. See the correspondence in BA R103/19.

107. Steinweis, *Art, Ideology, and Economics in Nazi Germany*, p. 170.

108. Letter from Hermann Fecht's daughter to the author, 3 March 1992.

109. I have not been able to view these letters, dated 30 June 1951 and 12 December 1951. They are briefly quoted in I. Bloth, *Adolf Wissel: Malerei und Kunstpolitik im Nationalsozialismus* (Gebrüder Mann Verlag, 1994), pp. 175–6, citing 'Nachlass Adolf Wissel, Velber/Hannover'.
110. *Badische Neuste Nachrichten*, 14 February 1953, p. 16.
111. See for example, Chef der Sicherheitspolizei und des SD, Amt III, Berlin, *Meldungen aus dem Reich*, 15 February 1943, BA R58/180–2, Nr. 359, frames 9–11; ibid., 22 February 1943, BA R58/180–2, Nr. 361, frames 67–72.
112. Ibid.
113. Feistel-Rohmeder, 'München 1941', p. 136.
114. Feistel-Rohmeder, 'München 1940', p. 122.
115. See *Das Bild*, March 1936, pp. 90–1 for the Sauter images; also F. Wilkendorf, 'Wilhelm Sauter', *Das Bild*, March 1939, pp. 74–7.
116. Member promotions, activities and deaths were often listed in the *German Art Report* supplement to *Das Bild*. See for example, 'Deutscher Kunstbericht', *Das Bild*, July 1940; 'Deutscher Kunstbericht', *Das Bild*, August 1940; 'Deutscher Kunstbericht', *Das Bild*, January 1942; 'Deutscher Kunstbericht', *Das Bild*, February/March 1943.

Bibliography

Archives

Berlin Document Center (BDC)
   Bühler, Hans Adolf
   Feistel-Rohmeder, Bettina
Bundesarchiv Berlin (BA Berlin)
   R32 Reichskunstwart
Bundesarchiv Koblenz (BA)
   NS8 Amt Rosenberg
   R31 Reichskunstwart
   R56 Reichskulturkammer
   R103 Reichsverband der deutschen Presse
Generallandesarchiv Karlsruhe (GLA)
   235 Volksbildungsministerium
   466/6094 Hans Adolf Bühler
Niedersächsisches Hauptstaatsarchiv Hannover (NHStAH)
   Hann. 180 Hannover E 8 Acc. 15/89 Nr. 48, Bd 2 (H. Blume)
   Nds. 171 Hannover Nr. 20260 (H. Blume)
Niedersächsisches Staatsarchiv Wolfenbüttel (NStAW)
   12 A Neu 13/18763 (Deutsche Kunstgesellschaft)
Sächsisches Hauptstaatsarchiv Dresden (SHStAD)
   Ministerium für Volksbildung, Nr. 14923 (Internationale Kunstausstellung
     Dresden 1926)
Thüringisches Hauptstaatsarchiv Weimar (ThHStAW)
   Thür Volksbildungsministerium (ThVBM) C 933
   Thür Volksbildungsministerium (ThVBM) C 936

Periodicals

*Das Bild: Monatsschrift für das Deutsche Kunstschaffen in Vergangenheit und
   Gegenwart*
Badische Neuste Nachrichten
Deutschbund Blätter

Deutschbund Nachrichten
Deutsche Bildkunst
Der Führer
Die Kunst für Alle
Die Kunst im Dritten (Deutschen) Reich
Kunst und Wirtschaft
Melsungen Tagblatt
Mitteilungen des Kampfbundes für deutsche Kultur
Völkischer Beobachter

Published Sources

Allgemeines Lexikon der bildenden Künstler: Von Antike bis zur Gegenwart,
   Leipzig: Verlag E. A. Seemann, 1915, etc.
Alt, T., *Die Herabwertung der deutschen Kunst durch die Parteigänger des*
   Impressionismus, Mannheim: Verlag F. Nemnich, 1911.
Chamberlain, S. H., *The Foundations of the Nineteenth Century*, 2 vols, John Lees
   trans, intro. George Mosse, New York: Howard Fertig, 1968.
Clauss, L. F., *Die nordische Seele: Eine Einführung in die Rassenseelenkunde*,
   Munich: Lehmannsverlag, 1933.
Deutsche Kunstgesellschaft, *I. Wanderausstellung Deutscher Kunst*, np, nd
   [1933].
——, *III. Wanderausstellung Deutscher Kunst der Deutschen Kunstgesellschaft*
   E. V., Karlsruhe: C. F. Müller Verlag, 1943.
Dresler, A. (ed.), *Deutsche Kunst und entartete 'Kunst': Kunstwerk und Zerrbild*
   als Spiegel der Weltanschauung, Munich: Deutscher Volksverlag, 1938.
Drey, P., *Die wirtschaflichen Grundlagen der Malkunst: Versuch einer Kunst-*
   ökonomie, Stuttgart: J. G. Cotta'sche Buchhandlung Nachfolger, 1910
Feistel-Rohmeder, B., *Das Frauenbildnis in der venezianischen Renaissance*, 3rd
   edn, Leipzig: Friedrich Rothbarth, 1905.
——, *Im Terror des Kunstbolschewismus: Urkundensammlung des 'Deutschen*
   Kunstberichtes' aus den Jahren 1927–1933, Karlsruhe: C. F. Müller Verlag,
   1938.
Fritzsching, L., 'Die wirtschaftliche Lage der bildenden Künstler seit Kriegs-
   ende', *Annalen der Deutschen Reichs für Gesetzgebung, Verwaltung und*
   Volkswirtschaft, Jahrgang 1921 und 1922, Munich: J. Schweitzer Verlag, 1923,
   pp. 133–97.
Gerstenhauer, M. R., *Der völkische Gedanke in Vergangenheit und Zukunft: Aus*
   der Geschichte der völkischen Bewegung, Leipzig: Armanen-Verlag, 1933.
Grosse Deutsche Kunstausstellung, Munich: Verlag Knorr & Hirth GmbH, 1937.
Günther, H. F. K., *Rassenkunde des Deutschen Volkes*, J. F. Lehmann, 1922.

Hellwag, F., 'Die derzeitige wirtschaftliche Lage der bildenden Künstler', in L. Sinzheimer (ed.), *Die geistige Arbeiter*, erster Teil, *Freies Schriftstellertum und Literaturverlag*, vol. 152, Schriften des Vereins für Sozialpolitik, Munich and Leipzig: Verlag von Duncker and Humblot, 1922, pp. 145–75.

Prinz zur Lippe, Friedrich Wilhelm, *Angewandte Rassenseelenkunde*, Leipzig: Adolf Klein Verlag, 1931.

Rosenberg, A., *Der Mythos des 20. Jahrhunderts: Eine Wertung der seelisch-geistigen Gestaltkämpfe unserer Zeit*, Munich: Hoheneichen-Verlag, 1939.

Schreiber, G., *Die Not der deutschen Wissenschaft und der geistigen Arbeiter: Geschehnisse und Gedanken zur Kulturpolitik des Deutsche Reiches*, Leipzig: Verlag von Quelle und Meyer, 1923.

Schultze-Naumburg, P., *Kunst und Rasse*, Munich: J. F. Lehmanns Verlag, 1928.

——, *Kampf um die Kunst,* Munich: Verlag Frz. Eher Nachf., GmbH, 1932.

Thode, H., *Böcklin und Thoma: Acht Vorträge über die neudeutsche Malerei*, Heidelberg: Carl Winter Universitätsbuchhandlung, 1905.

Weber, A., *Die Not der geistigen Arbeiter*, Munich: Duncker und Humblot, 1923.

Willrich, W., *Die Säuberung des Kunsttempels: Eine kunst-politische Kampfschrift zur Gesundung deutscher Kunst im Geiste nordischer Art*, Munich: J. F. Lehmanns Verlag, 1937.

Secondary Sources

Ankum, K. von (ed.), *Women in the Metropolis: Gender and Modernity in Weimar Culture*, Berkeley: University of California Press, 1997.

Backes, K., *Hitler und die bildenden Künste: Kulturverständnis und Kunstpolitik im Dritten Reich*, Cologne: DuMont Verlag, 1988.

Barron, S. (ed.), *'Entartete Kunst': Das Schicksal der Avantgarde im Nazi-Deutschland*, Munich: Hirmer Verlag, 1992.

Baumann, K., 'Kunstzeitschriften in Deutschland 1927–1939: Auf der Suche nach der "deutschen Kunst"', in L. Ehrlich, J. John and J. H. Ulbricht (eds), *Das Dritte Weimar: Klassik und Kultur im Nationalsozialismus*, Cologne: Böhlau Verlag, 1999, pp. 133–48.

Berding, H. (ed.), *Nationales Bewusstsein und kollektive Identität: Studien zur Entwicklung des kollektiven Bewusstseins in der Neuzeit 2*, Frankfurt am Main: Suhrkamp, 1994.

Bessel, R., and E. J. Feuchtwanger (eds), *Social Change and Political Development in Weimar Germany*, London: Croom Helm, 1981.

Blinkhorn, M. (ed.), *Fascists and Conservatives: The Radical Right and the Establishment in Twentieth-Century Europe*, London: Unwin and Hyman, 1990.

Bloth, I., *Adolf Wissel: Malerei und Kunstpolitik im Nationalsozialismus*, Berlin: Gebr. Mann, 1994.

Bollenbeck, G., *Tradition, Avantgarde, Reaktion: Deutsche Kontroversen um die Kulturelle Moderne, 1880–1945*, Frankfurt am Main; S. Fischer, 1999.

Bollmus, R., *Das Amt Rosenberg und seine Gegner: Studium zum Machtkampf im nationalsozialistischen Herrschaftssystem*, Stuttgart: Deutsche Verlags-Anstalt, 1970.

Braatz, W. E., 'The völkisch Ideology and Anti-Semitism in Germany', *Yivo Annual of Jewish Social Science* 15 (1974), pp. 166–87.

Bräunche, E. O., 'Die Entwicklung der NSDAP in Baden bis 1932/33', *Zeitschrift für die Geschichte des Oberrheins*, NF 86 (1977), pp. 331–75.

Brenner, H., 'Die Kunst im politischen Machtkampf, 1933–1934', *Vierteljahrshefte für Zeitgeschichte* 10 (1962), pp. 17–42.

——, *Die Kunstpolitik des Nationalsozialismus*, Reinbeck bei Hamburg: Rowohlt Taschenbuch Verlag, 1963.

Bridenthal, R., 'Beyond Kinder, Küche, Kirche: Weimar Women at Work', *Central European History* 6 (1973), pp. 148–66.

Brock, B., and A. Preiss, *Kunst auf Befehl? Dreiunddreizig bis Fünfundvierzig*, Munich: Klinkhardt und Biermann, 1990.

Broszat, M., 'Die völkische Ideologie und der Nationalsozialismus', *Deutsche Rundschau* 84 (1958), pp. 53–68.

Bullivant, K. (ed.), *Culture and Society in the Weimar Republic*, Totowa, NJ: Rowman and Littlefield, 1977.

Büsch, O., and J. J. Sheehan (eds), *Die Rolle der Nation in der deutschen Geschichte und Gegenwart*, Berlin: Colloquium Verlag, 1985.

Bussmann, G., '"Degenerate Art" – A Look at a Useful Myth', in C. Joachimides (ed.), *German Art in the Twentieth Century: Painting and Sculpture, 1905–1985*, Munich: Prestel-Verlag, 1985, pp. 113–24.

Chickering, R., *We Men Who Feel Most German: A Cultural Study of the Pan-German League, 1886–1914*, Boston, MA: George Allen & Unwin, 1984.

Childers, T., *The Nazi Voter: The Social Foundations of Fascism in Germany, 1919–1933*, Chapel Hill: University of North Carolina Press, 1983.

Dahm, V., 'Die Reichskulturkammer als Instrument kulturpolitischer Steuerung und sozialer Reglementierung', *Vierteljahrshefte für Zeitgeschichte* 34 (1986), pp. 53–84.

Denkler, H., 'Januskopfig: Zur ideologischen Physiognomie der Zeitschrift "Das Innere Reich" (1934–1944)', in H. Denkler and K. Prümm (eds), *Die deutsche Literatur im Dritten Reich: Themen-Traditionen-Wirkungen*, Stuttgart: Philipp Reclam jun, 1976, pp. 382–405.

Deshmukh, M. F., 'German Impressionist Painters and World War I', *Art History* 4 (1981), pp. 66–79.

——, 'Max Liebermann: Observations on the Politics of Painting in Imperial Germany, 1870–1914', *German Studies Review* 3 (1980), pp. 171–206.

Diehl, J. M., *Paramilitary Politics in the Weimar Republic*, Bloomington, IN: Indiana University Press, 1977.

——, 'Von der "Vaterlandspartei" zur "nationalen Revolution": Die "Vereinigten Vaterländischen Verbände Deutschlands (VVVD)" 1922–1932', *Vierteljahrshefte für Zeitgeschichte* 33 (1985), pp. 617–39.

Dupeux, L., 'La version "volkisch" de l'alternative, 1830–1933', *Revue d'Allemagne* 22 (1990), pp. 381–9.

Eley, G., *Reshaping the German Right: Radical Nationalism and Political Change after Bismarck*, New Haven, CT: Yale University Press, 1980.

Favorat, J., 'Theodore Fritsch ou la conception "völkisch" de la propagande', *Revue d'Allemagne* 16 (1984), pp. 521–32.

Feldman, G. D., *The Great Disorder: Politics, Economics, and Society in the German Inflation, 1914–1924*, New York: Oxford University Press, 1993.

Fischer, J. M., '"Entartete Kunst": Zur Geschichte eines Begriffes', *Merkur* 38 (1984), pp. 346–52.

Fritzsche, P., *Rehearsals for Fascism: Populism and Political Mobilization in Weimar Germany*, New York: Oxford University Press, 1990.

Fröhlich, E., 'Die kulturpolitische Pressekonferenz des Reichspropagandaministeriums', *Vierteljahrshefte für Zeitgeschichte* 22 (1974), pp. 347–81.

—— (ed.), *Die Tagebücher von Joseph Goebbels, Sämtliche Fragmente*, Part 1, *Aufzeichnungen 1924–1941*, vol. 4, Munich: K. G. Saur, 1987.

Funke, M., H. Jacobsen, H. Knütter, and H. Schwarz (eds), *Demokratie und Diktatur: Geist und Gestalt politischer Herrschaft in Deutschland und Europa*, Düsseldorf: Droste Verlag, 1987.

Gay, P., *Weimar Culture: The Outsider as Insider*, New York: Harper and Row, 1968.

Gossler, A., 'Friedrich Lange und die "völkische Bewegung" des Kaiserreichs', *Archiv für Kulturgeschichte* 83 (2001), pp. 377–411.

Grill, J. H., *The Nazi Movement in Baden, 1920–1945*, Chapel Hill: University of North Carolina Press, 1983.

Grossmann, A., 'Feminist Debates about Women and National Socialism', *Gender and History* 3 (1991), pp. 350–8.

Härtl, U., B. Stenzel and J. H. Ulbricht (eds), *Hier, hier ist Deutschland…: Von nationalen Kulturkonzepten zur nationalsozialistischen Kulturpolitik*, Wallstein Verlag, 1997.

Hering, R., '"Des deutschen Volkes Wiedergeburt": Völkischer Nationalismus und politische Erneuerungspläne', *Zeitschrift für Geschichtswissenschaft* 42 (1994), pp. 1079–84.

Hermand, J., *Old Dreams of a New Reich: Völkisch Utopias and National Socialism*, P. Levesque trans, in collaboration with S. Soldovieri, Bloomington, IN: Indiana University Press, 1992.

——, and F. Trommler, *Die Kultur der Weimarer Republik*, Munich: Nymphenburger Verlagshandlung, 1978.

Hettling, M., and P. Nolte (eds), *Nation und Gesellschaft in Deutschland*, Munich: Verlag C. H. Beck, 1996.

Heusinger von Waldegg, J., *Die Hochschule der bildenden Künste Karlsruhe im Dritten Reich*, Karlsruhe: Staatliche Akademie der Bildenden Künste Karlsruhe, 1987.

Hinz, B., *Art in the Third Reich*, R. and R. Kimber, trans, New York: Pantheon, 1979.

Jacobi, W., *Bildersturm in der Provinz: Die NS-Aktion 'Entartete Kunst' 1937 in Südbaden*, Freiburg i. B.: Dreisam-Verlag, 1988.

Jarausch, K., 'Die Not der geistigen Arbeiter: Akademiker in der Berufskrise 1918–1933', in W. Abelshauser (ed.), *Die Weimarer Republik als Wohlfahrtsstaat*, Stuttgart, 1987, pp. 280–300.

——, *The Unfree Professions*, New York: Oxford University Press, 1990.

Jones, L. E., *German Liberalism and the Dissolution of the Weimar Party System: 1918–1933*, Chapel Hill: University of North Carolina Press, 1988.

——, 'Culture and Politics in the Weimar Republic', in George Martel (ed.), *Modern Germany Reconsidered 1870–1945*, London: Routledge, 1992, pp. 74–95.

Kaes, A., 'Die ökonomische Dimension der Literatur: Zum Strukturwandel der Institution Literatur in der Inflationszeit (1918–1923)', in G. D. Feldman et al. (eds), *Konsequenzen der Inflation/Consequences of Inflation*, Berlin: Colloquium Verlag, 1988, pp. 307–29.

——, and M. Jay and E. Dimendberg (eds), *The Weimar Republic Sourcebook*, Berekeley, CA: University of California Press, 1994.

Kater, M. H., *Das 'Ahnenerbe' der SS 1935–1945: Ein Beitrag zur Kulturpolitik des Dritten Reiches*, Stuttgart: Deutsche Verlags-Anstalt, 1974.

——, 'Frauen in der NS-Bewegung', *Vierteljahrshefte der Zeitgeschichte* 31 (1983), pp. 202–41.

——, *The Nazi Party: A Social Profile of Members and Leaders 1919–1945*, Cambridge, MA: Harvard University Press, 1983.

Ketelsen, U., 'Kulturpolitik des III. Reichs und Ansätze zu ihrer Interpretation', *Text und Kontext* 8 (1980), pp. 217–42.

Klein, I., *Vom kosmogonischen zum völkischen Eros: Eine sozialgeschichtliche Analyse bürgerlich-liberaler Kunstkritik in der Zeit von 1917 bis 1936*, Munich: tuduv, 1991.

Kolb, E., *Die Weimarer Republik*, 2nd edn, Munich: R. Oldenbourg Verlag, 1988.

Koonz, C., *Mothers in the Fatherland: Women, the Family, and Nazi Politics*, New York: St. Martin's Press, 1987.

——, 'Nazi Women before 1933: Rebels against Emancipation', *Social Science Quarterly* 56 (March 1976), pp. 553–63.

Koshar, R., *Social Life, Local Politics, and Nazism: Marburg, 1880–1935*, Chapel Hill: University of North Carolina Press, 1986.

Die Kunst der Dritten Reich, Dokumente der Unterwerfung, Frankfurt am Main: Frankfurter Kunstverein, 1976.

Kunst in Karlsruhe 1900–1950, Karlsruhe: C. F. Müller Verlag, 1981.

Lane, B. M., *Architecture and Politics in Germany, 1918–1945*, Cambridge, MA: Harvard University Press, 1968.

Laqueur, W., *Weimar: A Cultural History, 1918–1933*, New York: Putnam, 1974.

Lehmann-Haupt, H., *Art under a Dictatorship*, New York: Oxford University Press, 1954.

Lenman, R., 'A Community in Transition: Painters in Munich, 1886–1914', *Central European History* 6 (1982), pp. 3–33.

——, *Die Kunst, die Macht und das Geld: Zur Kulturgeschichte des kaiserlichen Deutschland 1871–1918*, R. Grundmann trans, vol. 23, Edition Pandora, Frankfurt: Campus Verlag, 1994.

——, 'Painters, Patronage and the Art Market in Germany 1850–1914', *Past and Present*, No. 123 (1989), pp. 107–40.

Lewis, B. I., *Art For All? The Collision of Modern Art and the Public in Late Nineteenth-century Germany*, Princeton, NJ: Princeton University Press, 2003.

Loham, U., *Völkischer Radikalismus: Die Geschichte des Deutschvölkischen Schutz-und Trutzbundes 1919–1923*, Hamburg: Leibnitz-Verlag, 1970.

Mallmann, M., *'Das Innere Reich': Analyse einer konservativen Kulturzeitschrift im Dritten Reich*, Bonn: Bouvier Verlag Herbert Grundmann, 1978.

McKale, D. M., *The Nazi Party Courts: Hitler's Management of Conflict in his Movement, 1921–1945*, Lawrence: University Press of Kansas, 1974.

Merker, R., *Die bildenden Künste im Nationalsozialismus: Kulturideologie, Kulturpolitik, Kulturproduktion*, Cologne: DuMont Buchverlag, 1983.

Meskimmon, M., and S. West (eds), *Visions of the 'Neue Frau': Women and the Visual Arts in Weimar Germany*, Brookfield, CT: Scolar, 1995.

Milfull, J. (ed.), *The Attractions of Fascism: Social Psychology and Aesthetics of the Triumph of the Right'*, New York: Berg, 1990.

Mittenzwei, W., *Der Untergang einer Akademie oder die Mentalität des ewigen Deutschen: Der Einfluss der nationalkonservativen Dichter an der Preussischen Akademie der Künste, 1919–1947*, Berlin: Aufbau-Verlag, 1992.

Mohler, A., *Die konservative Revolution in Deutschland 1918–1932: Ein Handbuch*, 2nd edn, Darmstadt: Wissenschaftliche Buchgesellschaft, 1972.

Mommsen, W. J., *Bürgerliche Kultur und politische Ordnung: Künstler, Schriftsteller und Intellektuelle in der deutschen Geschichte 1830–1933*, Frankfurt am Main: Fischer Taschenbuch Verlag, 2000.

Mosse, G. L., *The Crisis of German Ideology: Intellectual Origins of the Third Reich*, New York: Grosset and Dunlap, 1964.

Müller, J., *Mythen der Rechten: Nation, Ethnie, Kultur*, Berlin: Edition ID-Archiv, 1995.

Müller-Mehlis, R., *Die Kunst im Dritten Reich*, 2nd edn, Munich: Wilhelm Heyne Verlag, 1976.

Naumann, M., 'Bildung und Gehorsam: Zur ästhetischen Ideologie des Bildungsbürgertums', in K. Vondung (ed.), *Das wilhelminische Bildungsbürgertum: Zur Sozialgeschichte seiner Ideen*, Göttingen: Vandenhoeck und Rupprecht, 1976, pp. 34–52.

Nipperdey, T., 'Nationalidee und Nationaldenkmal in Deutschland im 19. Jahrhundert', in idem (ed.), *Gesellschaft, Kultur, Theorie: Gesammelte Aufsätze zur neueren Geschichte*, Göttingen: Vandenhoeck und Rupprecht, 1976, pp. 133–73.

Paret, P., *The Berlin Secession: Modernism and Its Enemies in Imperial Germany*, Cambridge, MA: The Belknap Press of Harvard University, 1980.

Petropoulos, J., *Art as Politics in the Third Reich*, Chapel Hill: University of North Carolina Press, 1996.

——, 'A Guide through the Visual Arts Administration of the Third Reich', in G. R. Cuomo (ed.), *National Socialist Cultural Policy*, New York: St. Martin's Press, 1995, pp. 121–53.

Petsch, J., *Kunst im 'Dritten Reich': Architektur – Plastik – Malerei. Alltagsästhetik*, 2nd edn, Cologne: Vista Point Verlag, 1987.

Puschner, U., W. Schmitz and J. H. Ulbricht (eds), *Handbuch zur 'Völkischen Bewegung' 1871–1914*, Munich: K. G. Saur, 1996.

Rave, P. O., *Kunstdiktatur im Dritten Reich*, U. M. Schneede (ed.), Berlin: Argon, 1988.

Rogoff, I. (ed.), *The Divided Heritage: Themes and Problems in German Modernism*, Cambridge: Cambridge University Press, 1991.

Roh, F., *'Entartete' Kunst: Kunstbarbarei im Dritten Reich*, Hanover: Fackelträger Verlag, 1962.

Rothe, W., 'Gesundes Volksempfinden – Entartete Kunst: Ein Kapitel bürgerlicher Kunstphilosophie', *Museen der Stadt Köln Bulletin* 3 (1981), pp. 26–34.

Rupp, L. J., 'Mother of the *Volk*: The Image of Women in Nazi Ideology', *Signs: Journal of Women in Culture and Society* 3 (1977), pp. 362–79.

Schraeder, B., and J. Schebera, *The 'Golden' Twenties: Art and Literature in the Weimar Republic*, K. Vanovich trans, New Haven: Yale University Press, 1988.

Seydewitz, M., *Dresden: Musen und Menschen: Ein Beitrag zur Geschichte der Stadt, ihrer Kunst und Kultur*, Berlin: Buchverlag Morgen, 1973.

Snitow, A. B., C. Stansell and S. Thompson (eds), *Powers of Desire: The Politics of Sexuality*, New York. Monthly Review Press, 1984.

Stachura, P. D., 'Der Kritische Wendepunkt? Die NSDAP und die Reichstagwahlen vom 20. Mai 1928', *Vierteljahrshefte für Zeitgeschichte* 26 (1978), pp. 66–99.

Stark, G., *Entrepreneurs of Ideology: Neoconservative Publishers in Germany, 1890–1933*, Chapel Hill: University of North Carolina Press, 1981.

Steinweis, A. E., *Art, Ideology, and Economics in Nazi Germany: The Reich Chambers of Music, Theater, and the Visual Arts*, Chapel Hill: University of North Carolina Press, 1993.

——, 'Conservatism, National Socialism, and the Cultural Crisis of the Weimar Republic', in L. E. Jones and J. Retallack (eds), *Between Reform, Reaction, and Resistance: Studies in the History of German Conservatism from 1789 to 1945*, Providence, RI: Berg, 1993, pp. 329–46.

——, 'Weimar Culture and the Rise of National Socialism: The *Kampfbund für deutsche Kultur*', *Central European History* 24 (1991), pp. 402–23.

Stern, F., *The Politics of Cultural Despair: A Study in the Rise of the Germanic Ideology*, Berkeley, CA: University of California Press, 1961.

Thomae, O., *Die Propaganda-Maschinerie: Bildende Kunst und Öffentlichkeitsarbeit im Dritten Reich*, Berlin: Gebrüder Mann, 1978.

Todorow, A., 'Frauen im Journalismus der Weimarer Republik', *Internationales Archiv für Sozialgeschichte der deutschen Literatur* 16 (1991), pp. 84–103.

Turner, H. A. Jr., 'Hitler's Secret Pamphlet for Industrialists, 1927', *Journal of Modern History* 40 (1968), pp. 349–74.

Ulbricht, J. H., 'Die "Deutsche Heimatschule" in Bad Berka: Ein vergessenes Kapitel regionaler Schulgeschichte', *Heimat Thüringen: Kulturlandschaft, Lebensraum, Umwelt* 3 (1996), pp. 22–3.

——, 'Kulturrevolution von rechts: Das völkische Netzwerk 1900–1930', in D. Heiden and G. Mai (eds), *Nationalsozialismus in Thüringen*, Weimar: Böhlau Verlag, 1995, pp. 29–48.

Verboten, Verfolgt: Kunstdiktatur im Dritten Reich, Duisburg: Wilhelm Lehmbruck Museum, 1983.

Vondung, K., 'Zur Lage der Gebildeten in der wilhelminischen Zeit', in idem (ed.), *Das wilhelminische Bildungsbürgertum: Zur Sozialgeschichte seiner Ideen*, Göttingen: Vandenhoeck und Rupprecht, 1976, pp. 20–33.

Walter, F., *Schicksal einer deutschen Stadt: Geschichte Mannheims 1907–1945*, vol. 1 (1907–1924), Frankfurt am Main: Fritz Knapp Verlag, 1949.

West, S., *The Visual Arts in Germany 1890–1937: Utopia and Despair*, New Brunswick, NJ: Rutgers University Press, 2001.

Widdig, B., *Culture and Inflation in Weimar Germany*, Berkeley, CA: University of California Press, 2001.

Wulf, J., *Die bildenden Künste im Dritten Reich: Eine Dokumentation*, Gütersloh: Siegbert Mohn Verlag, 1963.

Zuschlag, C., *'Entartete Kunst': Austellungsstrategien im Nazi-Deutschland*, Worms: Wernersche Verlagsgesellschaft, 1995.

Zwischen Widerstand und Anpassung: Kunst im Deutschland, 1933–1945, Berlin: Akademie der Künste, 1980.

Index

Page numbers in italics refer to illustrations.

Index